THE THREE CS OF HIGHER EDUCATION

The Three Cs of Higher Education

*Competition, Collaboration
and Complementarity*

Edited by

ROSALIND M. O. PRITCHARD,
MARK O'HARA,
CLARE MILSOM,
JAMES WILLIAMS
and
LIVIU MATEI

Central European University Press
Budapest–New York

Published in 2019 by

Central European University Press

Nádor utca 9, H-1051 Budapest, Hungary
Tel: +36-1-327-3138 or 327-3000
E-mail: ceupress@press.ceu.edu
Website: www.ceupress.com

224 West 57th Street, New York NY 10019, USA

ISBN 978-963-386-327-5

On the cover: The Atrium of Central European University, Budapest. Image credit – CEU, György Petrók.

Library of Congress Cataloging-in-Publication Data

Names: European AIR Forum (40th : 2018 : Budapest, Hungary) | Pritchard, Rosalind M. O., editor. | O'Hara, Mark, editor. | Milsom, Clare, editor. | Williams, James, 1971– editor. | Matei, Liviu, editor.
Title: The three C-s of higher education : competition, collaboration and complementarity / edited by Rosalind Pritchard, Mark O'Hara, Clare Milsom, James Williams and Liviu Matei.
Description: Budapest ; New York : Central European University Press, 2019. | „This book brings together thirteen papers from the 40th annual forum of the European Association of Institutional Research (EAIR) hosted in August 2018 by the Central European University (CEU) in Budapest"— Introduction. | Includes bibliographical references and index.
Identifiers: LCCN 2019020885 | ISBN 9789633863275 | ISBN 9789633863282 (ebook)
Subjects: LCSH: Education, Higher—Europe—Congresses. | Education, Higher—United States—Congresses.
Classification: LCC LA628 .E95 2019 | DDC 378.4—dc23
LC record available at https://lccn.loc.gov/2019020885

Printed in Hungary

Table of Contents

List of Tables and Figures ix
List of Abbreviations xiii

Introduction
James Williams 1

THE HIGHER EDUCATION SYSTEM: THE 'THREE Cs'

Policies and Values

Chapter 1. Competition, Collaboration and Complementarity:
Higher Education Policies in Europe
Frank Ziegele and Lisa Mordhorst 11

Chapter 2. Current Challenges to Academic Freedom: Academic
Capitalism and Neo-nationalism
Sheila Slaughter 27

Institutional Identity and Ownership

Chapter 3. Investigating Organisational Identity in HEIs
Lise Degn 51

Chapter 4. Gender Imbalance in Higher Education: A Comparison
between Academic Positions, European Countries and Study Subjects
Caroline Friedhoff, Deborah Werner and John Roman 71

Rankings, Evaluation and their Impact on Academia

Chapter 5. Do Classifications and Rankings Improve or Damage
Institutions?
Victor M. H. Borden, Cynthia Cogswell and Fox Troilo 89

Chapter 6. National Evaluation Systems and Universities' Strategic
Capacities: Case Studies among European Universities
Laura Behrmann and Thorben Sembritzki 107

STUDENT EXPERIENCE AND 'THE THREE Cs'

Recruiting and Managing Students

Chapter 7. Searching for the Perfect Match: Evaluation of Personal
Statements Using a Multi-method Approach
Julia Zeeh, Karl Ledermüller and Michaela Kobler-Weiß 131

Chapter 8. 'Learning to Fly': Higher Education Students' and
Institutional Leaders' Perceptions of the Relevance of Institutional
Support Mechanisms in their Integration Process
Maria José Sá, Teresa Carvalho and Maria de Lourdes Machado-Taylor 151

Internationalisation and the Student

Chapter 9. The Perceived Impact of Intercultural Awareness on Peer
Interaction: Study of a UK University
*Ming Cheng, Olalekan Adeban Adekola, Gayle Pringle Barnes and
Linghui Tian* 169

Chapter 10. The Development of Intercultural Competencies During
a Stay Abroad: Does Cultural Distance Matter?
Joris Boonen, Ankie Hoefnagels and Mark Pluymaekers 185

Engaging Student Diversity

Chapter 11. Cultivating Voter Participation among First-generation College Students: The Relationship of Study Abroad Participation to Post-college Voting Behaviour
Radomir Ray Mitic 205

Encouraging Entrepreneurial Spirit among Students

Chapter 12. Developing Students' Innovation Capacities: A Comparison between US and Germany
Benjamin S. Selznick, Lini Zhang, Matthew J. Mayhew, Carolin Bock and Daniel Dilmetz 233

CONCLUSION: THE 'THREE CS' IN PRACTICE

Chapter 13. The Virtues of Cooperation, Complementarity and Competition in Higher Education in Time of Crisis
Liviu Matei 253

List of Contributors 267
Index 269

List of Tables

Table 4.1 Female graduates per 100 male graduates 78

Table 4.2 Average of gender balance indicator U-Multirank 2018 ... 83

Table 6.1 Comparison of NES 110

Table 6.2 Sample for case studies 114

Table 6.3 Impact of NES on organisational strategic capacities 122

Table 7.1 Most frequent signals and social strata 143

Table 10.1 Principal component analyses sub scales: Global Mind
Monitor 193

Table 10.2 Linear regression models 197

Table 11.1 Descriptive statistics of study variables 210

Table 11.2 Estimated general effects predicting study abroad 215

Table 11.3 Estimated general effects predicting post-college voting .. 217

Table 11.4 Estimated effects predicting post-college voting by first-
generation college student status 221

Table 12.1 Descriptive statistics of the sample 236

Table 12.2 Properties of measurement items 238

Table 12.3. Correlation matrix of model constructs 240

Table 12.4 SEM analysis results for US students 241

Table 12.5 SEM analysis results for German students 243

List of Figures

Figure 3.1 Proposed theoretical framework 63

Figure 4.1 Percentage of women by degree/position
(2011 and 2014) 77

Figure 4.2 Percentage of female students in U-Multirank subjects
2017/ 2018 80

Figure 4.3 Female graduates per field—as percent of all graduates
(2007 and 2012) 81

Figure 7.1 Most frequent words 137

Figure 7.2 Reduction to 35 signals 138

Figure 7.3 Most frequent signals 139

Figure 7.4 Linear model study success and signals 140

Figure 7.5 Comparison wordcloud of social strata and most frequent
words 142

Figure 7.6 Signals and social strata 145

Figure 7.7 Study success and social strata 147

Figure 10.1 Mean scores sum scales Wave 1 and Wave 2 194

Figure 10.2 Positive (significant) effects of cultural distance
(beta coefficients from multivariate regression models) 196

Figure 11.1 Proposed conceptual model on the effects of study
abroad on post-college civic engagement 208

Figure 12.1 Summary of SEM results from US data 245

Figure 12.2 Summary of SEM results from German data 246

List of Abbreviations

AAU   Association of American Universities

AAUP   American Association of University Professors

ACT   One of two popular standardised college entry examinations used in the United States. Originally represented an abbreviation of American College Testing but now just the initials are used. See SAT.

AERES   See HCERES

AKP   *Adalet ve Kalkinma Partisi*: Justice and Progress Party (Turkey)

ALEX   American Legislative Exchange Council

ARWU   Academic Ranking of World Universities produced by the Shanghai Consultancy

Big 10   Athletic Conference and general affiliation group consisting of 14 large, Midwestern and Atlantic Coast Universities (USA)

CCC   Competition, Collaboration and Complementarity

CCIHE   Carnegie Classification of Institutions of Higher Education

CEU   Central European University

CQ   Cultural Intelligence

EAIR   The European Higher Education Society

ECTS	European Credit Transfer and Accumulation System
EHEA	European Higher Education Area
EIGE	European Institute for Gender Equality
ELS	Educational Longitudinal Survey
ERT	European Round Table of Industrialists
ESF	European Social Fund
ETER	European Tertiary Education Register
EU	European Union
EUA	European University Association
FCT	Foundation for Science and Technology
FGCS	First-Generation College Student
FSU	Florida State University
GDP	Gross domestic product
GMAT	Graduate Management Admission Test
GPA	Grade-point average
HCERES	*Haut conseil d'évaluation de la recherche et de l'enseignement supérieur.* High Commission for the Evaluation of Research and of Higher Education (formerly AERES, France)
HE	Higher Education
HEFCE	Higher Education Funding Council for England
HEI	Higher Education Institution
HERD	Higher Education Research and Development
HOD	Head of Department
IRS	Internal Revenue Society
ISCED	International standard classification of education
IU	Indiana University (USA)
IUB	Indiana University Bloomington (USA)
IUPUI	Indiana University-Purdue University Indianapolis (USA)

IUSoM	Indiana University School of Medicine (USA)
KIT	Karlsruhe Institute of Technology
LOM	*Leistungsorientierte Mittelvergabe:* performance-related funding (Germany)
M.Ed.	Master of Education degree
MBA	Master of Business Administration
MOU	Memorandum of Understanding
MPQ	Multicultural Personality Questionnaire
NES	National Evaluation System
NGOs	Non-governmental organisations
Non-S&E	Non-Science and Engineering
NRW	North Rhine-Westphalia (Germany)
OECD	Organisation for Economic Co-operation and Development
OIR	Office of Institutional Research (Dartmouth College)
OSUN	Open Society University Network
PhD	Doctor of Philosophy
PiS	*Prawo i Sprawiedliwość*: Law and Justice Party (Poland)
QR	Quality-related Research
QS	Quacquarelli Symonds
R&D	Research and Development
R1	Research 1, reference to the 'Very High Research' category of the Carnegie Classification of Institutions of Higher Education
RAE	Research Assessment Exercise
REF	Research Excellence Framework
S&E	Science and Engineering
SAR	Scholars at Risk

SAT	One of two popular standardised college entry examinations used in the United States. At various times it was an abbreviation for Scholastic Aptitude Test and Scholastic Achievement Test, but is now referred to only by initials. See ACT.
STC	Scale enlargement, Task division and Concentration
STEM	Science, Technology, Engineering, Mathematics
UAS	University of Applied Science
UGA	University of Georgia (USA)
UK	United Kingdom
UNESCO	United Nations Educational, Scientific and Cultural Organisation
UOA	Unit of Assessment
US	United States
USNWR	US News & World Report
VBA	Visual Basic for Applications
WU	Vienna University of Economics and Business

Introduction

James Williams

This book brings together thirteen papers from the 40th annual Forum of the European Association of Institutional Research (EAIR) hosted in August 2018 by the Central European University (CEU) in Budapest. It is the fifth in a series of books drawn from the annual Forums of EAIR from 2013 onwards. The books are a valuable contribution to current debates on higher education because they highlight the important work presented at the conferences. EAIR has its origins in a shared interest in institutional research, an interdisciplinary field that aims at collecting, analysing and using data about higher education institutions to inform policy and practice. EAIR has provided the main arena for sharing experience of institutional research in a European context for four decades. The Association has proved remarkably persistent, having been established in 1979, and is still going strong. It has, admittedly, expanded its remit to become Europe's main conference for bringing together researchers and practitioners. The series of which this volume is a part, is designed to share the important work undertaken by members of the Association.

Each year, the EAIR Forum takes as its theme a contemporary challenge facing higher education, usually one that is close to the heart of the host institution. Holding the Forum at the Central European University was appropriate because it highlighted the very real challenges that higher education faces at the moment. It is currently being pulled in two directions: there is increasing competition between institutions and even between academics for both students and resources; at the same time, there is increasing expectation that institutions and stakeholders will act in a collaborative manner (Teixeira et al. 2014). At the same time, institutions try to, and are expected to be distinctive and have clear 'unique selling points', attempting to provide different approaches to research and teaching. This is part of a wider notion of complementarity in higher education and it is a notion that applies to law, social and natural sciences. The problem, however, is that institutions often tend to uniformity and mediocrity: institutional mission statements seldom differ to any great extent. The theme of the CEU forum was therefore the triad of inter-related, inter-connected and controversial features of higher education today: competition, collaboration and complementarity.

Contemporary higher education is characterised by competition at all levels as highlighted by Musselin in a recent article (2018). There is competition between institutions for all the key resources: students, both from home and abroad; staff; funding. Competition between institutions has found expression in an explosion of ranking systems, some of which appear to drive institutional improvement programmes as well as funding. There is competition within institutions and between departments for staff and funding. Between staff, there is competition for research funding; there is competition for resourcing of programmes and research. There is much criticism of competition in higher education on the basis that there are always losers in any competition which can lead to loss of jobs for individuals; closure of departments; even the collapse of universities. However, competition is not wholly viewed as a bad thing: it has been credited with improving productivity and forcing institutions to take the student experience more seriously than they had ever done before.

Collaboration is a well-established feature of much of the work of higher education. Collaboration can be between individuals and institutions. Collaborative research projects involve partners; teaching programmes often involve a team of academics; in some cases, the students are beginning to take a more engaged role as 'partners' in the academic endeavour. However, collaboration is not simply a potentially positive approach: it is now a political principle. At the European level, collaboration is the basis of all funded activity in higher education. Partnership is a fundamental principle of such programmes as Erasmus+. Collaboration is now part of the agenda of research councils.

Complementarity is a term that is used in a number of distinct contexts and as such needs careful definition. The broad dictionary definition is: 'a relationship in which two or more different things improve or emphasise each other's qualities.' (Oxford English Dictionary). In physics, the theory of complementarity is where two contrasted theories can explain a set of phenomena whereas individually, they can only explain some aspects of them. Complementarity in higher education can refer to a range of its characteristics. It can refer to the way in which universities bring together a range of expertise to strengthen their work in a particular field; it can be where institutions merge to create new, different institutions. Complementarity clearly owes much to a Hegelian view that the whole is more than the sum of its parts and it is perhaps rooted in systems theory. Arguably, too, complementarity can be seen as being core to peer review, one of the long-standing principles of higher education.

The chapters in this book range widely and reflect the perennial and contemporary issues discussed at the EAIR Forum in 2019. They cover issues such as university missions; ranking systems; intercultural awareness and attracting students internationally; student participation; institutional identity. The first part of the book focuses on the three Cs and broader aspects of the higher education system. The second part of the book focuses on students and staff and the impact of the three Cs on their experience.

The Higher Education System: The 'Three Cs'

This part of the book focuses on aspects of competition, collaboration and complementarity relating to the wider higher education system. In particular, it focuses on policies and values, identity and ownership, ranking and evaluation and its impact on academia.

POLICIES AND VALUES

The notion of the 'Three Cs' is discussed in the opening chapter by Frank Ziegele and Lisa Mordhorst. Their chapter, based on the CEU Forum keynote on the so-called 'Three Cs', argues that competition, collaboration and complementarity are highly interconnected and provide a valuable perspective on contemporary higher education policy and practice. Their analysis of the design and outcomes of higher education policies in national higher education systems in Europe suggests that each of the three Cs comes to dominate at different periods and in specific ways. They also argue that national policies tend to stimulate all three Cs at the same time but that they form transient configurations, owing to changes in policy and in institutional reactions to them. Ziegele and Mordhorst argue that national governments need to practise a careful instrumental design and the European Commission needs to balance potential negative effects of national policies.

One of the major negative effects of the three Cs on higher education, argues Sheila Slaughter, is a fundamental challenge to academic freedom. At the heart of this argument is that organisations funding academic activity threaten their independence and autonomy. At the same time, the new nationalisms are associated with a dislike of academic expertise and this sometimes leads to targeting and harassment of individual academics. Slaughter highlights the need to view academic freedom as a fragile and precious thing and argues that problematising it is perhaps the best way to protect it.

INSTITUTIONAL IDENTITY AND OWNERSHIP

At the heart of the discussion of the three Cs is a concern with identity and ownership of higher education. Lise Degn discusses the multifaceted dimensions of organisational identity in higher education institutions that are in a state of constant change. Caroline Friedhoff, Deborah Werner, and John Roman explore the extent of the continuing gender imbalance in European higher education. In their meta-analysis of three existing large-scale datasets, the authors find that fewer women than men study science and technology subjects, fewer women achieve higher positions in academia and fewer women are in positions to form higher education policy. Although the situation is slowly changing, the findings suggest that recent policy-initiatives are not very successful.

RANKINGS, EVALUATION AND THEIR IMPACT ON ACADEMIA

As competition between institutions intensifies, league tables and evaluation systems of various sorts have grown in number and influence. Although there is much debate about the efficacy of such ranking systems, few scholars have explored their impact on academia (Hazelkorn 2017; 2015). In this book, Victor Borden, Cynthia Cogswell and Fox Troilo address this gap by exploring the ways in which research universities in the United States respond to and manage classifications and rankings. The authors discuss how rankings influence HEI behaviour, leadership, and planning. They ask whether classification and ranking systems add value to or detract from the 'mission critical' activities of higher education institutions. In the succeeding chapter, Laura Behrmann and Thorben Sembritzki explore the impact of research evaluations on university governance. Reflecting the notion that academics and institutions respond in a spirit of 'dramaturgical' compliance to quality assurance (Barrow 1999), the authors argue that evaluations can help organisational 'actors' to operate strategically and that they foster the emergence of an organisational actorhood.

Student Experience and the 'Three Cs'

Part 2 focuses on what happens to students before, during and after their admission into higher education viewed through the lens of competition, collaboration and complementarity. Following a relatively chronological approach, the section begins with recruitment of students and the ways institutions manage them once they have arrived. It then moves on to explore issues relating to internationalisation. The chapter then explores issues relating to stakeholder diversity, particularly socio-economic inequality.

RECRUITING AND MANAGING STUDENTS

With intensified competition among higher education institutions, the recruitment of the 'best' students, as well as managing them once they have arrived, has become increasingly important. Two chapters in this volume reflect on ways in which institutions recruit students and manage them during their studies. Julia Zeeh, Karl Ledermüller and Michaela Kobler-Weiß focus on the recruitment process prior to admission and explore the relationship between different signals of social class and study success. Maria José Sá, Teresa Carvalho and Maria de Lourdes Machado-Taylor discuss the ways in which students are managed during their course and stress the importance of integrating students into the life of the institution. Higher education institutions, they argue, provide actions aimed at integrating their students, and have a wide range of services to support and monitor students' experience. They believe that the relationship between the students' traits and culture, and the institutional culture will determine the students' degree of integration, commitment and success.

INTERNATIONALISATION AND THE STUDENT

Higher education institutions are strongly investing in international exchange programmes and other internationalisation experiences that foster the development of intercultural competencies among students. In this volume, two chapters explore intercultural competencies from two different angles. Ming Cheng, Olalekan Adeban Adeko, Gayle Pringle Barnes and Linghui Tian explore the impact of intercultural awareness on students' interaction with their peers, taking as their case study a group of Chinese students and their peers from a range of different international backgrounds at a British university. The distinct experiences of these two groups of students offer invaluable insights into the challenges that students often encounter in a multicultural learning environment. Joris Boonen, Ankie Hoefnagels and Mark Pluymaekers explore the impact on students of study abroad programmes and the implications for institutions in preparing their students for such programmes. They find that students who have experienced a bigger cultural difference from their host country learnt more than those who had not.

ENGAGING STUDENT DIVERSITY

Higher education institutions have wrestled with the issue of diversity for many years and the debate still rages. Inclusivity is a key element of most political agendas regarding higher education. The European Union states that inclusivity is a key to higher education maintaining its competitiveness. For scholars such as Radomir Ray Mitic, inclusion of students from poorer socio-economic backgrounds has implications not only for higher education but for democratic development. In this volume, Mitic explores issues of democratisation and social class in the behaviour of first-generation students and argues that there is a link between having a study abroad experience and post-college voting behaviour.

ENCOURAGING ENTREPRENEURIAL SPIRIT AMONG STUDENTS

Higher education institutions are increasingly expected to prepare their students for employment after graduation, both as a result of students having to pay higher tuition fees and the development of a widespread 'entrepreneurship agenda' in the sector. This agenda has been an important part of the European Union's higher education vision since the development of the Lisbon Strategy and is a fundamental part of the Europe 2020 strategy. Entrepreneurship education is now a particular focus for many higher education institutions. Indeed, it has come under the purview of the quality assurance process in countries such as the United Kingdom since 2012. However, significant regional and institutional variations exist in the extent of such programmes, as highlighted in a much-quoted survey that was undertaken at the request of the European Commission in 2008 (NIRAS 2009). In this volume, Benjamin Selznick, Lini Zhang and Matt Mayhew tease out the relationship between education, personality and innovation. In a comparative analysis of US and German universities, they ask where innovators come from and what role universities can play in supporting innovators' beneficial connections to regional and national ecosystems.

The 'Three Cs' in Practice

The contributions to this volume provide varied perspectives on the 'three Cs'. The themes emerging from these chapters are drawn together by Liviu Matei in a concluding chapter that reviews the virtues of the three Cs in higher education. He focuses on the case of the Central European University (CEU) at a time when it has found itself at the centre of a fight for academic freedom and institutional autonomy in a context not unlike those discussed by Sheila Slaughter in this volume. The chapter highlights the political nature of the three Cs and their potential for interference from outside forces: however, it points to potential benefits of cooperation within higher education.

References

Barrow, Mark. 1999. 'Quality-management Systems and Dramaturgical Compliance'. *Quality in Higher Education* 5 (1): 27–36.

Hazelkorn, Ellen. 2017. *Rankings and Higher Education: Reframing Relationships within and between States.* Centre for Global Higher Education. Working paper no. 19 May 2017 (accessed on 3 July 2018).

Hazelkorn, Ellen. 2015. *Rankings and the Reshaping of Higher Education: The Battle for World-Class Excellence.* London: Palgrave Macmillan.

Musselin, Christine. 2018. 'New Forms of Competition in Higher Education'. *Socio-Economic Review* 16 (3): 657–683. Available at https://academic.oup.com/ser/article/16/3/657/5067568 (accessed 24 March 2019).

NIRAS. 2009. *Survey of Entrepreneurship Education in Higher Education in Europe.* Cambridge: NIRAS Consultants.

Teixeira, Pedro, Vera Rocha, Ricardo Biscaia, and Margardida F. Cardoso. 2014. 'Public and private higher education in Europe: competition, complementarity or worlds apart?' In *Knowledge, Diversity and Performance in European Higher Education: a Changing Landscape,* edited by Andrea Bonaccorsi, 84–106. Cheltenham and Camberley: Edward Elgar Publishing.

Turri, Matteo. 2014. 'The New Italian Agency for the Evaluation of the University System (ANVUR): a Need for Governance or Legitimacy?' *Quality in Higher Education* 20 (1): 64–82.

The Higher Education System:
The 'Three Cs'

Policies and Values

CHAPTER 1

Competition, Collaboration and Complementarity: Higher Education Policies in Europe

Frank Ziegele and Lisa Mordhorst

Megatrends such as globalisation or digitalisation have deeply influenced higher education policies in Europe during recent decades and led to many changes (de Boer et al. 2017, 1–28). Structural reforms but also smaller change programmes and the use of 'new' steering instruments in the context of new public management play a crucial role in government initiatives. According to de Boer et al. (ibid., 3) structural reforms can be defined as 'government-initiated or supported reforms aimed at affecting a significant part of the higher education system and its structure'. Higher education policies cause different parallel and interlinked dynamics. In this chapter, their design and outcomes in national higher education systems in Europe are analysed using the 'lenses' of *competition, collaboration and complementarity* (CCC). The main questions posed are, which national settings result from policies in terms of CCC? How are different instruments used? Which instruments can be used in order to foster which C? We suggest how to assess effects of the developments in CCC and reflect briefly on the role of the European Union (EU).

This chapter is organised as follows: first, we describe the drivers of CCC and their effects on higher education systems. Second, we use these three lenses to analyse what kind of settings result from policies combining CCC in higher education systems in Europe. Third, we depict which national policy instruments are used to influence CCC. Fourth, we describe and analyse the effects of the policy instruments and developments in CCC. Fifth, we outline the role of the EU in the CCC context.

Analytical Approach

This chapter is based on a keynote held at the 40th Annual EAIR Forum in 2018 at the Central European University. It refers to the conference theme 'Competition, Collaboration and Complementarity in Higher Education' (EAIR 2018) by using CCC as lenses through which to explore higher education policies in Europe.

Competition can be defined as 'a situation in which people or groups are trying to get something which not everyone can have' (Sinclair 1989, 185). In the current European higher education landscape, this notion plays a crucial role due to the expansion of higher education. For instance, in terms of funding—although new financial sources are constantly appearing—there are more higher education institutions who want a share of available funds or available human resources, thus creating a competitive environment for these resources (Deiaco, Gren and Melin 2009, 19). In the course of new public management reforms, governments foster competition among universities as an instrument targeted at efficiency and effectiveness (Hüther and Krücken 2016, 59).

Cooperation means 'to work closely together' (Sinclair 1989, 206). In the competitive context described above, collaboration may be one way for higher education institutions 'to lower the risk of missing out on resources' (Deiaco, Gren and Melin 2009, 19).

'Two or more different things are complementary if they form a complete or better unit when they are brought together' (Sinclair 1989, 186). Complementarity in a higher education system means that it 'incorporates a diverse group of institutions with different objectives, characteristics, and organisational structures' (Orange 2017, 91). Thus, higher education systems with a high level of complementarity are characterised by diverse institutional profiles, leading to '"horizontal" diversity' (Teichler 2007, 6). The term addresses differences in the missions and profiles of higher education institutions without any normative connotation (Teichler 2007; Ziegele 2013; Ziegele and van Vught 2018).

Our hypothesis is that competition, cooperation and complementarity can always be found to varying extents in higher education systems and serve as lenses to analyse the systems' situations and changing patterns. CCC are used as descriptors for governance configurations in higher education systems, but they will also turn out to be normative concepts of higher education policies. Forces in all three directions work simultaneously and their combination determines the system development. To understand these forces, we need to know the drivers of CCC.

Drivers of Competition, Collaboration, Complementarity

CCC are influenced by megatrends which are not bound to the higher education sector but do have strong influence on it. Relevant driving forces of this category are globalisation, digitalisation and global challenges such as climate change. Additionally, megatrends within the higher education systems play a crucial role. For instance, 'massification' leads to a diverse student body. Furthermore, a growing number of university activities have an impact on society or economy (and vice versa). This is often called 'Third Mission' (Roessler, Duong and Hachmeister 2015)[1]. Through a revue of literature on these trends, the effects they have on the CCC can be described in a simplified manner.

Since the 1990s globalisation has come to be seen as a major theme for higher education. Although universities were always embedded in the global environment, today they are more affected by circumstances beyond the campus and across national borders (Altbach 2016, 81). Globalisation has induced an increase in higher education competition (McKelvey and Holmén 2009, 1; Strike 2017, 3). Higher education institutions 'compete for students, staff and resources, be they material (financial) or symbolic (prestige). In the age of globalisation and knowledge societies, competition is imposed upon universities by external forces, including the markets, regulators and policy makers, funders and ranking agencies' (EAIR 2018). The increase in competition with universities abroad tends to reduce national competition, as on the national level for example universities see the need to merge in order to be prepared for the world 'market'. As mentioned above, a strategy for higher education institutions to survive in this context can be collaboration. In order to form an impactful cooperation in a globalised world, the size and quality of the critical mass needed to do so has shifted to higher levels. For instance, certain universities with a research profile need to build strong networks with other similarly strong

---

[1] 'Third Mission' can be seen as a new trend in some countries like Germany. Other countries, for instance Spain or the United Kingdom, have a long tradition of activities and policies in this field (Berthold, Meyer-Guckel and Rohe 2010; Newcastle University 2009, 43-47).

(foreign) research institutions in order to maintain their global impact. In terms of complementarity, globalisation causes segmentation of 'world-class universities' (Salmi 2009) which compete with other global players instead of competing with the institutions in their country.

The second megatrend to be addressed is digitalisation, especially in the context of teaching and learning. In the field of competition, it is important to note that digitalisation can make it easier to access higher education; it lowers the barriers to enter the higher education 'market' and increases the number of competitors. New formats of teaching based on learning software are leading to new ways of achieving university degrees. Digitalisation promotes new modes of collaboration, e.g., recognition of prior learning outcomes from online classes or joint investments of higher education institutions in learning infrastructure. Digitalisation also fosters complementarity by fuelling the emergence of new types of university profiles such as the open online university or the 'recognition university' only providing services in recognition and certification of competences instead of offering their own teaching. The latter does not exist yet but could possibly emerge considering the current trends (Dräger et al. 2017, 243–257).

Global challenges once more depict the need for interdisciplinary research (Luijten-Lub et al. 2005) and question how long we can continue to work and compete in administrative, research and teaching structures that are bound to disciplines. Joint international research efforts of different disciplines (cooperation), topic-oriented university profiles and research institutes (complementarity) such as the Eberswalde University of Sustainable Development (2018) or the GEOMAR Helmholtz Centre for Ocean Research Kiel (2019) already go beyond these categories.

Torben Schubert and Henning Kroll (2013, 6) show a positive impact of higher education institutions' regional activities on the GDP, on employment rates and the number of patents in a region. According to the so called 'new regionalism' economic competition is no longer pushed by national states, but rather by regions which need to be innovation-supportive. In this context Henke, Pasternack and Schmid (2017, 41) highlight the importance of higher education institutions for the region. It can be assumed that especially Third Mission activities are relevant in this regard since they focus on transfer. The transfer of ideas, knowledge and technologies from universities to society as well as the economy and vice versa fosters collaboration. Partners in society and economy become relevant, e.g., for research cooperation (ibid., 11–12). This trend also leads to higher specialisation of universities and different university profiles arising from regional engagement and transfer (complementarity) (ibid., 106).

The 'massification' of higher education has become the international normality and has increased the diversity of students (Altbach 2016, 44; Dräger et al. 2014). In some countries, for instance Germany, this has led to the emergence of a new private higher education sector especially in the field of universities of applied science (UAS). In Germany, it has contributed to competition between higher education and vocational training by 'academisation' (development of academic programmes in areas such as early childhood education which used to be completely covered by vocational training) (Wolter 2017, 100–105). However, it has also led to cooperation between universities, UAS and vocational training, to allow permeability of learning paths between institutions (Krone 2015; von Lojewski 2015). Furthermore, heterogeneous student needs require a well-differentiated, complementary higher education system with opportunities for students' choices and therefore emphasise horizontal diversity (Altbach, Reisberg and de Wit 2017, 9–13).

These examples demonstrate that global and common trends within higher education in general push all the CCCs forward at the same time. However, there are some more specific developments in higher education and research that could also have an impact. If for example funding mechanisms in research change from individual researchers' project funding to institutional funding of research excellence, the whole nature of competition for research funding changes. If technological change requires regular updates of skills in a lifelong learning process, new 'markets' for lifelong learning programmes emerge (with effects on complementarity through specialised institutions for further education and effects on competition between universities and further education providers). Many more examples could be added.

National governments take up the rationales from the global trend analysis to promote CCC and implement policies to foster CCC. General developments and government policies mostly reinforce each other. However, the national priorities and settings combining CCC show a large variation. Governments promote vertical differentiation and quality, reward excellence, create performance incentives, set 'market' rules, and listen to rankings, all of which emphasises competition. Governments strive for economies of scale, large units, critical masses, joint efforts, synergies, regional and stakeholder orientation and therefore promote collaboration. Governments create university typologies, want to avoid duplication, promote systems with diversity of tasks and profiles, require institutional strategies and promote horizontal diversity to foster complementarity.

National CCC Settings

Before analysing what kind of settings result from trends and policy interventions which combine CCC in higher education systems, a general remark on the effects of policies is necessary. As de Boer et al. (2017, 2–3) point out: '[G]oal achievement as the result of the reform initiatives is not to be taken for granted. [...] Evidently, system-level reform processes are complex due to multitudes of actors, interests, overlapping and potential conflicting political initiatives, path dependencies and "local" situations.' Furthermore, 'the unique nature of higher education and its institutions contributes to the challenge' (ibid., 2).

Germany provides an illustrative example of policy outcome at different phases of development. Up to the 1990s, regulated complementarity dominated. At this stage, the system of universities, UAS and non-university research institutions such as Max-Planck institutes were marked by a clear legal typology with different tasks, low competition and cooperation, as well as a high homogeneity within each sector.

Reforms starting in the 1990s (Hüther and Krücken 2016, 50–51), led to an increase in various forms of competition within and also between the complementary sectors of the system. Public formula funding and performance-oriented salaries were introduced in the university and UAS sector. Competition between universities and non-university research institutions for research funds emerged. Universities and UAS started to compete for students, due to financing policies with a money-follows-students-approach (Mayer and Ziegele 2009, 54–61).

At the beginning of the new century, a counterbalance to competition became stronger: cooperation within and between sectors with different purposes. Mergers even created hybrids such as the Karlsruhe Institute of Technology (KIT), arising from a merger between a university and a Helmholtz research institution (KIT 2019). Examples for collaboration are joint PhD-programmes between universities and UAS as well as regional alliances or excellence clusters between universities and non-university research institutions (Mayer and Ziegele 2009, 61–62).

In recent years, cooperation led to effects on complementarity and competition, as the following examples show. In this phase new sub-types of institutions emerged, universities and research institutions engaged in competition for new 'markets' and the competition within groups of institutions was reduced. The *Hochschulallianz für den Mittelstand* (2018) [Higher Education Alliance for Small and Medium Enterprises] and the excellence universities as part of the *Exzellenzinitiative* (Bundesministerium für Bildung und Forschung 2018a) [Excellence Initiative][2] are examples of new complementary subtypes of the older types, 'university' and 'university of applied sciences', which reduced competition within these groups on the national level. The international collaboration of universities changes the nature of global competition. Cooperation of former competitors can of course reduce competition, but it can also lead to new competitive constellations, as institutions are now able to enter 'markets' they could not access before, for instance 'markets' for international research funds.

The German example shows how CCCs work together and demonstrates that at different periods in time one or two of the three mechanisms could dominate in a specific way, leading in the next period to a shift in balances again. The three Cs happen at the same time and form a specific non-permanent configuration, as the trends influencing CCC and governmental policies continue to induce changes.

In other European countries, system changes are also motivated and determined by one or more of the three Cs. Some examples will be highlighted. Merger reforms play a crucial role in these cases and are classified here as a way of cooperation. These forms of reorganising higher education systems have been popular over the last decades (de Boer 2017, 4; Pruvot, Estermann and Mason 2015). 'The view that, by gaining mass, universities can find economies of scale and rationalise the use of resources, enabling them to function more cost-effectively, has been an important driver for merger and concentration processes' (ibid., 5). The dataset from the University Merger tool of the European University Association (EUA) which maps institutional mergers in the university sector across Europe shows that systematic and system-wide merger reforms are not common in all European countries (EUA 2018). For example, in the Czech Republic, Germany, Iceland, Italy, Poland, Portugal, and Slovakia, mergers are a rather isolated phenomenon. According to Pruvot, Estermann and Mason (2015, 16) mergers in England and Scotland too 'may be qualified as "isolated" in the sense that there is no political agenda on the topic'. The following examples will illustrate different types of 'system-wide restructuring processes' (ibid., 11).

---

[2] Now called *Exzellenzstrategie* [Excellence Strategy] with a slightly different approach (Bundesminsterium für Bildung und Forschung 2018b).

In the Netherlands, collaboration was intensified through a merger reform called 'Scale enlargement, Task division, and Concentration (STC)' (de Boer 2017, 1). The whole UAS sector was reorganised through that reform and larger entities were created by merging UAS. As a result, UAS reduced from 375 to 37 UAS between 1983 and 2015 (ibid.).

According to Pruvot, Estermann and Mason (2015, 11), Denmark introduced a government strategy and funding to stimulate mergers with the aim of preparing for global competition. This process was completed in 2007. The merger policy for universities and non-university research institutions was based on autonomous decisions of the institutions regarding the merger partners. Therefore, institutions chose partners from both sectors creating hybrids of universities and research institutions, but also mergers among universities (ibid.).

In Finland, the government stimulated local mergers within the university sector in order to foster international excellence, efficiency and autonomy (ibid., 11; EUA 2018). The university system was deeply reformed in 2010 through a new University Act, resulting in the number of universities being reduced from 20 to 14 (ibid.).

These three large-scale merger reforms represent fairly different outcomes of merger policies, which arise not only due to different national or local contexts but are also caused by varying approaches within a policy. While merger reforms might be a common approach in some countries 'diversity with regard to implementation and outcomes remains' (de Boer et al. 2017, 2). Although mergers are a form of cooperation, issues of competition and complementarity are also involved, and absorption plays a role in the example of Finland.

Two further specific examples of policy reforms related to CCC follow: in the Netherlands, strong competition led to an excellent and homogeneous university system in terms of profiles and performance. Since 2012 performance agreements with the ministry have been introduced to stimulate institutional profiling and strengthen complementarity. This attempt was partially successful (de Boer 2017; de Boer et al. 2015; Pruvot, Claeys-Kulik and Estermann 2015). In the United Kingdom the 1992 Higher Education Act led to a reduction of complementarity by assigning university status to all higher education institutions (Scott and Callender 2017, 123). However, complementarity was reintroduced completely bottom up by universities building alliances between institutions representing different profiles.

These cases reveal some insights and confirm some of the observations from the German example: national policies always create a mixture of CCCs. Political preferences for one or the other of the CCCs differ and change over time. Interventions regarding one C induce effects on others. Institutions react to policies and therefore have an effect on the CCCs too. The outcome is always a complex and differentiated structure. Good practice is required to ensure balances if serious problems are to be avoided. Strong movements in the direction of one of the CCC elements often induce counterbalancing trends afterwards. So, the systems may lurch around. Still a common observation is that policies always intend to increase CCC, we only find few interventions clearly targeted at CCC reduction.

National Policy Instruments Used to Influence the CCC

The previous section demonstrated the relevance of national policy instruments for the development of CCC. Now an overview of policy instruments and programmes which governments use to steer and promote CCC will be provided. The instruments are classified according to which category of CCC they are most likely to trigger.

In order to foster competition, performance-based public formula funding, 'market' simulation and regulation, competitive funding, excellence initiatives, transparency (including accreditation), rankings as well as performance-oriented salaries can all become the policy instruments of choice. If collaboration is to be induced, planned mergers or incentivised mergers, incentives for collaboration, target/performance agreements and legal settings for cooperation (e.g., joint degrees or PhDs) or public-private partnership funding can be helpful policy instruments. Complementarity can be triggered by sector consolidation processes (often supported by the advice from an expert group), target agreements, funding incentives for horizontal differentiation, classifications, legal regulation of institutional typologies and multidimensional performance measurement.

The example of competitive research funding stresses the specific arrangements with which governments implement policy tools. It needs 'fine tuning'. France implemented an excellence initiative called 'Investment for the Future' with research clusters and institutional strategies. This scheme was partly modelled on the German example. The German 'Excellence Initiative' was composed of graduate schools; research clusters including non-university research institutions; and institutional strategies. Competitive research funding in Norway and Poland also shows similarities. Both the 'Centres of Excellent Research' in Norway and the 'Leading

National Research Centres' in Poland feature clusters/ research consortia of smaller, sub-institutional entities such as laboratories. In Finland the 'Centres of Excellence in Research' are a new type of institution aiming to promote excellence. The Spanish 'Campus of International Excellence Programme' mainly promotes regional integration of universities. And finally, in the United Kingdom regular core funding is highly focused through the 'Research Excellence Framework' (European Commission 2009; Pruvot, Claeys-Kulik and Estermann 2015, 162–163). This means that in all these countries governments induce competition between institutions to achieve research excellence, at the same time triggering complementarity by creating a kind of 'elite' sector. In some countries this is strongly related to regional cooperation, in others to cross-sectoral collaboration. The details of implementation are highly diverse, leading to different CCC settings.

Summing up, extensive policy instruments and programmes exist. Some instruments can be used flexibly for different Cs, for instance target agreements. Others are clearly linked to a specific C, e.g., performance-based formula funding promotes competition. The design of instruments and programmes varies in detail, according to goals and national situations as is clear from the example of competitive funding of excellent research.

Effects of CCC Trends and Policies

There is no comprehensive analysis of the effects of CCC, so we have to focus on their potential impact. If CCC policies fulfilled their intentions, they would help governments to deal with the global trends mentioned above. A rational and well-reflected CCC policy would create dynamics and balances in higher education systems. However, there are also risks and potential problematic effects to be aware of; we have identified them as six in number:

1. Wrong instrumental design. One has to pay attention to implementation details. For example, state-controlled mergers, which are implemented with the aim of strengthening cooperation and complementarity, can cause unintended effects such as the absence of ownership and lack of real collaboration (Pritchard and Williamson 2008, 38–61). A counter-example is the Danish self-regulated example of mergers triggered by financial incentives which supports autonomy, ownership, strong internal reforms and effective cooperation. None

of the policy tools guarantees a positive and balanced development of CCC; this always depends on implementation and operationalisation of the instruments.

2. Erosion of basic funding. Funding incentives play a role for all CCC initiatives. If governments introduce targeted funding programmes they often redistribute money from the basic funding in order to generate a financial base for this. This has led to an erosion of core funding in many European countries.

3. Problems of big units. Big is not always beautiful. For instance, exaggerated mergers have to deal with the problems of big units in terms of comparability of cultures or going beyond critical masses.

4. Endangered university autonomy. After phases of dominance of one or two Cs, there is often a switch to the other C(s) in order to balance the system, but sometimes this goes too far. For instance, after phases of autonomy and competition, policies strengthening collaboration and complementarity sometimes largely restrict university autonomy. Also, the erosion of lump sum funding by the increase of specific funding programmes might endanger the autonomy of universities.

5. Reduction of national choice. A focus on international competition by more national cooperation and complementarity could reduce national choice, for instance by concentrating certain subjects in a specific region of the country to create critical mass. This could reduce accessibility to higher education for sedentary students.

6. Traditional excellence concept. It has a bias on competition and collaboration and is a merely research-focused notion of excellence, mergers, initiatives and league table rankings. It fosters a 'world-class' monoculture and the 'reputation race' (van Vught 2008, 151–174). The drift damages horizontal diversity and thus complementarity. It leads to the neglect of the university teaching and transfer function.

Thus, the CCCs have the potential to make higher education systems better, but also include substantial risks. Governments should have a balanced view of all university missions and should orientate CCC policies towards a vertical and horizontal diversity of higher education systems. Governments should see CCC policies as a top down and bottom up process, balancing policy intervention and self-regulation of higher education institutions. Policy instruments, which influence the CCC, need careful and detailed instrumental design.

The Role of the European Union

The EU could assume a variety of subsidiary functions to frame and support national CCC policies and already does so. The Bologna structure jointly created by the member states sets a framework for national CCC policies. The EU Commission supports national governments in finding appropriate solutions for their higher education systems using the 'open method of coordination', for instance by peer counselling. The 'European Universities Initiative' (EU Commission 2019) takes CCC to the transnational level. With an innovation focus on regional development the EU aims to counterbalance national CCC policies targeted exclusively at research excellence. Too much focus on vertical diversity is already amended by EU transparency initiatives which focus on horizontal diversity. For instance the European transparency tool U-Multirank (2018) is an instrument to promote complementarity and competition in a balanced way. It depicts performance indicators of universities and UAS, worldwide, in the fields of research, teaching and learning, internationalisation, regional engagement and knowledge transfer.

CCC is an interesting perspective on EU policies. The EU should take a complementary role in promoting it, since there is a need to support CCC balance on national and European level(s). The examples illustrate that steps in this direction have already been taken by the EU. This role could include stimulating frameworks, transnational upscaling of CCC by setting linkages and also taking into account already existing linkages between CCC on a transnational level, counterbalancing interventions and supporting national governments. Some open questions remain: is a European complementarity policy desirable? Do we need European mergers? The European University Initiative may stimulate an answer to the latter.

Summary

Analysing higher education policies in Europe through the lenses of CCC reveals some important aspects of current policy approaches. It is worth noting that CCC and therefore policies are pushed forward by common global trends within higher education. These tendencies and government policies mostly reinforce each other. However, the national priorities and settings, combining CCCs, show a large variation. Political preferences for the CCCs differ and change over time, although most governments address all three CCC elements. Sometimes this is intended but sometimes it is due to uncalculated (side) effects. The outcome is always a complex and, in most cases, differentiated higher education system structure.

Although policy effects are hard to calculate—due to varying national and local contexts, the specific nature of higher education institutions as well as the institutional reactions to reforms—instruments can be classified according to their main outcomes. Some tools can be used flexibly for different Cs, e.g., target agreements. Others are clearly linked to a specific C, for instance performance-based formula funding to promote competition. The design of instruments varies in detail, according to goals and national situations—as the examples of the excellence schemes and of merger policies demonstrates. Policy tools need careful and detailed instrumental design. The substantial risks described above should always be kept in mind. In order to promote differentiated higher education systems, CCC policies need to address vertical and horizontal diversity and balance policy intervention and self-regulation of higher education institutions.

The EU can support national governments in this regard by assuming a complementary role in promoting CCC, which includes for example stimulating frameworks, transnational upscaling of CCC, correcting interventions and supporting national governments. The question of the types and amounts of interventions needed will be a crucial topic for the next decades.

References

Altbach, Philip G. 2016. *Global Perspectives on Higher Education*. Baltimore: JHU Press.

Altbach, Philip G., Liz Reisberg, and Hans de Wit. 2017. 'Executive Summary'. In *Responding to Massification. Differentiation in Postsecondary Education Worldwide*, edited by Philip G. Altbach, Liz Reisberg and Hans de Wit, 9–13. Rotterdam: Sense Publishers.

Berthold, Christian, Volker Meyer-Guckel, and Wolfgang Rohe. 2010. *Mission Gesellschaft—Engagement und Selbstverständnis der Hochschulen. Ziele, Konzepte, internationale Praxis. Edition Stifterverband* (Mission society—dedication and self-concept of higher education institutions. goals, concepts, international practice). https://www.stifterverband.org/mission-gesellschaft.

Bundesministerium für Bildung und Forschung. 2018a. Exzellenzinitiative (Excellence Initiative). Accessed December 03, 2018. https://www.bmbf.de/de/die-exzellenzinitiative-staerkt-die-universitaere-spitzenforschung-1638.html.

Bundesministerium für Bildung und Forschung. 2018b. Exzellenzstrategie (Excellence Strategy). Accessed July 14, 2018. https://www.bmbf.de/de/die-exzellenz-strategie-3021.html.

De Boer, Harry. 2017. 'Higher Education Systems and Institutions. The Netherlands'. In *Encyclopedia of International Higher Education Systems and Institutions*, edited by Pedro Teixeira and Jung Cheol Shin. Dordrecht: Springer.

De Boer, Harry, Jon File, Jeroen Huisman, Marco Seeber, Martina Vukasovic, and Don F. Westerheijden. 2017. *Policy Analysis of Structural Reforms in Higher Education. Palgrave Studies in Global Higher Education.* Cham: Springer International Publishing. Doi: 10.1007/978-3-319-42237-4.

De Boer, Harry, Jon File, Jeroen Huisman, Marco Seeber, Martina Vukasovic, and Don F. Westerheijden. 2017. 'Structural Reform in European Higher Education: An Introduction'. In *Policy Analysis of Structural Reforms in Higher Education. Palgrave Studies in Global Higher Education*, edited by Harry de Boer, Jon File, Jeroen Huisman, Marco Seeber, Martina Vukasovic and Don F. Westerheijden, 1–28. Cham: Springer International Publishing. Doi: 10.1007/978-3-319-42237-4_1.

Deiaco, Enrico, Ana M. Gren, and Göran Melin. 2009. 'Exploring University Alliances and Comparable Academic Cooperation Structures'. In *Learning to Compete in European Universities. From Social Institution to Knowledge Business*, edited by Maureen McKelvey and Magnus Holmén, 19–47. UK: Edward Elgar Publishing Limited.

Dräger, Jörg, Frank Ziegele, Jan Thiemann, Ulrich Müller, Melanie Rischke, and Samira Khodaei Dolouei. 2014. *Hochschulbildung wird zum Normalfall - Ein gesellschaftlicher Wandel und seine Folgen* (Higher education is becoming the normality – a societal chance and its consequences). Gütersloh: CHE.

Dräger, Jörg, Julius-David Friedrich, Lisa Mordhorst, Ulrich Müller, and Ronny Röwert. 2017. 'Higher Education Institutions Need Strategies for the Digital Age'. In *Prospects and Future Tasks of Universities. Digitalization – Internationalization – Differentiation*, edited by Austrian Council for Research and Technology Development, 243–257. Vienna: Lit Verlag.

EAIR – The European Higher Education Society. 2018. 'Forum Theme: Competition, Collaboration & Complementarity in Higher Education.' Accessed November 6, 2018. https://www.eairweb.org/forum2018/2018-forum-theme/.

EUSD – Eberswalde University of Sustainable Development. 2018. 'HNE Eberswalde. Hochschule für nachhaltige Entwicklung' (University of Applied Science for Sustainable Development). Accessed November 29, 2018. https://www.hnee.de/en/Startseite/Eberswalde-University-for-Sustainable-Development-E1016.htm?0,760235

European Commission. 2019. 'European Universities Initiative'. Accessed January 16, 2019. https://ec.europa.eu/education/education-in-the-eu/european-education-area/european-universities-initiative_en

European Commission. 2009. 'CREST OMC working group report on mutual learning on approaches to improve the excellence of research in universities'. Accessed July 14. 2018. doi: 10.2777/34314.

European University Association (EUA). 2018. 'University Mergers in Europe'. Accessed July 6, 2018. http://www.university-mergers.eu/

GEOMAR Helmholtz Centre for Ocean Research Kiel. 2019. 'About GEOMAR'. Accessed February 1, 2019. https://www.geomar.de/en/centre/about-geomar/

Hochschulallianz für den Mittelstand e.V.. 2018. 'Hochschulallianz für den Mittelstand' (Alliance of higher education institutions for SME). Accessed December 3, 2018. http://www.hochschulallianz.de/ueber-uns.html

Henke, Justus, Peer Pasternack, and Sarah Schmid. 2017. *Mission, die Dritte. Die Vielfalt jenseits hochschulischer Forschung und Lehre: Konzept und Kommunikation der Third Mission* (Third Mission. The diversity beyond higher educational research and teaching: concept and communication of the Third Mission). Berlin: BWV Berliner Wissenschafts-Verlag GmbH.

Hüther, Otto, and Georg Krücken. 2016. *Hochschulen. Fragestellungen, Ergebnisse und Perspektiven der sozialwissenschaftlichen Hochschulforschung* (HEI. Questions, findings and perspectives of the social scientific higher education research). Wiesbaden: Springer Fachmedien.

Karlsruhe Institute of Technology – KIT (2019). *History.* Accessed February 5, 2019. https://www.kit.edu/kit/english/history.php

Krone, Sirikit. 2015. *Dual Studieren im Blick. Entstehungsbedingungen, Interessenlagen und Umsetzungserfahrungen in dualen Studiengängen* (Focusing on dual studies. Circumstances, interests and experiences of establishing dual study programs). Wiesbaden: Springer.

Luijten-Lub, Anneken, Marijk van der Wende, and Jeroen Huisman. 2005. 'On Cooperation and Competition: a Comparative Analysis of National Policies for Internationalisation of Higher Education in seven Western European Countries'. *Journal of Studies in International Education* 9: 147–163. http://journals.sagepub.com/doi/10.1177/1028315305276092.

McKelvey, Maureen, and Magnus Holmén. 2009. *Learning to Compete in European Universities. From Social Institution to Knowledge Business.* UK: Edward Elgar Publishing Limited.

Newcastle University. 2009. *Characterising modes of university engagement with wider society. A literature review and survey of best practice.* Newcastle upon Tyne: Newcastle University. https://talloiresnetwork.tufts.edu/wp-content/uploads/Characterisingmodesofuniversityengagementwithwidersociety.pdf.

Orange, Sophie. 2017. 'Democratization of Postsecondary Education in France: Diverse and Complementary Institutions'. In *Responding to Massification. Differentiation in Postsecondary Educations Worldwide*, edited by Philipp G. Altbach, Liz Reisberg and Hans de Wit, 91–99. Hamburg: Transnational University Leaders Council.

Pritchard, Rosalind, and Arthur Williamson. 2008. 'Long-Term Human Outcomes of a "Shotgun" Higher Education Marriage: An Anatomy of a Merger Two Decades Later'. In *Higher Education Management and Policy*, edited by the OECD. Vol. 20, No. 1: 38–61.

Pruvot, Enora Bennetot, Anna-Lena Claeys-Kulik, and Thomas Estermann. 2015. 'Strategies of Efficient Funding of Universities in Europe'. In *The European Higher Education Area: Between Critical Reflections and Future Policies*, edited by Adrian Curaj, Liviu Matei, Remus Pricopie, Jamil Salmi and Peter Scott, 153–168. Springer, 2015. doi: 10.1007/978-3-319-20877-0.

Pruvot, Enora Bennetot, Thomas Estermann, and Peter Mason. 2015. *DEFINE thematic report: University mergers in Europe.* Brussels: European University Association. https://eua.eu/resources/publications/363:define-thematic-report-university-mergers-in-europe.html

Roessler, Isabel, Sindy Duong, and Cort-Denis Hachmeister. 2015. *Welche Missionen haben Hochschulen? Third Mission als Leistung der Fachhochschulen für die und mit der Gesellschaft.* (What are the missions of HEIs? 'Third Mission' as an achievement of universities of applied science for and with the society). Gütersloh: CHE.

Salmi, Jamil. 2009. *The Challenge of Establishing World-Class Universities*. Washington: World Bank. https://openknowledge.worldbank.org/handle/10986/2600

Sinclair, John. 1989. *English Dictionary*. London: Collins.

Schubert, Torben, and Henning Kroll. 2013. *Endbericht zum Projekt 'Hochschulen als regionaler Wirtschaftsfaktor'*. (Final report for the project 'HEIs as regional economic factor'). Karlsruhe: Frauenhofer-Institut für System- und Innovationsforschung ISI.

Scott, Peter, and Claire Callender. 2017. 'United Kingdom: From Binary to Confusion'. In *Responding to Massification. Differentiation in Postsecondary Education Worldwide*, edited by Philip G. Altbach, Liz Reisberg and Hans de Wit, 141–152. Rotterdam: Sense Publishers.

Strike, Tony. 2017. 'Introduction. Macro-Level Competition and Collaboration'. In *Collaboration, Communities and Competition*, edited by Samuel Dent, Laura Lane and Tony Strike, 3–13. Rotterdam: Sense Publishers.

Teichler, Ulrich. 2007. *Higher Education Systems. Conceptual Frameworks, Comparative Perspectives, Empirical Findings*. Rotterdam: Sense Publishers.

U-Multirank. 2018. 'Universities Compared. Your Way'. Accessed November 30, 2018. https://www.umultirank.org/

van Vught, Frans. 2008. 'Mission Diversity and Reputation in Higher Education'. *Higher Education Policy*, 21(2): 151–174. https://doi.org/10.1057/hep.2008.5

von Lojewski, Ute. 2015. 'Erfolgsfaktoren der Kooperation Universität–Fachhochschulen. HWM - Jahrestagung "Der Streit um die Promotion"' (Success factors of cooperation between universities and universities of applied science. Annual conference of higher education and science management 'The argument about the doctoral degrees'). Presented at the annual conference of the University of Applied Science Osnabrück. https://www.hs-osnabrueck.de/fileadmin/HSOS/Studium/Studienangebot/Studiengaenge/Masterstudiengaenge/WiSo/Hochschul-und_Wissenschaftsmanagement/Kolloquium/12/von_Lojewski_Promotion_Erfolgsfaktoren_der_Kooperation.pdf

Wolter, Andrä. 2017. 'The Expansion and Structural Change of Postsecondary Education in Germany'. In *Responding to Massification. Differentiation in Postsecondary Education Worldwide*, edited by Philip G. Altbach, Liz Reisberg and Hans de Wit, 100–109. Rotterdam: Sense Publishers.

Ziegele, Frank, and Frans van Vught. 2018. 'Understanding Institutional Diversity'. In *Encyclopedia of International Higher Education Systems and Institutions*, edited by Pedro Teixeira and Jung Cheol Shin. Dordrecht: Springer. doi: https://doi.org/10.1007/978-94-017-9553-1_538-1

Ziegele, Frank. 2013. 'Classification of Higher Education Institutions: The European Case'. *Pensamiento Educativo. Revista de Investigación Educacional Latinoamericana* 50 (1): 76–95. Accessed December 3, 2018. doi:10.7764/PEL.50.1.2013.7

Ziegele, Frank, and Peter Mayer. 2009. 'Competition, Autonomy and New Thinking: Transformation of Higher Education in Federal Germany'. *Higher Education Management and Policy* 21 (2): 51–70. Accessed February 4, 2019.

CHAPTER 2

Current Challenges to Academic Freedom: Academic Capitalism and Neo-nationalism

Sheila Slaughter

Academic freedom in the US and the EU is surrounded by different histories, norms and legal scaffolding, yet professors in US and Europe would likely agree that at the minimum, academic freedom should include the right of faculty to follow research where it leads, to have their research judged by their peers, to have a strong voice in setting the curricula in their areas of expertise, to select and promote their colleagues, and to select and evaluate students. However, professors in many colleges and universities in the US and Europe find it difficult, if not impossible to realise fully this conception of academic freedom. Despite professors' hopes and struggles for academic freedom, history shows us that it is not an absolute, nor a human right, not even an academic privilege, but a construct developed by professors over centuries to protect their fragile autonomy from church, state, political parties, industrialists and financiers (Veblen 1918; Lazersfeld and Thielens 1958; Metzger 1969; Goldstein 1978; Schrecker 1986; Lewis 1988; Baez and Slaughter 2001; Slaughter 2011; LeRoy 2016). Academic freedom is always in the making, often honoured officially, yet undercut by the many organisations and institutions that now seek to profit from knowledge; or undermined by leaders and their followers who would reshape the higher learning to protect their power, policies and parties.

As in earlier eras, broad shifts in economics, politics and technology create new challenges for academic freedom. Although the challenges are many, the focus of this chapter is primarily on two: challenges created by intermediating organisations and by neo-nationalism. Intermediating organisations are non-profit foundations, think-tanks, and non-governmental organisations (NGOs) the members of which bring together elites from corporations, political parties, the state and universities to shape higher education policy. These come with very different social, political and economic agendas: some professors may esteem, like the McArthur Foundation which disperses genius grants to deserving faculty, and others may be viewed with opprobrium, such as Donors Trust which funds groups that lobby against climate science (Hickey 2013). Some intermediating organisations specifically work to uphold academic freedom. For example, the American Association of University Professors (AAUP) is a non-profit that seeks to protect academic freedom by investigating violations, engaging in dialogue with university administrators, submitting friends of the court briefs and sometimes lobbying the US congress. However, these intermediating organisations do not have deep pockets and usually cannot convene elites across sectors. Others have extensive resources, can bring elite leaders together to shape higher education policy, and in the process sometimes re-shape academic freedom. Examples are the Business-Higher Education Forums in both the US and the EU, which seek to bring about closer relations with business and higher education, and in the process may shift research in directions professors might not pursue of their own accord, thereby changing research agendas developed and promoted over many years by communities of scholars through their journals and associations. Still other intermediating organisations pose much greater challenges to academic freedom. These are far-right or 'dark money' family foundations that bring together wealthy conservative business leaders, leaders of universities, and sometimes politicians or leaders of state to reduce or redirect the influence of the intelligentsia, primarily as embodied by professors at elite universities. Examples are the family foundations of Scaifes, the Olins, and the Koch brothers in the US. Whether left, right, or centre intermediating organisations try to shape various types of policy by bringing their influence to bear on the state and social institutions, such as universities. Historically, foundations and non-profits were viewed positively, as charitable entities representing civil society. Presently, some foundations and non-profits with massive resources are engaging in activities that may be neither charitable nor representative of the citizenry, and these can present powerful new challenges to professors' academic freedom.

Neo-nationalism is the opposite side of the coin. Neo-nationalists are often unhappy with the global capitalism created by persons such as the Scaifes, Olins, and Kochs as well as more liberal globalist entrepreneurs. Neo-nationalists critique global institutions such as the United Nations, the World Trade Organisation, the International Monetary Fund, as well as supranational ones such as the EU for infringing upon national sovereignty. Often they see only some ethnic groups as deserving of full rights of citizenship or free college tuition. They are frequently against migration, for tighter borders, and increased militarisation. As in the past, neo-nationalists frequently view faculty with suspicion, seeing them as focused on global and liberal issues rather than on nationalist concerns. Neo-nationalists in some countries are targeting faculty who produce academic knowledge that challenges neo-nationalism, and faculty have been dismissed, harassed or subjected to other punishments, and universities closed, shattering beliefs that professors are entitled to even a modicum of academic freedom.

Background

The idealism of professors' shared beliefs about academic freedom in the EU and the US was captured by Merton's norms of science. Merton (1942) argued that the norms of faculty knowledge creation were characterised by communism, universalism, disinterest, and organised scepticism. By communism or communalism, Merton meant that ownership of scientific goods belonged to the scientific community because they depended on the work of scientists past as well as on current collaboration with others: thus, discoveries could not be considered as intellectual property held exclusively by individuals or their heirs, and the possibility of university ownership of Intellectual Property was not even considered. Universalism meant that science should be judged objectively, by impersonal criteria, such as competence. Writing on the eve of World War II, Merton was specifically concerned about the rising tide of nationalism, which he called ethnocentric particularism, and argued against making judgements on the basis of personal or social attributes of scientists or subjects because this violated the universalism essential to science. Disinterested knowledge meant that scientists acted for the benefit of the scientific community, not for personal gain. Organised scepticism was a habit of mind that led scientists to question everything, whether sacred or profane, and to subject their work to scrutiny and critique by their peers

Academic freedom defends the norms of science. Although these norms have come under a good deal of scrutiny and critique themselves (Anderson et al., 2010), they likely capture scholars' and professors' ideals of academic freedom, if not the reality, during World War II and the postwar period. As such they offer a benchmark by which to evaluate current conditions, understanding that norms are liminal and likely to change as institutions do. Changes in the norms of science became noticeable in the mid-1980s (Slaughter and Leslie 1997). Norms such as communism, disinterested science and related ideas of knowledge as a public good have shifted now that both individual scientists and universities share patents and profit from intellectual property. Universalism has been undercut by prefer-ences for markets in scientific knowledge that are external to the university and its scholarly and professional communities: like the global economy, university knowledge production is increasingly 'managed by the market' (Davis 2009) and is being monetised. Universalism has been challenged by ethnocentric particularism, which currently takes the shape of neo-nation-alism. The legitimacy of organised scepticism has been called into ques-tion as criteria other than evidence-based scientific judgment are increas-ingly used to inform consequential public policy decisions. Neo-nationalists often prefer ideology unchallenged by evidence. The legitimacy of organised scepticism has been undermined by the politicisation of knowledge.

Academic capitalism provides the theoretical background for ways that intermediating organisations work to accelerate universities' ties to markets. Concrete cases are analysed that shed light on the rise of interme-diating organisations, and special attention is paid to far right, dark money foundations and their implications for academic freedom. Theories of state formation, deformation and migration are used to understand the rise of neo-nationalism and its effects on academic freedom, again by analysis of specific cases. The cases are selected for their heuristic value to help problematise academic freedom, rather than to lead to predictive certainty about its future.

Intermediating Organisations

Neoliberalism (see Blyth 2002, Harvey 2005) and financialisation (Palley 2007, Eaton et al., 2016) are preconditions for the changing relations be-tween research universities and markets. These theories see policies de-veloped by elites, particularly elites in the financial sector, as normalising conceptions of the political economy that favour free global markets, sub-stantial government subsidies and contracting opportunities for capital, lower taxes for the wealthy, labour market flexibility, all of which contracts the parts of government serving the majority of voters and likely lowers wages for the citizenry as a whole. It stands Marx's labour theory of value on its head, instead seeing leaders of finance and industry as due special concessions because they produce value in the economy. These policies, ini-tiated in the 1980s, have been remarkably successful and have been accom-panied by the rise of finance as the dominant global industry (Davis 2009).

Many scholarly works explore faculty and university relations with the market, but very few are mechanism based. An exception is academic capitalism, which identified many mechanisms that move universities toward the market (Slaughter and Leslie 1997; Slaughter and Rhoades 2004; Slaughter and Cantwell 2012; Slaughter and Taylor 2016). However, time and space limitations led to focusing on a single mechanism: intermediating organisations.

INTERMEDIATING ORGANISATIONS IN THE US AND THE EU

Academic capitalism makes the case that in the US, beginning in the 1980s, a number of intermediating organisations—non-profit foundations and think-tanks—brought together state leaders, economic leaders, and universities to shape research policy that promoted entrepreneurial research to stimulate economic growth: for example, the Carnegie Commission on Science, Technology and Government; the Belfer Center for Science and International Affairs; the Brookings Institution; the American Enterprise Institute and the Council on Competitiveness, and the Business-Higher Education Forum (Slaughter and Rhoades 2005). These foundations and think tanks produced position papers and lobbied Congress to create Bayh-Dole type legislation, which allowed universities to hold patents on faculty research, as well as curricula and research for what came to be called knowledge economies (Slaughter 1990).

Similar organisations developed at the level of the EU. Beginning in the 1980s, groups of European political and business elites began to lobby and operate within European institutions to enact neoliberal policies and establish a discourse on European global competitiveness (Bieler and Morton 2001). For example, the European Round Table of Industrialists (ERT), a group composed of around 50 CEOs and chairmen from large European corporations convened to influence the European policy agenda. ERT lobbied heavily before and after the Treaty of Maastricht to establish EU-wide consensus for public institutions to aid the private sector in the efficient allocation of labour within the common European market (van Apeldoorn 2000). In February 2008, the European Union held the first meeting of a newly created Higher Education-Business Forum. The Forum brought together university administrators, European Commissioners, representatives from chambers of commerce, and business executives, to network and coordinate the activities of academia and industry for Europe's educational institutions to better serve the smart economy. In justifying the forum, European Commissioner Ján Figel' explained, 'Europe has been too weak for too long in bringing the worlds of university academia and business enterprise together, to achieve successful commercial exploitation of academic excellence' (Europa 2008).

Intermediating organisations span public, non-profit and for-profit sectors and have policy payoffs. The competitiveness narrative became so normalised that by 2009, the Obama White House could issue the following bulletin without any questions as to the implications for universities, science and technology, or academic freedom:

> Scientific discovery and technological innovation are major engines of increasing productivity and are indispensable for creating economic growth, safeguarding the environment, improving the health of the population and safeguarding our national security in the technology driven 21st century. To this end, the administration is already investing in: high-risk, high-payoff research; making permanent the Research and Experimentation tax credit; targeting investment in promising clean air technologies; improving health outcomes while lowering costs; and nurturing a scientifically literate population as well as a world-class, diverse science, technology, engineering and mathematics workforce (Orszag and Holdren 2009).

The same was the case in the EU. The oft-cited Lisbon Agenda aims were to make Europe the most competitive region in the world (European Commission 2000). Higher education was integral to the Lisbon Agenda which called for economic competitiveness through the interaction between the state, industry, and universities in networks of innovation driven by application and production of knowledge. Lisbon goals included expanding public and private funds for research and development, industry-university partnerships, establishing EU-wide networks of lifelong learning, and boosting tertiary participation, especially in science and technology fields. In 2006, the EC made the case that 'European universities have enormous potential, but this potential is not fully harnessed and put to work effectively to underpin Europe's drive for more growth and more jobs' (European Commission 2006, 3). In response, a nine-point plan for 'modernising' Europe's universities, which largely focused on further market reforms, was announced: (1) funds for increased researcher and student mobility; (2) new management systems for greater accountability; (3) incentives for academy-industry partnerships; (4) education programs geared to meet labour market demands; (5) funds for increased research and development funding and generation of external revenues; (6) encouragement of interdisciplinary research; (7) engagement in stakeholder dialogue; (8) reward of 'excellence' through differential pay; (9) plans for marketing the European research area through global initiatives.

While faculty were always involved with markets, historically they pursued market relations through associations of learned disciplines and professional associations, setting the rules for certification and evaluation of the bodies of knowledge for practising professionals, researchers, and graduates. Now the intermediating organisations discussed above often have a stronger voice than faculty in shaping faculty relations with markets, and frequently these relations are structured around economic development. The shift to academic capitalism has undercut norms of communalism and disinterested knowledge. Once proprietary knowledge becomes a preferential form of academic knowledge, faculty and universities often become invested in specific profit generating knowledge trajectories, making their pronouncements within these knowledge communities suspect.

David R. Johnson's study (2017) contrasted scientists involved in commercialisation with those who were not located at elite high patenting universities. His work illustrates what a preference for proprietary knowledge means. A well-known scientist who eschewed commercial work said the following about a professor successful with patents and commercialisation:

> Let me just give you an example that illustrates that there is not one hundred percent consensus about [commercialisation]. You know [Campbell] is the [technology] guy here. He brings in a lot of money. The tech transfer office loves him, and they take care of him. He is not young anymore, so a few years ago the tech transfer office decided that in case [he] were to croak off, we needed to have an expert in place here who knew [his technology]. The technology transfer office actually put up the money for us to hire a new professor, but the string attached to that money was that it had to be somebody who worked with [Campbell's technology]. People didn't like that. They didn't like the idea that the department would let its future direction be dictated by commercial needs. The new faculty member didn't exactly get a resounding majority. We hired him, but it was not something we did cheerfully or wholeheartedly (34).

Another very successful scientist who was nearing the end of his career had refused to engage in commercial activity, found himself unable to give up basic research, and was uncertain that he would be able to continue to get funding. However, he was unwilling to compromise.

I have a fairly pessimistic view from my own experience, and you know
it makes me [...] I'm not looking forward to retiring but this is one of
the reasons why I think that I might like to retire—that I see the kinds of
science that I love and am good at being choked off. So I'm pretty pessimistic, and at some point, it will be the thing that leads me to say, okay,
I'm turning off the lights in my lab (126).

Rather than supporting the academy as a public space for education, the
free flow of ideas, and curiosity driven research—all key components of
academic freedom—many intermediating groups intervened to redefine
state supported universities as engines of economic development, steering
funds to fields and disciplines deemed to have entrepreneurial capacity,
most often in STEM fields.

NEW FORMS OF INTERMEDIATING ORGANISATIONS IN THE US

A new form of intermediating organisation has emerged in the US. These
are 'dark money' foundations and think tanks that are tied to the rise of
the radical right. They were able to give millions upon millions of dollars to colleges and universities and professors that were anti-government,
anti-regulation, and saw the unfettered accumulation of private wealth as
the key to liberty (Mayer 2016). These foundations differ from those described above because they often operate through billionaire's personal
foundations that contribute money to universities without disclosing the
source of the funding. US tax law now allows families such as the Scaifes,
the Olins, and the Kochs to design large trusts that donate all net income
to non-profit charities for 20 years, after which the principal passes to the
offspring without any inheritance taxes. To illustrate, if your family set up
a $50 million dollar trust for you and each of your 4 siblings, together you
would have $250 million that you could use to set up 5 foundations, and
after 20 years, you could keep the principal ($50 million each), having
in the meantime spent the money, and the returns from the money, on
'charitable' causes that you thought worthy, such as funding economics
departments that promote free market ideology, or law schools that promote assessment of the economic impact of all laws. The only regulator
of these trusts are the states attorneys general and the Internal Revenue
Society (IRS) which rarely question the 'charitable' claims made by such
foundations.

Much of the money from these intermediating organisations was
directed toward achieving conservative political outcomes—for example,

the Scaife Foundation funded the American Legislative Exchange Council (ALEX) that wrote conservative legislation for state legislators and worked with them to get it passed. However, some foundations aimed their funding at colleges and universities, using a 'beachhead' strategy, whereby the radical right made a landing at elite college and universities to begin its war against what John Olin, president of the Olin Foundation and Cornell grad and trustee, 'regarded as campus[es] overrun by scholars with "definite left-wing attitudes and convictions"' (Mayer 2016, 100). Olin agreed with Friedreich Hayek, the radical right Austrian economist, that to conquer politics, one must first conquer the intellectuals. The Bradley Foundation agreed, and, in the words of one of its managers, 'the key…was to fund the conservative intelligentsia in such a way that it would not "raise questions about academic integrity"' (Mayer, 103). Rather than trying to buy a Chair or 'dictate a faculty appointment, both of which would "generate fierce controversy," [the manager] [...] suggested that conservative donors [should] look for like-minded faculty members whose influence could be enlarged by outside funding' (Mayer, 103).

Among the Olin Foundation's major successes were its Law and Economics program, which, according to Teles (2008) was 'the most successful intellectual movement in the law of the past thirty years, having rapidly moved from insurgency to hegemony' (3). Funders claimed that the Law and Economics did no more than support jurisprudence that took into account economic impacts of legislation. However, Law and Economics promoted free market ideology. According to Mayer:

> …the Olin Foundation spent $68 million underwriting its growth. Like an academic Johnny Appleseed, the Olin Foundation underwrote 83 percent of the costs for all Law and Economics programs in American law schools between the years of 1985 and 1989. Overall, it scattered more than $10 million to Harvard, $7 million to Yale and Chicago, and over $2 million to Columbia, Cornell, Georgetown, and the University of Virginia (107).

Olin's largest donation was $18 million to Harvard for the John M. Olin Center for Law, Economics, and Business at Harvard Law School, a donation happily accepted by Harvard President Derek Bok.

Over time, radical right foundations became less cautious in their approach to academe and demanded more in return for their money. Between 2001 and 2013, the Koch brothers' multiple foundation gave almost $70 million to US colleges and universities (Associated Press, 2018;

Strauss 2014). Generally, this money funded programs that promoted libertarian and free market ideology. Recently the foundations have begun to employ Memorandums of Understanding (MOU), as was the case at Florida State University and Clemson, that gave the Kochs influence over the hiring of professors and the development of curriculum (Jordan 2015). Details from the FSU MOU show that a three-member advisory board that the Koch Foundation helped select was responsible for hiring the professors supported by the grant. In response to criticism, the MOU was revised to have only a single Koch representative on the board, and the board no longer hired. However, the board decided after a professor was hired whether it would pay his or her salary (NPR 2018). George Mason University, which has received more than $34 million from the Kochs since 2011, has an MOU with the Kochs, but the campus community is unable to discover what is in it because GMU keeps these grants in an armslength private foundation. Students at some campuses that have received funding from the Koch brothers' foundations have started a movement called UnKoch my Campus.

The Olin Foundation and Koch Foundations are only a few of many that seek beachheads in colleges and universities. These foundations share strategies and approaches through conferences and radical right organisations. The challenges they pose to academic freedom are many. Radical right foundations are hardly disinterested when they fund programs and professors—they favour free market ideology and global capitalism. They have no problem with the monetisation of knowledge, and they seek to undermine professors' ability to be arbiters of sciences and professions, replacing professors whose primary allegiance is to their disciplines and fields with professors who have a preference for the market.

NEW FORMS OF INTERMEDIATING ORGANISATIONS IN EUROPE

The European 'third sector', refers to organisations that are neither state nor proprietary organisations; they are quite different to those in the US. The third sector developed later, gaining ground in the 1990s, and was primarily concerned with delivering or supplementing social services for various states. In marked contrast to the US, the third sector is usually closely governed by national laws and regulations, and Non-Governmental Organisations (NGOs) are often state funded. There are private foundations that focus on science, education and research—for example, the Wellcome Trust in the UK, the Robert Bosch Stiftung Foundation in Germany, and the Knut and Alice Wallenbergs Foundation in Sweden—but these do not usually receive large tax breaks and are often regulated by more than the tax authority. In Europe, the third sector is separate from the state, perhaps a source of innovation for social services, but not far from the state and not likely to attack the state in the way that far-right foundations do in the US.

The UK is the exception. Like the US, the most universities in the UK are exempt charities, and govern autonomously, subject to oversight by the Office for Students. This allows them greater freedom to restructure creatively to engage markets while preserving tax free status in some endeavours, such as education of foreign students (Wright 2016). Like the US, the UK has a number of think tanks that are charities: they receive donations and are tax-exempt. To date, the way they interact with universities has not been extensively documented. The majority of UK think tanks are very transparent or broadly transparent, and likely similar to the intermediating foundations in the US—Carnegie, Brookings, the Business-Higher Education Forum—that influenced higher education in the US in the 1990s. However, seven UK foundations were identified as 'highly opaque and deceptive' and are fuelled by dark money (unidentified donors from unidentified countries): four of the seven are charities, which means they are tax exempt (Transparify 2017, 7). In other words, the UK has the potential for think tanks to act like dark money foundations and think tanks in the US.

The challenges to academic freedom posed by far-right foundations in the US are many. Far-right foundations use money with the deliberate intent of re-shaping academic knowledge by funding professors who support their viewpoints. When they receive adverse publicity, they argue that they possess the right to use their funds to create a diverse campus climate. Few universities have turned down dark money gifts or gifts from family foundations, nor have professors been reluctant to take positions in departments and institutes funded by them. This means knowledge is both monetised in that market fundamentalism is promoted and politicised in that ideology is the test for support by these radical right intermediating organisations.

Neo-Nationalism and Academic Freedom

As shifts in the political economy create new challenges for academic freedom, so do changes in politics. When war, violence, immigration and ethnic conflict—and one often follows from the other—are at play for many nations, 'things fall apart; the centre cannot hold', as W.B. Yeats wrote about the wrenching birth of modern Ireland. In the aftermath of World War II, the initial impulse for EU was to end war in Europe, moving beyond nationalism to modern, rationalised, democratic societies based on individual achievement. However, nationalism has remained strong.

The theories that inform this chapter are based on the work of scholars who study state formation and migration (Nordman 1997, Wimmer and Schiller 2002; Wimmer 2013; Anderson 2006). Among the elements they see as giving rise to neo-nationalism are war or violence, followed by migration that leads elements within states where migrants flee to develop ideas about 'the [legitimate] people [...] as a group of obligatory solidarity, an extended family knit together by obligations of mutual support; and the people as an ethnic community knit together, undifferentiated by distinctions of honour and prestige, but united through a common destiny and shared culture' (Wimmer & Schiller 2002, 308). It is these people who own the state and deserve its services and rewards (Van Bruegan 2011–2012). The migrants are the 'other'. The 'sacralisation of the national territory' arising from nation-state formation linked together then leads to beliefs about 'the nation as a sanctuary that deserves to be defended by the blood of the people' (Nordman 1997). These ideas of peoplehood and the state create a tinder box easily ignited by immigrants crossing national borders or global entities that threaten national culture.

NEO-NATIONALISM IN EUROPE

Neo-national parties in Europe have proliferated, morphing from far-right to neo-national. The distinction is important. Eger and Valdez (2015) traced political parties and their platforms from the 1970s to the present in the EU and find that radical right parties once favoured free market ideology, reduction of state economic interventions in markets, small government, and neoliberal taxation. And some far-right parties still do. But others have shifted to become anti-immigrant, anti-EU parties that favour more social welfare for 'co-ethnics', but not for others. These are neo-nationalist parties. The variables that increased likelihood of voting for a neo-nationalist party between 2002–2010 were: anti-immigrant/anti-multiculturalist sentiment; beliefs in the importance of traditions/customs; a strong state that protects its citizens; support for welfare chauvinism; anti-EU enlargement. Variables that decreased the likelihood of voting for a neo-nationalist party were: trust in the European Parliament; caring about human rights; more years of education.

The problems neo-nationalism poses in Europe for academic freedom are familiar. During World War II, fascism did more than challenge academic freedom, it destroyed it (Ringer 1969). Rather than intermediating organisations—although these may play a part—it is the state and political parties that now challenge academic freedom. In most cases, political parties seeking to expand their hold on nation states approaching the brink of war, at war, or threatened by waves of immigration have tried to stop critique and dissent in academe on the part of both students and faculty. In many instances, it did not turn out well for dissenters, despite their invocation of academic freedom.

Recent challenges to academic freedom in the EU have occurred in Hungary, Poland and Turkey, an aspirant to EU membership. First, a word about the relationship between institutional autonomy and academic freedom. In a provocative article Matei and Iwinska (2018), both from the Central European University, make the case that institutional autonomy and academic freedom have had different policy trajectories in the European Higher Education Area from 1999–2000 to the present. The two should work together. Instead, Matei and Iwinska (2018) argue that the idea of institutional autonomy, as championed and defined by various European level groups and the European University Association, has had remarkable success, whereas academic freedom has been ignored by the European level groups and EUA, and has sometimes been treated regressively in the legislation of specific nations. Matei and Iwinska make the case that the idea of autonomy is defined by EAU's Autonomy Scorecard that measures organisational, financial, and staffing practices as well as academic autonomy, all with elaborate sub categories. These scholars argue that the epistemology of institutional autonomy, as inferred from European narratives touching upon it, makes a European wide model of autonomy necessary, that organisations such as the EUA are working to create it, and that this rendition of institutional autonomy invokes neoliberal policy narratives because its justifying purpose is to create policies and tools that will increase the efficiency of the university to deliver its mission or product. Steering is still accomplished by governments, but the language of rights and democracy is not used. In contrast, academic freedom is understood as the freedom for individual faculty and students to 'teach, study and pursue education and research without undue interference or restriction from law, institutional regulations or public pressure' (Beiler and Morton 2001, 349).

According to Matei and Iwinska (2018), there are no intermediating organisations in the European Higher Education Area that promote academic freedom as does the AAUP in the US, nor are there are any comprehensive registers of academic freedom cases. There are some organisations that attempt to publicise violations of academic freedom—such as Scholars at Risk, Free-to-Think, and the Academic Freedom Index. However, they do not speak for the academic profession or for specific countries, let alone for the EU as a whole.

Unsurprisingly, given the concern with institutional autonomy, the most recent highly publicised academic freedom cases in the EU involve institutions. All involve states with neo-nationalist leaders or strong neo-nationalist parties enacting or trying to enact legislation against universities. They are Hungary, Poland, and Turkey.

Viktor Orbán's Fidesz party espouses most of the neo-nationalist beliefs and attitudes described above. He has targeted liberal billionaire George Soros as using the CEU and his money to promote massive immigration from Africa, which he sees as threatening Hungarian people's customs and values. After a two-year legal battle with Orbán that ended when he refused to sign an agreement with the CEU in early December, 2018, CEU announced it would move its US accredited degree programs to Vienna the following September, although some Hungarian accredited courses will continue to be taught (Walker 2018).

The Lex CEU action was directed against the CEU, not against specific professors or students. However, it certainly challenges academic freedom as well as institutional autonomy in that professors and students will now lose the university that supported them. After Orbán's victory in the 2018 April elections, academics generally were put under more pressure. *Figyelő*, a pro government paper, published a list of 200 persons it accused of being Soros 'mercenaries', thirty of whom were academics at CEU. The government has also been funding nationalist research institutes, such as the Migration Research Institute, which produces studies that affirm many government positions. It created the László Gyula Institute, which may focus on a version of 'the people' at odds with that of most historians (Karath 2018).

Analysis of the situation in Turkey, a country that allegedly still aspires to full EU membership, again shows a neo-nationalist leader, or rather the neo-Ottomanist leader, Recep Tayyip Erdoğan, and his party, Adalet ve Kalkınma Partisi (AKP) that espouses Islamist cultural values, is suspicious of the EU, and is extremely socially conservative. Like other neo-nationalist leaders and parties, the AK is trying to consolidate state power and is deeply suspicious of higher education, professors and students. Scholars at Risk (SAR), a group funded by New York University and various foundations runs a monitoring project that concentrates on attacks on academic freedom at the individual level—professors and students—that include 'killings, violence, and disappearances; wrongful persecution and imprisonment; loss of positions and expulsion from study; improper travel restrictions; and other severe or systemic issues (including military closure or occupation of a campus)' (Free to Think 2017, 4). Turkey was singled out as an exceptional, ongoing case. In 2016, scholars who signed the Academic Petition for Peace in Turkey were investigated, detained, fired, and had their travel restricted. After the coup, over 7,000 academic and administrative personnel were targeted for firing, and hundreds of students dismissed. Almost 1000 professors, staff and students were detained or arrested, and warrants were issued for more than 300 others. Usually those at risk were accused of having connections with Fethullah Gulen, a Muslim cleric who resides in the US and is suspected by Erdoğan of masterminding the coup. The report goes on to detail specific charges and actions against various professors.

Poland is yet another case where another neo-nationalist leader, Andrzej Duda, and another neo-nationalist party, Law and Justice (PiS), is trying to consolidate state power by restoring national pride. According to Freedom House (2017), a human rights organisation, the PiS worked throughout 2017 to put pressure on Holocaust historians and to allow a stronger government voice in government institutions that deal with Polish history. The PiS wants to promote patriotic education that emphasises heroic and glorious episodes of history. It definitely does not want to remember Poland's participation in atrocities against Jews during World War II (Zerofsky 2018). President Duda started proceedings to strip a Princeton professor, Jan Gross, a historian of the holocaust, of the Order of Merit that he had received for his opposition to the Communist regime. Gross published *Neighbors* in 2001, which told the story of a small town in Poland that brutalised its Jewish population and then burned them alive. The government is also championing a law that will call for 5 years' imprisonment for anyone who blames Poland for Nazi or Stalinist atrocities.

Lest we think that neo-nationalist parties are confined to the former East or Africa, we need to remember that most European countries have these parties, and they are not fringe parties: Germany has Alternative fur Deutschland, which is anti-Islam and Eurosceptic; France, the National Front; Greece, the Golden Dawn; Austria, Freiheitiliche Partei Osterreich; Finland the True Finns; Sweden, the Sweden Democrats; Denmark, the Danish People's Party; the Netherlands, the Dutch Nationalists; and Italy, Lega Nord, a Neo-Fascist party (Chakelian 2017).

NEO-NATIONALISM IN THE US

In the US, as in Europe, neo-nationalism is familiar, known from the Red Scare, McCarthyism, the Vietnam War and post-9/11 (Goldstein 1978; Lewis 1988; Schrecker 2010; Heins 2013). Currently, Donald Trump and his 'base' are acting as neo-nationalists seeking to consolidate state power, sometimes through actions that challenge academic freedom. In contrast to the EU, the cases that have been most publicised are against individual professors. After 9/11, as in the EU, academic freedom cases were tied to neo-nationalism that stems from war, violence, the rise of anti-immigration sentiments, and in Trump's case, a call to make 'America great again', which evokes a past remembered as less multi-cultural and politically correct, as well as a search for security that depends on closed borders.

The first dismissal of a professor after 9/11 was that of Sami al-Arian at the University of South Florida. Al-Arian was a computer scientist and a Palestinian nationalist whose case was a test of the new powers associated with the US Patriot Act. He was accused of giving money to the Palestinian Islamic Jihad, which the US had categorised as a terrorist organisation. Al-Arian was tried and retried on many counts, held under house arrest from 2008–2014, and finally deported to Turkey in 2015 after pleading guilty to a single count of conspiracy related to donating money to Islamic Jihad (AAUP 2003; Schrecker 2010; Gerstein 2014). Al-Arian's case was a hot-button issue for Republicans and likely dragged on because they were invested in using it as a symbol of border insecurity and anti-Arab sentiment.

The Ward Churchill case at the University of Colorado-Boulder illustrated the way the state and the university, also a state entity, as well as the academic profession participated in Churchill's dismissal. After 9/11 Churchill, a professor of Ethnic Studies, wrote an article in which he argued that the attacks were blowback for American involvement in Iraq specifically, and the Middle East generally, and called those working in the World Trade Center technocratic 'little Eichmanns'. The university did not move against Churchill until the state, through regents and politicians, began to call for his dismissal, and for an investigation of his department, Ethnic Studies. The University of Colorado administration did not want to risk bringing dismissal charges against Churchill for fear of losing the case if it were cast as a free speech issue. Instead, the University brought controversial charges against him for research misconduct. Correctly constituted faculty committees found against him on the research misconduct issue after several split votes. Churchill was dismissed in 2007, and in turn, sued the University of Colorado, arguing he was not fired for research misconduct but for his article following 9/11. In 2009, a Denver jury awarded Churchill $1 million in damages, but a district court denied him the money. In 2010, Churchill appealed, and, after more appeals and counter-charges, in 2012 the Colorado Supreme Court upheld the University of Colorado's position, leaving Churchill with neither a monetary award nor an academic position. In 2013, the Supreme Court declined to hear the case (Schrecker 2010, Slaughter 2011).

In December 2017, in a special report of Committee A, the AAUP targeted the Trump administration for threatening academic freedom in two areas: international scientific exchange and climate science. The first was related to national security and economic (in)security, and the second to politicisation of knowledge linked to economic interests. An egregious violation of academic freedom stemmed from US accusations of espionage against a Chinese scientist. In 2015, Xiaoxing Xi, a naturalised US citizen and interim chair of the physics department at Temple University, was in his home when a dozen federal agents entered, guns drawn, with a warrant for his arrest. He was handcuffed in front of his family and taken away. He was an expert on superconducting thin films that are very useful in industrial processes and he was accused of industrial espionage based on information acquired by federal agents' search of emails to colleagues in China with whom he was collaborating. If the charges were substantiated, Xi could have spent eight years and prison and been fined $1 million. However, the charges proved unfounded and were dropped (Committee A, AAUP 2017).

Michael Mann, a Penn State professor of atmospheric physics who successfully made the case for climate change, was harassed continually by members of radical-right groups via the post, phone and email, even to the point of receiving a letter filled with white powder that was at first taken as anthrax. The Virginia Attorney General, together with the American Traditional Institute, a far-right foundation, sought Mann's Penn State emails relating to climate change on the grounds that they would show he distorted or changed evidence. After a lengthy legal fight, Mann was cleared of all charges against him. However, as the Climate Legal Defense Fund, which assisted in Mann's defence, noted, harassment can continue indefinitely. Recently, the Energy & Environment Legal Institute (aka American Traditional Institute, see above) demanded that two University of Arizona climate scientists release all their email correspondence with Mann for a six-year period (Wihbey 2014).

While these two cases were won with the help of various non-profit organisations and foundations, the toll they take on the involved scientists is great, and may discourage other scientists from engaging in areas of politicised science. And there are many more cases in progress. According to the Union of Concerned Scientists (2018), an intermediating organisation:

> A clear pattern has emerged over the first six months of the Trump presidency: multiple actions by his administration are eroding the ability of science, facts and evidence to inform policy decisions, leaving us more vulnerable to threats from public health and the environment. The Trump administration is attempting to delegitimise science, it is giving industries more ability to influence how and what science is used in policy making, and it is creating a hostile environment for federal agency scientists who serve the public (2).

The challenges neo-nationalism poses to academic freedom are great, and can have serious repercussions for faculty and students who challenge 'ethnocentric particularism', to use Merton's phrase. The repercussions can include jail time, deportation, and death. Although more abstract, the undercutting of scientific authority is equally consequential. Criteria other than evidence based scientific judgment are increasingly used to inform far-reaching public policy decisions. Neo-nationalists often prefer ideology unchallenged by evidence. In other words, the legitimacy of organised scepticism has been undermined by the politicisation of knowledge, and increasingly all knowledge is politicised.

Discussion

Academic capitalism analyses mechanisms that move universities toward competition for external resources which are often managed by markets. Analysed here were intermediating organisations, a specific mechanism through which this occurred. From the mid-1980s forward, some intermediating organisations worked to bring academe, industry and sometimes the state closer together to promote discovery that leads to technology and business innovation. Like other mechanisms (new circuits of knowledge, new narratives and discourses, new funding sources, expansion of managerial capacity within higher education) that support a shift toward academic capitalism, the agendas of the intermediating organisations discussed above, whether traditional types of foundations and think tanks (Carnegie, Brookings and the Business-Higher Education Forum) or new forms of intermediating organisations (new right, dark money foundations) see knowledge as raw material and promote the monetisation of knowledge. This creates challenges for academic freedom because multiple market-based actors are quite literally invested in academic knowledge production.

Theorists of neo-nationalism see war, violence and ensuing economic instability, often exacerbated by waves of migration, as leading to neo-nationalism. The resulting 'ethnocentric particularism', leads some groups within the state to claim ownership of its benefits and seeks to exclude others. In defence of 'the people' and its state, knowledge that critiques or contradicts the regime is attacked and 'alternative facts' are presented that justify the politics of those in power: knowledge is politicised. When professors or universities challenge politicised knowledge, they are sometimes fired, universities occasionally closed, and academic freedom ignored.

For analytic purposes, I separated academic capitalism, which looks at mechanisms that move universities and faculty toward the market, from neo-nationalism and politicisation of knowledge. However, the two are entwined. As the Mann case demonstrates, global corporate capitalism as represented by the fossil fuel industries seeks to delegitimise the great majority of academic scientists who present evidence of global warming by calling on a small number of academic scientists who disagree. Global oil and gas profits are then protected in the political arena by alleged disagreement among scientists. Economics and politics are never very far apart.

In the US, the AAUP and the courts are often regarded as guardians of academic freedom. The AAUP has sometimes made case that the Supreme Court has recognised academic freedom, but recently has acknowledged that rather than protecting academic freedom, the Court has at best used 'positive language' about academic freedom (AAUP 2018). Public universities, drawing on institutional autonomy, also present themselves as defenders of academic freedom. However, a recent, widely cited meta-analysis of academic freedom cases (LeRoy 2016) reveals that when faculty litigate against their universities about speech rights, universities win in almost three-quarters of the cases. When cases involve free speech, he concludes that 'First Amendment jurisprudence does not protect the most controversial ideas expressed by faculty in higher education' (42). Overall, he sees the courts as treating faculty less like a protected group and 'more like a government agency than a laboratory of experimentation' (44).

Similarly, Matei and Iwinska (2018) make the same case about the European Higher Education Area. They note that there is no codification of academic freedom such as that provided by the AAUP and no endorsement of academic freedom like that made by Association of American Universities and Colleges. There are international treaties that have provisions, usually without binding legal authority at the national level, but these have tried very few cases. Overall Matei and Iwinska make the case that since 1999–2000 there is more institutional autonomy and less academic freedom in the European Higher Education Area.

Faculty are presumed to be champions of academic freedom, but sometimes are not. Segments of the professoriate have embraced commercialisation, profiting from a percentage of patents owned by their universities, and are differentially and highly rewarded by their institutions (Slaughter and Rhoades 2004; Johnson 2017). Universities and professors have contributed to what Friedman (2018) calls 'everyday nationalism' when they present their countries as the source of civilisation and accepted knowledge, or take the state to be a given and not a problematic entity (Wimmer and Schiller 2002).

Conclusion

The Mertonian conception of the norms of science, defended by academic freedom, took knowledge to be a public good, essential to the health of a democratic society. These ideas are difficult to sustain now that knowledge has become rivalrous and monetised—the raw material of innovation—and politicised, so that the communities of academic scientists' claims to expertise are weakened if not delegitimated when political controversy arises. Challenges to academic freedom also have been exacerbated by the rapid growth of higher education in the EU and the US: the greater the numbers of institutions, the greater the number of faculty and students, the greater the potential for challenges to academic freedom. The higher order thinking skills acquired by those attending colleges and universities have contributed to a broad understanding that all knowledge can be monetised and that a new app can lead to a new industry, like ride sharing services or Amazon. When global corporate profit depends on universities, professors and colleges and departments are drawn into the whirlpool of conflict and contention about how the fruits of science are deployed, creating challenges for academic freedom. So too most college graduates know that all knowledge has a standpoint and thus potential for politicisation and observe daily how information and analyses, theories and hypotheses are deployed in power struggles among contending parties. Concepts like objectivity—always problematic—have been undermined. As indicated above, many groups of concerned scientists, and many organisations and research projects have spoken out against these challenges to academic freedom. However, the organisations and institutions that are supposed to protect academic freedom no longer seem to be able to do the job now that knowledge is central to economic growth and political success. Professors like you and me are divided about how our disciplines and professions should intersect the market and the political arena. I invite you to think with me about we might change this.

References

American Association of University Professors. 2018. Legal cases affecting academic speech. https://www.aaup.org/get-involved/issue-campaigns/speak-speak-out-protect-faculty-voice/legal-cases-affecting-academic.

American Association of University Professor. 2017. National security, the assault on science, and academic freedom. https://www.aaup.org/report/national-security-assault-science-and-academic-freedom.

American Association of University Professors. Committee A. 2003. Academic freedom and tenure: University of South Florida. Academe May–June. https://www.aaup.org/report/academic-freedom-and-tenure-university-south-florida

Anderson, Benedict. 2006. *Imagined Communities: Reflections on the Origin and Spread of Nationalism*. Revised edition. London & NY: Verso.

Anderson, Melissa S., Emily A. Ronning, Raymond De Vries, and Brian C. Martinson. 2010. 'Extending the Mertonian Norms: Scientists' Subscription to Norms of Research'. *Journal of Higher Education*. 81 (3): 366–393.

Baez, Benjamin, and Sheila Slaughter. 2001. 'Academic Freedom and Federal Courts in the 1990s: The Legitimation of the Conservative Entrepreneurial State'. In *Handbook of Theory and Research in Higher Education*, edited by John Smart and William Tierney, 73–118. Bronx, NY: Agathon Press.

Associated Press, 2018. 'Koch's University Donations bought influence in hiring, firing faculty'. New York Post. https://nypost.com/2018/05/01/kochs-university-donations-bought-influence-in-hiring-firing-faculty/

Bieler, Andreas, and A. Morton, ed. 2001. *Social Forces and the Making of the New Europe: Restructuring European Social Relations in the Global Political Economy*. Basingstoke, UK: Palgrave Macmillan.

Blythe, Mark. 2002. *Great Transformations: Economic Ideas and Institutional Change in the Twentieth Century*. Cambridge: Cambridge University Press.

Chakelian, Anoosh. 2017. 'Rise of the Nationalists: A Guide to Europe's Far Right Parties'. *New Statesman*. https://www.newstatesman.com/world/europe/2017/03/rise-nationalists-guide-europe-s-far-right-parties

Davis, Gerald F. 2009. *Managed by the Markets: How Finance Reshaped America*. Oxford: Oxford University Press

Eaton, Charlie, Jacob Habinek, Adam Goldstein, Cyrus Dioun, Daniela García Santibáñez Godoy, and Robert Osley-Thomas. 2016. 'The Financialization of US Higher Education'. *Socio-Economic Review* 14 (3): 507–535.

Eger, Maureen A., and Sarah Valdez. 2015. 'Neo-nationalism in Western Europe'. *European Sociological Review*, 31 (1): 115–130.

Europa. 2008, February 28. Commission organises forum to foster university–business cooperation (Press release IP/08/343) http://www.europa.eu/rapid/pressReleasesAction.do?reference=IP/08/343&format=HTML&aged=1&language=EN &guiLanguage=en. Accessed 16 February 2010

European Commission. 2000. Presidential Conclusions: Lisbon European Council 23 and 24 March 2000. *Resource document.* http://www.europarl.europa.eu/summits/lis1_en.htm. Accessed 20 May 2010.

European Commission. 2006. Delivering on the Modernization Agenda for Universities. *European Commission.* http://ec.europa.eu/education/policies/2010/lisbon_en.html. Accessed 17 May 2010

Free to think, 2017. Report of the Scholars at Risk Monitoring Project. *Scholars at Risk.* https://www.scholarsatrisk.org/resources/free-to-think-2017/. Special section on Turkey, 12–19.

Freedom House. 2017. Freedom of the Press 2017. Poland Profile. *Freedom House.* https://freedomhouse.org/report/freedom-press/2017/poland

Friedman, Jonathan Z. 2018. 'Everyday Nationalism and Elite Research Universities in the USA and England'. *Higher Education* 76 (2): 247–261.

Gerstein, Josh. 2014. 'Feds Drop Al-Arian Prosecution'. *Politico,* 2014 June 06. https://www.politico.com/story/2014/06/sami-al-arian-prosecution-108404?o+=1

Goldstein, Robert J. 1978. *Political Repression in Modern America, 1870 to the Present.* Cambridge, MA.: Schenkman.

Harvey, David. 2005. *A Brief History of Neoliberalism.* Oxford: Oxford University Press.

Heins, Marjorie. 2013. *Priests of Our Democracy: The Supreme Court, Academic Freedom, and the Anti-Communist Purge.* New York: New York University Press.

Hickey, Walter. 2013. 'Inside the Secretive Dark Money Organisations that's Keeping the Lights on for Conservative Groups'. *Business Insider.* https://www.businessinsider.com/donors-trust-capital-fund-conservative-dark-money-2013-2

Jordan, Kalin. 2015. Koch Funding of Universities is Shrouded in Secrecy. https://billmoyers.com/2015/04/24/koch-funding-universities-shrouded-secrecy/

Johnson, David R. 2017. *A Fractured Profession: Commercialization and Conflict in Academic Science.* Baltimore: Johns Hopkins University Press.

Karath, Kata. May 10, 2018. 'Hungarian Scientists are on Edge as Country is Poised to Force out Top University'. *Science* http://www.sciencemag.org/news/2018/05/hungarian-scientists-are-edge-country-poised-force-out-top-university

Lazersfeld, Paul F. and Wagner Thielens Jr. 1958. *The Academic Mind: Social Scientists in Times of Crisis.* Glencoe: Free Press.

LeRoy, Michael H. 2016. How Courts View Academic Freedom, 42 *J.C. & U.L.* 1

Lewis, Lionel. 1988. *Cold War on Campus: A Study of the Politics of Organisational Control.* New Brunswick, NJ: Transaction Press

Matei, Liviu, and Julia Iwinska. 2018. 'Diverging Paths? Institutional Autonomy and Academic Freedom in the European Higher Education Area'. In *European Higher Education Area: The Impact of Past and Future Policies,* edited by A. Cruaj et al., 345–368. https://doi.org/10.1007/983-3-319-77407-7_22

Mayer, Jane. 2016. *Dark Money: Hidden History of Billionaires and the Rise of the Radical Right.* NY: Doubleday.

Merton, Robert K. 1973 (1942). 'The Normative Structure of Science'. In *The Sociology of Science: Theoretical and Empirical Investigations,* by R.K. Merton, 267–281. Chicago: University of Chicago Press.

Metzger, Walter P. 1969. *The Development of Academic Freedom in the United States.* NY: Columbia University Press.

National Public Radio. 2018. Koch foundation criticized again for influencing Florida State. https://www.npr.org/2014/05/23/315080575/koch-foundation-criticized-again-for-influencing-florida-state

Nordman, Daniel. 1997. 'Des limites d'état aux frontières nationales'. In *Les lieux de mémoire: la nation,* vol. 1, edited by Pierre Nora, 1125–1146. Paris: Gallimard.

Orszag, Paul R., and John P. Holdren. 2009. *Memorandum for the Heads of Executive Departments: Science and Technology Priorities for the FY 2011 Budget.* Washington, D.C.: The White House.

Pally, Thomas I. 2007. *Financialization: What It Is and Why It Matters.* Washington, D.C.: The Levey Economic Institute and Economics for Democratic and Open Societies.

Ringer, Fritz K. 1969. *The Decline of the German Mandarins: The German Academic Community 1890–1933.* Cambridge, MA: Harvard University Press.

Scholars at Risk. 2017. *Free to think 2017* https://www.scholarsatrisk.org/resources/free-to-think-2017

Schrecker, Ellen W. 1986. *No Ivory Towers: McCarthyism and the Universities.* NY: Oxford University Press.

Schrecker, Ellen. 2010. *The Lost Soul of Higher Education: Corporatization, the Assault on Academic Freedom and the End of the American University.* NY & London: New Press.

Slaughter, Sheila. 1990. *The Higher Learning and High Technology: The Dynamics of Higher Education Policy Formation.* Albany: SUNY Press.

Slaughter, Sheila. 2011. 'Academic Freedom, Professional Autonomy, and the State'. In *The American Academic Profession: Changing Forms and Functions,* edited by Joseph Hermanowicz, 241–279. Baltimore: The Johns Hopkins University Press.

Slaughter, Sheila, and Brendan Cantwell. 2012. 'Transatlantic Moves to the Market: Academic Capitalism in the US & EU.' *Higher Education* 63 (5): 583–606.

Slaughter, Sheila, and Larry L. Leslie. 1997. *Academic Capitalism: Politics, Policies and the Entrepreneurial University.* Baltimore: Johns Hopkins University Press.

Slaughter, Sheila, and Gary Rhoades. 2004. *Academic Capitalism and the New Economy: Markets, State and Higher Education.* Baltimore: Johns Hopkins University Press.

Slaughter, Sheila, and Gary Rhoades. 2005. 'From endless frontier to basic science for use: Social contracts between science and society'. *Science, Technology and Human Values* 30 (4): 1–37.

Slaughter, Sheila, and B.J. Taylor, eds. 2016. *Higher Education, Stratification, and Workforce Development: Competitive Advantage in Europe, the US, and Canada.* Switzerland: Springer International Publishing.

Strauss, Valerie. 2014. 'How a Koch Foundation influenced a university economics department.' *Washington Post.* https://www.washingtonpost.com/news/answer-sheet/wp/2014/09/12/how-a-koch-foundation-influenced-a-university-economics-department/?utm_term=.9fb0b0b4cf61

Teles, Stephen M. 2008. *The Rise of the Conservative Legal Movement: The Battle for Control of the Law.* Princeton: Princeton University Press.

Union of Concerned Scientists. 2018. 'Abandoning Science Advice: One Year In, the Trump Administration is Sidelining Science Advisory Committees'. *The*

Union of concerned Scientists. Center for Science and Democracy. Washington, D.C. https://www.ucsusa.org/center-science-and-democracy/abandoning-science-advice-trump-administration-sidelines-advisory-committees#.XGBFt89Kj0d

Transparify. 2017. 'Think Tanks in the UK 2017: Transparency, Lobbying, and Fake News in Brexit Britain'. *Transparify*. Bristol, UK and Tbilisi, Georgia.

van Apeldoorn, Bert. 2000. 'Transnational Class Agency and European Governance: The Case of the European Round Table of Industrialists'. *New Political Economy* 5: 157–181.

Van Bruggen, Anne. 2011–12. 'The Rise of Dutch Neo-Nationalism: Analysis of Three Explanations for the Recent Upsurge in Nationalism Mobilization'. *The Yale Review of International Studies* 2 (1): 92–99.

Veblen, Thorstein. 1918. *A Memorandum on the Conduct of Universities by Business Men*. New York: Viking.

Walker, Shaun. 2018. 'Dark Day for Freedom: Soros Affiliated University Quits Hungary'. *The Guardian* https://www.theguardian.com/world/2018/dec/03/dark-day-freedom-george-soros-affiliated-central-european-university-quits-hungary

Wihbey, John. 2014. 'Strange Bedfellows…and Fear of Broad Impacts of Mann/UVa Court Ruling'. *Yale Climate Connections*. https://www.yaleclimateconnections.org/2014/02/strange-bedfellows-and-fear-of-broad-impacts-of-mann-uva-court-ruling/

Wimmer, Andreas. 2013. *Nationalism, State Formation, and Ethnic Exclusion in the Modern World*. NY: Cambridge University Press.

Wimmer, Andreas, and Nina Glick Schiller. 2002. 'Methodological nationalism and beyond: nation state building, nationalism and the social sciences'. *Global Networks* 2 (4): 301–334.

Wright, Susan. 2016. 'The Imaginators of English University Reform'. In *Higher Education, Stratification, and Workforce Development: Competitive Advantage in Europe, the US, and Canada* edited by Slaughter, S. and B.J. Taylor, 127–150. Cham: Springer International Publishing.

Zerofsky, Elisabeth. 2018. Is Poland Retreating from Democracy? *The New Yorker*. June https://www.newyorker.com/magazine/2018/07/30/is-poland-retreating-from-democracy

Institutional Identity and Ownership

CHAPTER 3

Investigating Organisational Identity in HEIs

Lise Degn

Introduction

Organisational identity has been a rising concept in the study of Higher Education Institutions (HEIs) for several years, not least due to the ever-lasting conundrum of change vs. stability in highly institutionalised organisations such as universities. Organisational identity is often understood and studied as the central, enduring and distinctive characteristics of an organisation, but in this chapter the aim is to refine this definition by treating organisational identity as processes of identification and sensemaking. Identification describes the process through which organisational members come to see themselves as belonging to a certain organisation, and are as such argued here to be processes of sensemaking: processes where individuals infuse their lives and actions with meaning, while building and maintaining their individual and social self. This chapter ties these concepts closer together and suggests an alternative framework for studying the formations of organisational identity in HEIs.

Organisational change is a recurring theme in studies of higher education institutions and one which also reaches beyond higher education studies and into wider organisational theory—although often with HEIs as the empirical base (Gioia and Thomas 1996; Elsbach and Kramer 1996). And exactly this focus on change in HEIs has also led to the interest in organisational identity. MacDonald (2013) claims that organisations articulate their identities in times of organisational change, and this connection between change and the importance of identities is echoed in many studies. Organisational change can be seen as the *antecedent* of identity construction, e.g., in merger processes where new, composite identities are introduced and negotiated. However, it may also be seen as the *consequence* of identity transformation, for example when the construed external image—

what organisation members believe that others think of their organisation—is deteriorating; this may lead to changes in organisational structures (Dutton and Dukerich 1991; Balmer 2008).

Despite this interest in the identity concept, particularly in studies of organisational change, literature on organisational identity is highly heterogeneous and conceptually disparate (Whetten 2006; He and Brown 2013; Gioia et al. 2013); it also tends to study organisational identity through vision and mission statements, strategic plans, and other organisational documents that are assumed to represent central identity claims (Seeber et al. 2017; Morphew et al. 2018; Strike and Labbe 2016).

In this chapter the aim is, as mentioned, to outline an approach which addresses organisational identity from a process perspective by conceptualizing it as an interactional process which plays out continually in organisations, rather than a strategic management tool or as an essential feature of an organisation. To do this, the chapter discusses how the study of organisational identity in HEIs could be strengthened by integrating more process-sensitive concepts such as identification and sensemaking. In doing this, an alternative framework for studying processes of 'organisational identity building' is suggested, using empirical examples from HEIs undergoing transformation. It is hoped that this will provide insight into how organisational identity is constructed in and through sensemaking processes within HEIs.

Background

Organisational identity has over the past decades become a central focus within organisational studies generally, often with higher education as a case study (Czarniawska and Wolff 1998; Elsbach and Kramer 1996; Gioia and Thomas 1996; Gioia et al. 2013). Organisational identity literature often builds upon the seminal work of Albert and Whetten (1985) which defines organisational identity as that which is *central, enduring* and *distinctive* about an organisation's character. Recognizing the difficulty in determining important concepts such as *centrality*, newer works on organisational identity have adopted a more dynamic understanding of the construct, namely what organisation members *perceive to be* central, enduring and distinctive about their organisation (Whetten 2006; Gioia, Schultz, and Corley 2000; Ravasi and Schultz 2006). Most of these approaches, however, to some extent neglect to explore or conceptualise how organisational identity may be constructed and translated from the bottom up—

that is, how organisational identity is made sense of and reshaped by organisational members, and how this influences the modes of action that are possible within an organisation. The present chapter argues that in order to understand how organisational identity is created and maintained, we need to explore how individuals infuse it with meaning and relate to such creations through identification processes. Organisational identification is understood here as the degree to which individuals describe themselves as belonging to a specific organisation and feel a sense of oneness with it (Haslam 2004).

The chapter thereby builds on the work of Stensaker (2015), He and Brown (2013), and others, attempting to build bridges across the literature on organisational identity and organisational identification (Humphreys and Brown 2002; Ashforth and Mael 1989, Dutton, Dukerich, and Harquail 1994), academic identity (Henkel 2005) and sensemaking (Weick 1995; Degn 2013; 2015). The aim is to disentangle (some of) the many dynamics of building organisational identity in changing HEIs.

In the following sections, the research approach will be outlined and the empirical studies which are used as examples in the unfolding of the framework will be introduced.

Subsequently, the challenges organisational identity literature face, as well as the usefulness of a new approach, are discussed. This approach is then introduced through a presentation of the sensemaking framework, and its connections with the identification concept. Finally, the possibilities and limitations of the approach are discussed.

Research Approach

In this chapter, insights from disparate literature on organisational identity and organisational identification, as well as theories of sensemaking and sensegiving, and social (and academic) identity, are drawn together in order to suggest a framework for investigating processes of building organisational identity and identification, through a sensemaking perspective.

The chapter—while being more conceptual than empirical—still highlights examples from previous empirical studies of sensemaking in higher education institutions. The examples are drawn from two qualitative studies primarily of teachers and researchers, but also of top- and middle level management. The examples stem from studies of Danish universities (see also Degn 2013; 2015; 2018), but the chapter is not meant as an in-depth national case study of organisational identity building. The examples serve to illuminate the potential of the suggested framework by highlighting how processes of sensemaking reshape and remould organisational narratives of identity in changing higher education institutions.

Organisational Identity in the Literature

As mentioned above, organisational identity literature (whether focused on organisations in general or HEIs specifically) tends to begin with the definition proposed by Albert and Whetten (1985), where organisational identity is seen as that which is *central, distinctive* and *enduring* about an organisation. As the concept and theorisation of organisational identity has gained importance over past decades, reviews of the literature have been conducted (Brown 2016; He and Brown 2013; Gioia et al. 2013), all highlighting the definitional pluralism in the literature. As He and Brown somewhat glumly state: 'While there are as yet no signs that interest in OI is declining, neither are there overwhelming grounds for optimism that definitional, ontological, epistemological or methodological disputes between scholars are likely to be resolved any time soon' (He and Brown 2013, 11). They arrive at this discouraging statement after categorising the organisational identity literature into four strands: functionalist (e.g., new institutional) approaches, social constructionist approaches, psychodynamic perspectives and postmodern (or non-standard) perspectives on organisational identity. These perspectives in some way represent a continuum: from realist approaches where identity is seen as a feature of organisations which may be studied via its representation in artefacts, for example, to anti-realist approaches where identity is studied as an illusion or an image of the organisation, captured via discourse or narratives. Glynn (2008) similarly describes two traditions—the *essentialist* and *strategic*—which refer to two different ways of approaching organisational identity. The key difference, according to Glynn, is that scholars tend to see organisational identity as something inherent to the organisation (essentialist) or as something which is attributed to the organisation and therefore subject to strategic 'manipulation' (strategic). Brunninge (2005) mentions that these diverse approaches, which all have their starting point in the same definition, namely the one put forth by Albert and Whetten, might be due to a misinterpretation and mis-citing of the original work, but another explanation might also simply be varying ontological conceptions and standpoints.

These categorisations, however, highlight the challenges to working with organisational identity, as they clearly illustrate how underspecification of the central concept, namely identity, may lead to disparate approaches to studying it. In other words, if scholars do not agree on whether identity is a metaphor or a real organisational feature, then it is hard to claim that they are indeed studying the same phenomenon.

In HE literature, the conceptual disparity also prevails, and even a brief search for organisational identity studies in a few established higher education journals confirms the picture of highly diverse conceptualisations of the core concept, e.g., defining it as: 'the perception among organisational stakeholders that their membership in a given organisation defines themselves and their beliefs' (Bastedo, Samuels, and Kleinman 2014) as narratives aimed at gaining (or maintaining) legitimacy, while optimally balancing 'similarity for legitimacy and competitive differentiation' (Seeber et al. 2017); or inspired by systems theory, as the 'joint construct of its self-observation and self-description' (Lenartowicz 2015).

However, in this, still burgeoning, literature on organisational identity in HEIs, we also see attempts to address this disparity and build bridges between various kinds of literature. Some of the recent studies of organisational identity, in this way, address the disparity and suggest new ways of approaching organisational identity, e.g., by focusing on the central activities in higher education and their links to organisational identity (Stensaker 2015) or by addressing factors affecting identity narratives seen as symbolic representations of the organisation (Seeber et al. 2017). The present chapter builds on these studies, and elaborates on them by defining organisational identity as *both* an antecedent of identification and as an artefact of the very same identification. Organisational identity within this definition thus becomes visible through the identification processes, and is not seen as something which is static enough to define solely through organisational documents or other formal identity claims.

The Challenges and the Need for Another Approach

There are thereby good reasons to turn identity studies on their head. As mentioned in the introduction, HEIs and HE systems in general are facing substantial challenges, and the competition between HEIs is now stronger than ever. So in times of an increasingly accelerated academy (Vostal 2016) and the rise of an academic 'precariate', it is crucial to increase our knowledge of how organisational identity is formed—that is, how understandings of centrality, distinctiveness and continuality are selected and moulded inside the HEIs.

The suggested approach that will be outlined and discussed in the remainder of the chapter thus rests on two assumptions; 1) that we need to embrace the assertion made by Albert and colleagues almost two decades ago that: 'Increasingly, an organisation must reside in the heads and hearts of its members' (Albert, Ashforth, and Dutton 2000), and 2) that we must also be aware that claims about organisational identity are also purposefully designed by top level management, or imposed from the outside-in.

In order to build bridges between these two assumptions, the mechanisms of *identification* and *sensemaking* are in the following sections linked closer to the identity concept.

Organisational Identification

First, let us explore identification as a process of organisational identity building. Organisational identification is often described in the literature as the sense of belonging that members feel towards their organisation, a conceptualisation mainly stemming from social identity theory (Ashforth and Mael 1989). The overall argument of social identity theory is that any individual's identity is a dual construct: 'the self-concept is comprised of a personal identity encompassing idiosyncratic characteristics (e.g., bodily attributes, abilities, psychological traits, interests) and a social identity encompassing salient group classifications' (Ashforth and Mael 1989, 21). The organisation, within which you work, then provides you with a readily available classification to identify with. However, as the definition above indicates, a social identity comprises various sources of identification, that is, not only the organisational. This also means that organisational identification is not an automatic process which comes with organisational membership. As several studies have pointed out, members may dis-identify or partially identify with the organisation with which they are associated without actually leaving this organisation (Humphreys and Brown 2016; Degn 2018). Moreover, as Henkel has already noted, an HEI 'has more power to affect academic working lives, but it may be a weaker source of identification' (Henkel 2005, 164), not least due to internal differentiation in HEIs. In HEIs, other salient group classifications may thus be at play, most notably the disciplinary communities or professional groups that may not be delimited to the department. Other HE scholars (El-Khawas 2008; Moscati 2008) have pointed out the importance of these sources of identification, but the dynamics and actual workings of these identifications are rarely studied empirically.

The work of Hekman and colleagues (2009) represents a notable exception, as they studied medical doctors (a professional group which can in many ways be compared to academics in HEIs) and their behaviour in small-scale organisational change processes. The study indicated that the degree of organisational identification and strength of professional identity affect organisational behaviour and social exchange in more intricate ways than expected.

A key finding, which is quite relevant for HE scholars interested in organisational change processes, is that doctors who demonstrated high organisational identification and lower professional identification tended to perform higher, even when the organisation did not act supportively. Conversely, low performance was demonstrated by those who identified mainly with their profession (and less with the organisation)—even when the organisation acted in a supporting manner (Hekman et al. 2009). Transferred to HE, this finding suggests that academics who identify primarily with their 'professional group' (their peers) and less so with their organisation (the HEI) may not respond with higher performance, measured on whatever scale, even when the organisation supports them, as social exchange theory (Cook et al. 2013) would otherwise suggest.

A key point made by He and Brown (2013) supports this focus on identification, namely that while perceived organisational identity attributes may influence organisational identification, so do relational and interactional factors. Therefore, instead of attempting to change identity claims to enhance identification, organisations might benefit more from changing leadership styles and other cultural mechanisms. This is particularly relevant for organisations such as HEIs, where leadership has come to play a more significant role in formal organisational processes, but where strategy, performance and other classic managerial terms tend to be regarded with suspicion.

An example of this can be found in a recent, small-scale study (Degn 2018), where the relational identification with top- and middle-level management emerged as a key component in the analysis of how academic employees responded to change processes. This study indicated that middle level leaders (department heads) were often protected from negative classification by the academic staff, by framing them as 'one of us', 'not a real manager' or a 'manager like in the old days' (Degn 2018). Negative identification, however, was a clear pattern when looking at the relation between academics and top-level leaders, and as the quote below indicates, this was seen to affect academic work and motivation:

> ... the further you get up to that political level, the Dean's level, there you have the feeling that they simply have no sense of what we are doing.

And they have no respect for it, and that's what makes you tired right?
And demotivated... (Excerpt from focus group interview) (Degn 2018)

Identification processes, then, can be seen to affect the *reception* of an attempt to change identity. To return to the basic assumptions of this chapter, the way from the formal identity claims to the heads and hearts of the organisation members is enacted through identification processes.

However, most literature on organisational identification focuses on antecedents and outcomes of identification, but qualitative explorations of processes are rarer. To present a framework for analysing identification as it plays out in HEIs, the concepts of sensemaking and sensegiving will now be introduced.

Sensemaking and Sensegiving

Sensemaking, as it is unfolded by Weick (1995; Weick, Sutcliffe, and Obstfeld 2005); and Helms-Mills (Helms Mills, Thurlow, and Mills 2010; Helms-Mills 2003), is a concept which describes how members of organisations continually work to infuse their organised life with meaning, and how these processes of making meaning are affected by perceptions of identity. The fundamental thesis is that individuals create meaning continuously, through the ongoing selection of cues. The sensemaker selects salient cues from the vast mass of available information, and processes these cues by connecting them to a frame, or what Weick (1995) calls 'past moments of socialization'. It is this basic operation of connecting a cue to a frame, which creates meaning. A central point is that these processes of constructing meaning are guided by identity-needs (Erez and Earley 1993) such as the need for self-enhancement or self-efficacy. These needs direct one's attention towards cues that support feelings of self-efficacy, for example, and mask other cues (events, characteristics etc.) that do not support such feelings.

In this way, sensemaking concerns the formation of identity in relation to the social world and describes some of the mechanisms involved in this formation. Sensemaking may then also be seen as the continual formation of collective, or organisational, identity, because the individual, through sensemaking, enacts a certain perception of the world, which becomes the basis of future sensemaking and action. In plainer words: the perceptions of who I am, and the social categories I belong to, affect the options I believe I have, and thus my actions. These actions and perceptions then become the frames of reference in future sensemaking. It is thereby a process of creating stories out of a flux of, sometimes contradictory, input which allows for continuous action.

Sensegiving, which describes the more intentional side of sensemaking, is defined by Gioia and Chittipeddi (1991) in yet another study of an HEI going through change processes, as being: 'concerned with the process of attempting to influence the sensemaking and meaning construction of others toward (sic) a preferred redefinition of organisational reality' (442). This may then, in the terminology of the present framework be seen as the formal identity claims, or the organisational identity which is put forward in formal documents from the HEI, and may then serve as a frame for ensuing sensemaking processes—or not.

Though the sensemaking perspective/concept has been used to study organisational/organised behaviour for many years, it is rarely linked firmly with other aspects of organisational theory, such as organisational identity or identification. One might find this odd, as sensemaking is in essence about identity construction and organisation, and conversely, identity and organisation studies are essentially about meaning (Glynn 2008). As described above, however, organisational identity scholars have been occupied with studying formal identity claims, whereas the formation of identity has been somewhat neglected (Gioia et al. 2010).

The sensemaking framework nevertheless has great potential for investigating how organisational change is navigated inside the HEI and the impact this has on academic work and performance. To highlight this potential, let us explore a few studies of sensemaking in HEIs and consider what they may contribute to the framework for studying the formation of organisational identity and identification in HEIs.

In a study of a radical organisational change process in a single HEI, Degn and colleagues demonstrated how sensegiving attempts of top-level management were navigated and imbued with sense at departmental level (Degn, Nielsen, and Smith 2016). The study illustrated that sensegiving attempts were perceived by middle management and academics as threatening to the established—yet somewhat ill defined—sense of identity, and that this sensegiving was seen as more threatening than external, more abstract, notions of competition such as New Public Management ideas. The study concluded that the formal identity claims put forth by top-level management, as part of a large scale organisational change process, could be seen as an attempt to maintain a single, authoritative organisational identity, whereas the sensemaking processes at departmental level revealed a more diversifying identity construction process, where multiple identities were maintained. This would in other words seem to support the traditionally dominant idea of the university as a loosely coupled organisation (Weick 1976; Bleiklie and Kogan 2007): an organisation consisting of smaller, independent units, which are mutually responsive, but each unit still 'preserves its own identity and some evidence of its physical or logical separateness' (Weick 1976, 3). In light of the identification perspective described above, we may interpret this as an example of dis-identification, where the organisation members reject the formal identity claims proposed by the top-level management. However, more importantly, by looking at it as a process of sensemaking, we see more clearly some of the mechanisms behind this type of dis-identification. In other words, by looking through a sensemaking lens, we may detect *why* organisation members dis-identify, or may discern the more precise 'nature' of this dis-identification. In the study in question, organisation members' feelings of self-efficacy were threatened by a perceived lack of recognition of professional knowledge:

> But maybe that was also some of the frustration: it seemed like they didn't want to use the competences that were present in the system [...] Why don't you ask, if you are at a university, where there are people with primary competences within organisation and management, why don't you ask these people? (Interview with Former Department head, Business School) (Degn, Nielsen, and Smith 2016)

The same connection between sensemaking dynamics and organisational identification was seen in another study of change processes in Danish HEIs, which was also mentioned earlier (Degn 2018). In this study, the analyses of academics' sensemaking demonstrated that sensegiving attempts from within the organisation might be perceived as more threatening than external impulses as they may 'damage' the sense of belonging. As the quote below illustrates, the managerial behaviour of the top-level management (in this case implementing an organisational centralisation) was seen as fundamentally incomprehensible to the academic staff:

> That experience that [...] the shocking experience that one of our own [...] I always imagined that they had their hands tied; I mean that it was all dictated from above [...] this standardisation [...] It was just going to be implemented, and 'if you want to keep your job, you'll do it, or we find someone else'[...] But of course, it is naïve to think it is that simple, but I think I lured myself into thinking it, because I simply couldn't understand [...] the lack of understanding [...]. (Excerpt from focus group interview) (Degn 2018)

These two studies, however, also demonstrate that dis-identification with the overall organisation opens up to other types of identification and the forging of new salient categorisations within the organisation. They thereby also show how constructions of personal and social identity influence how the formal organisational identity claims are transformed and sometimes rejected. The sensemaking and identification perspectives allow us to look more closely at these processes.

An Alternative Approach

In the preceding sections, two theoretical approaches have been presented as forming an alternative way of investigating organisational identity and its formation in HEIs. What has been suggested in the present chapter is thereby to begin with the process rather than with the product; the process of identification, which may be studied as sensemaking, rather than the formal identity claims, which are represented in the official documents of the HEIs. This does not exclude the formal claims from the study, but merely delineates such claims as potential cues in sensemaking processes. The suggested framework can be visualised as below in Figure 3.1.

Figure 3.1: Proposed theoretical framework

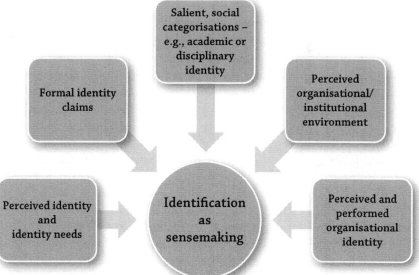

The key object of inquiry within such a framework becomes the sensemaking processes of academics, administrators, leaders etc. within the HEI. Sensemaking and identification is going on at all levels in the HEI, and one of the particularly interesting areas to investigate is how (or if) the organisation 'emerges' as a salient identification category in various ways across levels of responsibility or seniority.

In the following discussion, the analytical potential for scholars interested in organisational identity dynamics is outlined, and the question is addressed of how HEIs may (or should) work actively to strengthen organisational identification and thereby potentially commitment and performance.

Discussion

In this chapter, it has been argued that several sources of identification are available to HE organisation members, and that we need to be able to investigate how these are navigated and selected in order to understand how organisational identity *is built*. The argument here is that this is potentially more fruitful than attempting to pinpoint what an HEI's organisational identity *is*. One relevant way of investigating this is by exploring sensemaking and sensegiving, and how sources of identification are made salient through such processes. This may tell us more about organisational connects, disconnects, and the dynamics of organised life in HEIs than looking at formal structures and organisational missions and strategies. A few of the main potentials of the framework should be highlighted.

Firstly, the potential of investigating organisational identity building is evident in times of perpetual organisational change. As mentioned in the introduction to this chapter, change processes like mergers between HEIs are instances of identity building, conflict and articulation. Often these processes are studied via top-level management communication, e.g., the formulation of mission statements or other strategic documents. Such studies can be seen to study what in this chapter have been called formal identity claims. It is, however, much rarer to see processual studies of change processes. By linking the concept of organisational identification and the sensemaking perspective, this chapter has outlined a conceptual lens through which change processes emerge as instances where sensemaking becomes visible—and thereby also as examples of identity formation.

Secondly, the potential of this framework lies in its ability to shed light on the organised processes, wherein organisational structures and the nature and characteristics of their connections are continually constructed

(Orton and Weick 1990). HEIs are, as mentioned, traditionally described as loosely coupled organisations (Weick 1976), but as demonstrated in the present chapter and in other studies (Bleiklie, Enders and Lepori 2015), the state of coupling or connectivity is perhaps not as stable as it has been assumed. Focusing on how identification plays out through processes of sensemaking might also provide a more nuanced picture of the 'space for resistance' and the relations of power which influence the frames that are available for organisation members, and thereby also how the organisational couplings or connections are tightened and/or loosened. Further studies on these processes have the potential to shed new light on what has been called the actorhood of organisations (Krücken and Meier 2006).

Finally, the suggested framework has potential in studies of academic identity that is, the development of a professional academic identity with reference to both the discipline and the higher education institution (Winter 2009; Henkel 2005). By bringing in sensemaking as an identity formation concept, the framework suggested in this chapter opens up to the processes wherein these various 'defining communities' (Taylor 1989) are valued and balanced, and perhaps also challenged by other salient social groups. Academic identity has, in many studies (Deem 2004; Moscati 2008; Henkel 2000), come to equate an identification with the discipline at the expense of the HEI or the more managerial identification, but by exploring in detail the sensemaking processes of individual academics, we might provide ourselves with a more high-resolution picture of identity processes in HE and insight into how these may have changed as academia and HEIs have also evolved.

In conclusion, a short remark should be made on the potential implications for 'practice'; namely the question of whether the HEIs should—and can—support organisational identification? While the framework suggested in the present chapter does not provide a definite answer to this question, it does highlight some of the dynamics that HEI leaders and policy makers could take into account, for instance when implementing organisational change. As the examples demonstrated, acceptance of formal identity claims does not automatically happen—and perhaps an integrated organisational identity is not necessarily a goal to be pursued.

This leads to another key insight, namely the focus on the interplay between sources of identification. The framework suggests that if disciplinary identification among academic staff is high, then the non-research aspects of the HEI, e.g., teaching and other responsibilities, might suffer, because the motivation to 'help' the organisation is lower. More insight into how these balances are continually made and remade among organisation members, however, will be highly valuable for leaders of HEIs.

Concluding Remarks

The focus in the present chapter has been the development of an alternative approach to studying organisational identity as a process of identification and sensemaking, in order to provide a stronger conceptualisation of how identity is formed and transformed in higher education institutions.

The framework presented here obviously needs to be supported by more and larger empirical studies. The initial aim in this chapter has been to suggest an approach which will help scholars of HEIs and academic work in general with a more nuanced understanding of how sensemaking, identification and organisational identity interrelates, which may also help our understanding of the mechanisms of loose or tight coupling in HEIs.

With it, a final suggestion will also be for HE scholars to focus on more micro-oriented studies into the workings of identity construction processes in HEIs. Such studies will arguably also provide insights to practitioners of governance and leadership of higher education institutions, as they explore the complexities of the loosely coupled organisation and the implications for leaders of such an organisation.

References

Albert, Stuart, Blake E. Ashforth, and Jane E. Dutton. 2000. 'Organisational Identity and Identification: Charting New Waters and Building New Bridges'. *Academy of Management Review* 25 (1): 13–17. doi: 10.5465/amr.2000.2791600.

Albert, Stuart, and David A. Whetten. 1985. 'Organisational Identity'. *Research in Organisational Behavior* 7: 263–295.

Ashforth, Blake E., and Fred Mael. 1989. 'Social Identity Theory and the Organisation'. *Academy of Management Review* 14 (1): 20–39. doi: 10.2307/258189.

Balmer, John M. T. 2008. 'Identity Based Views of the Corporation: Insights from Corporate Identity, Organisational Identity, Social Identity, Visual Identity, Corporate Brand Identity and Corporate Image'. *European Journal of Marketing* 42 (9/10): 879–906. doi: 10.1108/03090560810891055.

Bastedo, Michael N., Elias Samuels, and Molly Kleinman. 2014. 'Do Charismatic Presidents Influence College Applications and Alumni Donations? Organisational Identity and Performance in US Higher education'. *Higher Education* 68 (3): 397–415.

Bleiklie, Ivar, and Maurice Kogan. 2007. 'Organisation and Governance of Universities'. *Higher Education Policy* 20 (4): 477–493.

Bleiklie, Ivar, Jürgen Enders, and Benedetto Lepori. 2015. 'Organisations as Penetrated Hierarchies: Environmental Pressures and Control in Professional Organisations'. *Organisation Studies* 36 (7): 873–896.

Brown, Andrew D. 2016. 'Organisation Studies and Identity: Towards a Research Agenda'. *Human Relations* 54 (1): 113–121. doi: 10.1177/0018726701541014.

Brunninge, Olof. 2005. *Organisational Self-understanding and the Strategy Process: Strategy Dynamics in Scania and Handelsbanken*. Jönköping: Jönköping International Business School.

Cook, Karen S., Coye Cheshire, Eric R.W. Rice, and Sandra Nakagawa. 2013. 'Social Exchange Theory'. In *Handbook of Social Psychology* edited by John DeLamater and Amanda Ward, 61–88. Dordrecht: Springer.

Czarniawska, Barbara, and Rolf Wolff. 1998. 'Constructing New Identities in Established Organisation Fields: Young Universities in Old Europe'. *International Studies of Management & Organisation* 28 (3):32–56.

Deem, Rosemary. 2004. 'The Knowledge Worker, the Manager-Academic and the Con-temporary UK University: New and Old Forms of Public Management?' *Financial Accountability & Management*, 20 (2): 107–128.

Degn, Lise. 2013. 'Making Sense of Management—A Study of Department Heads' Sensemaking Processes in a Changing Environment'. In *Resilient Universities: Confronting Changes in a Challenging World*, edited by Jan Erik Karlsen and Rosalind M.O. Pritchard, 191–211. Bern: Peter Lang.

Degn, Lise. 2015. 'Identity Constructions and Sensemaking in Higher Education—a Case Study of Danish Higher Education Department Heads'. *Studies in Higher Education* 40 (7): 1179–1193.

Degn, Lise. 2018. 'Academic Sensemaking and Behavioural Responses: Exploring how Academics Perceive and Respond to Identity Threats in Times of Turmoil'. *Studies in Higher Education* 43 (2): 305–321.

Degn, Lise, Jørn Flohr Nielsen and Pernille Smith. 2016. 'Transforming Identities in Higher Education: A Case Study of Organisational Change'. Consortium of Higher Education Researchers.

Dutton, Jane E., and Janet M. Dukerich. 1991. 'Keeping an Eye on the Mirror: Image and Identity in Organisational Adaptation'. *Academy of Management Journal* 34 (3): 517–554.

Dutton, Jane E., Janet M. Dukerich, and Celia V. Harquail. 1994. 'Organisational Images and Member Identification'. *Administrative Science Quarterly* 39 (2):239–263.

El-Khawas, Elaine. 2008. 'Emerging Academic Identities: A New Research and Policy Agenda'. In *From Governance to Identity. Festschrift for Mary Henkel*, edited by Alberto Amaral and Ivar Bleiklie, 31–44. Dordrecht: Springer.

Elsbach, Kimberly D., and Roderick M. Kramer. 1996. 'Members' Responses to Organisational Identity Threats: Encountering and Countering the Business Week Rankings'. *Administrative Science Quarterly* 41 (3): 442–476.

Erez, Miriam, and P. Christopher Earley. 1993. *Culture, Self-identity, and Work*. New York: Oxford University Press.

Gioia, Dennis A., and Kumar Chittipeddi. 1991. 'Sensemaking and Sensegiving in Strategic Change Initiation'. *Strategic Management Journal* 12 (6): 433–448.

Gioia, Dennis A., Shubha D. Patvardhan, Aimee L. Hamilton, and Kevin G. Corley. 2013. 'Organisational Identity Formation and Change'. *The Academy of Management Annals* 7 (1): 123–193.

Gioia, Dennis A, Kristin N. Price, Aimee L. Hamilton, and James B. Thomas. 2010. 'Forging an Identity: An Insider-Outsider Study of Processes Involved in the Formation of Organisational Identity'. *Administrative Science Quarterly* 55 (1): 1–46.

Gioia, Dennis A., Majken Schultz, and Kevin G. Corley. 2000. 'Organisational Identity, Image, and Adaptive Instability'. *Academy of Management Review* 25 (1): 63–81.

Gioia, Dennis A., and James B. Thomas. 1996. 'Identity, Image, and Issue Interpretation: Sensemaking during Strategic Change in Academia'. *Administrative Science Quarterly* 41 (3): 370–403.

Glynn, Mary Ann. 2008. 'Beyond Constraint: How Institutions Enable Identities'. In *The Sage Handbook of Organisational Institutionalism,* edited by Royston Greenwood, Christine Oliver, Roy Suddaby, and Kerstin Sahlin, 413–430. London: SAGE.

Haslam, S. Alexander. 2012. *Psychology in Organisations: The Social Identity Approach.* London: SAGE

He, Hongwei, and Andrew D. Brown. 2013. 'Organisational Identity and Organisational Identification: A Review of the Literature and Suggestions for Future Research'. *Group & Organisation Management* 38 (1): 3–35.

Hekman, David R., Gregory A. Bigley, H. Kevin Steensma, and James F. Hereford. 2009. 'Combined Effects of Organisational and Professional Identification on the Reciprocity Dynamic for Professional Employees'. *Academy of Management Journal* 52 (3): 506–526.

Helms-Mills, Jean. 2003. *Making Sense of Organisational Change.* London: Routledge.

Helms-Mills, Jean, Amy Thurlow, and Albert J. Mills. 2010. 'Making Sense of Sensemaking: The Critical Sensemaking Approach'. *Qualitative Research in Organisations and Management: An International Journal* 5 (2): 182–195.

Henkel, Mary. 2000. *Academic Identities and Policy Change in Higher Education.* London and Philadelphia: Jessica Kingsley Publishers.

Henkel, Mary. 2005. 'Academic Identity and Autonomy in a Changing Policy Environment'. *Higher Education* 49 (1–2): 155–176.

Humphreys, Michael, and Andrew D. Brown. 2002. 'Narratives of Organisational Identity and Identification: A Case Study of Hegemony and Resistance'. *Organisation Studies* 23 (3): 421–447.

Humphreys, Michael, and Andrew D. Brown. 2016. 'Narratives of Organisational Identity and Identification: A Case Study of Hegemony and Resistance'. *Organisation Studies* 23 (3): 421–447. doi: 10.1177/0170840602233005.

Krücken, Georg, and Frank Meier. 2006. 'Turning the University into an Organisational Actor'. In *Globalization and Organisation: World Society and Organisational Change,* edited by Gili Drori, John Meyer and Hokyu Hwang, 241–257. Oxford: Oxford University Press.

Lenartowicz, Marta. 2015. 'The Nature of the University'. *Higher Education* 69 (6): 947–961.

MacDonald, Ginger Phillips. 2013. 'Theorizing University Identity Development: Multiple Perspectives and Common Goals'. *Higher Education* 65 (2): 153–166.

Morphew, Christopher, Tatiana Fumasoli, and Bjørn Stensaker. 2016. 'Changing Missions? How the Strategic Plans of Research-intensive Universities in Northern Europe and North America Balance Competing Identities'. *Studies in Higher Education* 43(6): 1074–1088.

Moscati, Roberto. 2008. 'Transforming a Centralised System of Higher Education: Reform and Academic Resistance in Italy'. In *From Governance to Identity. Festschrift for Mary Henkel*, edited by A. Amaral and I. Bleiklie, 131–137. Dordrecht: Springer.

Orton, J. Douglas, and Karl E. Weick. 1990. 'Loosely Coupled Systems: A Reconceptualization'. *Academy of Management Review* 15 (2): 203–223.

Ravasi, Davide, and Majken Schultz. 2006. 'Responding to Organisational Identity Threats: Exploring the Role of Organisational Culture'. *Academy of Management Journal* 49 (3): 433–458.

Seeber, Marco, Vitaliano Barberio, Jeroen Huisman, and Jelle Mampaey. 2019. 'Factors Affecting the Content of Universities' Mission Statements: An Analysis of the United Kingdom Higher Education System'. *Studies in Higher Education* 44 (2): 1–15. doi: 10.1080/03075079.2017.1349743.

Stensaker, Bjørn. 2015. 'Organisational Identity as a Concept for Understanding University Dynamics'. *Higher Education* 69 (1): 103–115.

Strike, Tony, and Jacqueline Labbe. 2016 'Exploding the Myth'. In *Positioning Higher Education Institutions*, edited by Rosalind M.O. Pritchard, Attila Pausits, and James Williams, 125–140. Rotterdam: Sense Publishers.

Taylor, Charles. 1989. *Sources of the Self: The Making of the Modern Identity*. Cambride, MA: Harvard University Press.

Vostal, Filip. 2016. *Accelerating Academia: The Changing Structure of Academic Time*. New York: Palgrave.

Weick, Karl E. 1976. 'Educational Organisations as Loosely Coupled Systems'. *Administrative Science Quarterly* 21 (1): 1–19.

Weick, Karl E. 1995. *Sensemaking in Organisations*. London: Sage.

Weick, Karl E., Kathleen M. Sutcliffe, and David Obstfeld. 2005. 'Organizing and the Process of Sensemaking'. *Organisation Science* 16 (4): 409–421. doi: 10.1287/orsc.1050.0133.

Whetten, David A. 2006. 'Albert and Whetten Revisited: Strengthening the Concept of Organisational Identity'. *Journal of Management Inquiry* 15 (3): 219–234.

Winter, Richard. 2009. 'Academic Manager or Managed Academic? Academic Identity Schisms in Higher Education'. *Journal of Higher Education Policy and Management* 31 (2): 121–131. doi: 10.1080/13600800902825835.

CHAPTER 4

Gender Imbalance in Higher Education: A Comparison between Academic Positions, European Countries and Study Subjects

Caroline Friedhoff, Deborah Werner and John Roman

Introduction

Gender equality is a cross-sectional topic relating to several societal areas. In literature on gender equality, precedence is often given to violence and sexual harassment against women as well as to the gender pay gap. Yet in turn, gender equality in education as well as in a particular part of the labour market, namely that of Higher Education (HE), has not been accorded much attention so far. This is true in particular for quantitative analyses at the subject level. Addressing this gap in the gender equality literature, the present chapter focuses on the gender balance of students and staff in the tertiary education system. Authored by three members of the international university ranking project 'U-Multirank', it analyses the current representation of women in HE, in particular the imbalances existing between men and women concerning (a) subjects studied at university and (b) academic positions and the percentage of female and male academic staff across the pay scale from a European perspective.

According to the European Institute for Gender Equality (EIGE), gender balance refers to the 'equal participation of women and men in all areas of work, projects or programmes' (EIGE 2018). This means that in a gender equal society, 'women and men are expected to participate proportionally to their shares in the population' (ibid.). Yet in the HE sector, men still hold more top-level positions—both administrative and academic—than women when seen in relation to their respective shares in the population. As indicated by Index Mundi, there are slightly more women than men, with the sex ratio being 0.96 globally calculated as the overall total of the male population divided by the overall total of the female population. This means that to achieve gender balance in HE, slightly more women should hold top-level posts, achieve academic degrees and study subjects of all thematic areas (Index Mundi 2018).

In a worldwide bibliometric analysis, Larivière et al. (2013, 212) explore the question of whether there is an imbalance in the research output of men and women. They find that women have less research output than men do in most countries. Females dominate research output only in a few countries which in general have a low research output. In addition, the citation rate of women's research output is significantly lower than that of males (ibid., 213). They attribute this finding to the low numbers of female academic staff in comparison to male staff. Furthermore, data for the Australian HE system show the underrepresentation of women: while the proportion of female associate lecturers is 54 percent, the percentage of female professors at associate grade and above is significantly lower with only 19 percent (Carrington and Pratt 2003, 6). For the Italian case, Oppi et al. (2014, 12) focused on gender representation in Italian university boards and senates. For both these institutional bodies, women are highly underrepresented with 24 and 25 percent respectively.

Similar to Carrington and Pratt (2003), Oppi et al. found that only one quarter of academic board and senate members are female, despite Italian legislation asking to respect the constitutional principle of equal opportunity in the composition of the academic boards (2014, 13). The authors contend that this can be retraced to women's overall careers in academia ending after obtaining a doctoral degree (ibid., 14). The situation is similar in academic recruiting committees of Dutch universities. Few women form part of these, and when they do, they hold entry-level academic ranks (van den Brink, Benschop and Jansen 2010, 11–14).

Governance bodies such as academic boards, senates or recruiting boards are primarily formed by academics of the higher echelons. Hillman and Robinson (2016, 2) contend that women achieve better results at university. In spite of this, according to Goodall and Osterloh (2017, 2), fewer women than men are members of top-level academic governing bodies. This is partly because the authors find women to be less competitive than men despite often similar or higher qualification levels. Based on this, they suggest strategies to improve this situation such as random selection (ibid., 9). Similarly, Oppi et al. (2014) report on effective support structures for women such as maternity-related incentives, nurseries and flexible working hours—improving persisting gender imbalances at their faculty. Contrary to that, Shepherd (2017, 85) contends that women in fact do not lack agency, but that gender imbalances at the upper management levels of HE are due to structural impediments. This can include the hiring process being increasingly experience-based, risk-averse and dependent on a Vice Chancellor's personal and social preferences, sometimes keeping women from filling top positions. Particularly the latter mirrors the findings of Cohen and Hillbom (2015, 4) who showed that it was mostly down to homophily that women were severely underrepresented at a Swedish school of Economics and Management.

The improvement of gender balance and the associated actions for the case of Australia are described by Winchester and Browning (2015) 12 years after Carrington and Pratt (2003) analysed the situation: they monitored the gender balance in HE for three decades and showed in the mid-1980s only 20 percent of the academic staff of the 39 universities were female and six percent of women held senior positions. After 30 years in 2014 this dramatic imbalance was reduced to 44 percent female academic staff and 31 percent women in senior positions (Winchester and Browning 2015, 269). The authors argue that this change was caused not only by societal change, but also by the government and as well by the universities themselves. Government legislations, for example, the Affirmative Action (Equal Employment Opportunity for Women) Act from 1986 or the Workplace Gender Equality Act from 2012, decreased the gender inequality in the Australian HE system. In 1996 the Universities Australia Executive Women Group was formed by the Australian universities and their senior women, which also helped to reduce the gender imbalance in HE (ibid., 279).

Considering gender equality in tertiary education, there are two main forms of underrepresentation. Hillman and Robinson (2016), exploring education in the United Kingdom (UK), find a lack of men entering the tertiary system and an underrepresentation of women among HE staff. Women make up 45 percent of the academic staff, while the percentage of female senior academic staff is lower at 33 percent. Only 22 percent of professors in UK HE are women (ibid., 14). The Organisation for Economic Co-operation and Development's (OECD) data from 2015 show a gender gap in the tertiary education of students. On the one hand, the general percentage of women in most of the OECD countries is higher than that of men, despite female students being strongly underrepresented in the fields of Computing and Engineering programmes (OECD 2017, 24, 106). On the other hand, male students are dramatically underrepresented in the area of Health and Education (ibid., 122).

According to the *UNESCO Good Practice Handbook in Women in HE* from 2002, a multitude of actions have to come together to overcome the stalemate: the setting of specific targets and inclusion into strategic plans, the provision of scholarships specifically for women, transparency

of recruitment and promotion procedures, the visibility of schemes/proce-
dures, and most importantly backing up these measures by a legal framework and/or regular monitoring and reporting in order to raise visibility of
gender imbalances as well as decrease the impact of old 'boys' networks'. At
the lower degree levels, the participation and success of female students can
be furthered by teaching staff sensitive to the potentially different learning
and participation patterns of female students. Government legislation and
university actions towards gender equality are important to enable women
to participate in HE as men do. Additionally, to increase the probability for
women to achieve a doctorate at the university at which they are studying,
universities should consider implementing policies such as internal sponsor-
ships for women in the respective subjects (UNESCO 2002, 107).

This overview of research concerning gender in HE shows an imbalance of the genders in two areas: first, the subjects chosen by women and
men are different. Second, the higher the position in HE, the greater the
gender inequality. Moreover, there are no significant differences between
most countries—overall, the percentage of women in HE in most of its
aspects, such as research output as well as absolute staff numbers, is lower
than that of their male counterparts. The research questions of this chapter
therefore are: 1) What are the current predominant differences between
men and women in HE in terms of study subjects and academic career
positions? 2) How does the current participation of women and men in HE
compare to the gender imbalances portrayed by the literature?

Method and Data: Secondary Analysis of Higher Education Data

To answer the research question of gender imbalance in HE, this chapter executes a secondary analysis of data, parts of which are collected by
the authors, but it also includes publicly available data on the topics of
population and gender. The chapter aims at providing a meta-analysis of
the situation of women, both students and academic staff, in academia.
None of the datasets available cover all information necessary to answer
the above-mentioned research questions. This requires the combined use
of several datasets which contain information on the HE sector in Europe
and worldwide. For the secondary analysis, the chapter makes use of three
large quantitative datasets. The U-Multirank dataset provides information at HE institutional level as well as at subject level. Yet to widen the
data pool at institutional level, the chapter additionally draws on European Tertiary Education Register (ETER) data. In addition, it employs

Eurostat tertiary education data at country level to put the findings based on U-Multirank and ETER data into a Europe-wide context. As a consequence of providing a wider view on the topic of gender imbalance in HE, the chapter refers to datasets showing slight differences in terms of the subject areas and years covered. Whereas U-Multirank comprises a large variety of subjects, Eurostat presents data for the most common subject areas only. Moreover, Eurostat does not contain breakdowns by single subjects as U-Multirank does, but rather shows data per area of study. The chapter uses data with the least differences in reference years possible. However, no identical temporal coverage could be achieved across the three datasets employed.

The first dataset, U-Multirank, is a multi-dimensional global university ranking. Based on bibliometric data and data supplied by participating higher education institutions (HEIs) themselves, the results comprise more than 30 indicators in the five dimensions of 'Teaching & Learning', 'International Orientation', 'Knowledge Transfer', 'Research' and 'Regional Engagement' at both the institutional and subject levels. The data and the methodology of U-Multirank are publicly available. The 2018 results comprised more than 1,600 universities from 95 countries, with a focus on European HEIs. In its 2018 edition, U-Multirank covered 21 study subjects. The data used for this chapter were collected as part of the project's institutional and subject surveys conducted in 2017. In terms of gender balance, or rather imbalance, it uses U-Multirank data on female bachelor/undergraduate and master/postgraduate students, female academic staff and female professors at institutional level. At subject level, data are available for female students, albeit those not categorised by kind of degree, and on female PhD graduates (U-Multirank 2018a, 2018b).

Second, the chapter employs ETER data to complement the insights gained on the basis of U-Multirank data with a dataset currently containing more data at intuitional level in HE. Other than U-Multirank, which is interested in presenting HE data in a global perspective, ETER shows a focus on European HE data. It collects information on the number of students and graduates, staff, international doctorates, fields of education, income and expenditures and some descriptive information. ETER data from 2011 and 2014 are included to analyse the gender imbalance in HE (ETER 2018). These years were chosen because they were the most recent available data at the time of writing. The dataset includes more than 2,700 HEIs. The data for ETER are predominantly gathered from national statistical authorities, while a minor part comes from public sources (Lepori et al. 2018, 13).

Third, the chapter refers to Eurostat data on HE. Eurostat, being the statistical office of the European Union, collects data on a wide variety of aspects. For the purpose of this chapter, we draw on its tertiary education data (Eurostat 2018). Data are provided at country and regional levels for different areas of life. For this chapter, the most recent available data, that is, those of 2012 on the area of gender equality are used to identify female graduates in tertiary education by subject and country.

The analysis and results section contains descriptive and bivariate tables in order to answer the research questions of what are the current predominant differences between men and women in HE in terms of study subjects and academic career positions?

Analysis and Results

To give an overview of the gender imbalances in HE in Europe, the analysis is divided into three sections, (1) academic position, (2) countries and (3) subject areas, depending on the correlation of gender with the specific field of interest.

(1) Academic Position

For analysing the correlation of gender and the academic position, ETER data are used for the years 2011 and 2014. Considering these two points in time gives us the possibility to disclose changes in the percentage of men and women in different academic positions over the years. Academic position is defined according to the ETER classification, and includes the following categories: International standard classification of education ISCED 6 graduates referring to Bachelor and equivalent degrees, ISCED 7 graduates of Master and equivalent degrees, PhD graduates, academic staff and professors.

Figure 4.1 shows the percentage of women by academic position in 2011 and 2014. For 2014, the ISCED 6 graduates show the highest percentage of women out of the above groups with 58.6 percent. The ratio of women for ISCED 7 graduates is with 55.8 percent slightly lower. These numbers show that more women get a Bachelor's and/ or Master's degree in Europe than men. However, this overrepresentation of women turns into an underrepresentation when analysing further career steps of women in HE. Focusing on PhD graduates, the proportion of women is lower than 50 percent. This trend of underrepresentation of women in HE is compounded by the percentage of women in academic staff (42 percent) and professorships (26 percent). As a result, there is a negative correlation between the level of degree and gender, i.e. the higher the degree level, the fewer women achieve it.

Comparing the years 2011 and 2014, we also observe that there is no significant change in the percentages of the proportion of women in all categories of academic positions over time. It seems that except for ISCED 6 graduates, the percentage of women increased slightly over the years.

Figure 4.1: Percentage of women by degree/position (2011 and 2014)

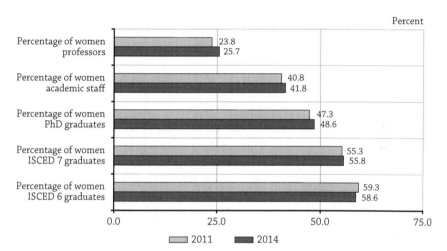

Source: Authors' own depiction based on ETER (2018) data from 2011 and 2014.

(2) Countries

According to Eurostat data, when comparing the number of female graduates per 100 male students within Europe, most European countries show an imbalanced distribution of women and men: women are overrepresented among postgraduates (Table 4.1). Just three countries make the exception: Liechtenstein, Switzerland and Turkey. Liechtenstein appears to be a special case as there is just one public university, Liechtenstein University, which has a strong focus on architecture, finance, entrepreneurship and information systems (Universität Liechtenstein, no year). Given that the subjects taught at this university are traditionally male-dominated, this could explain the imbalance in favour of men at this university. The reasons why more men than women graduate from Swiss and Turkish universities vary greatly and require further research that goes beyond the goal of this chapter, which is to provide an overview of the *status quo* of gender balances in HE. Like Index Mundi, we calculate the sex ratio as the number of men divided by the number of women in a given country. If a country has a higher number of female inhabitants, this can be one reason for the number of female graduates being high as well. The chapter finds that the low sex ratios of Estonia and Latvia partially explain the high figures of female graduates in these two countries.

In line with the global sex ratio indicating there are more women than men, the sex ratios of members of the European Free Trade Association and the European Union show more women in all countries except for Iceland and Norway. These two countries both feature an almost perfectly balanced sex ratio. The comparatively low sex ratios of Latvia (0.84), Lithuania (0.85) and Estonia (0.87) can be a reason for the high number of female graduates in these countries.

The European Union average is 143.2 women graduates per 100 male graduates. Latvia (207.7), Estonia (204.1) and Poland (193.3) show the highest number of female graduates; in these countries, women graduate twice as often as men do. In general, it seems there are more female graduates per 100 men in countries that are in the eastern part of Europe such as Slovakia, Lithuania and Hungary, than in most western European countries such as Austria, France, Germany and Ireland.

Table 4.1: Female graduates per 100 male graduates

Country	Female graduates per 100 male graduates	Country	Female graduates per 100 male graduates
European Union (27 countries in 2012)	143.2	Latvia	207.7
Belgium	145.7	Liechtenstein	26.3
Austria	122.2	Lithuania	176.8
Bulgaria	155.3	Luxembourg	137.8
Croatia	145.6	Malta	134.9
Cyprus	152.2	Netherlands	130
Czech Republic	164.5	Norway	156.2

Country	Female graduates per 100 male graduates	Country	Female graduates per 100 male graduates
Denmark	136.1	Poland	193.9
Estonia	204.1	Portugal	153.2
Finland	156.3	Romania	148.6
Former Yugoslav Republic of Macedonia	124.3	Slovakia	177.8
France	128.2	Slovenia	151.7
Germany	122.4	Spain	128.1
Greece	144.2	Sweden	160.3
Hungary	177.4	Switzerland	92.3
Iceland	181.7	Turkey	89.2
Ireland	120	United Kingdom	130.6
Italy	155.8		

Source: Authors' own depiction based on Eurostat (2018) data from 2012.

(3) Subject Areas

To complete the overview of gender imbalances in HE, subject areas must be taken into account. First, U-Multirank data from the publication years 2017 and 2018 for 17 different subjects are shown with the percentage of female students per subject in Figure 4.2. These data show that women are underrepresented in all engineering subjects; there is a higher percentage of male students in this subject area, while women are overrepresented in education, health and welfare related subjects. Yet, also when examining the subject area of engineering, we detect a high variation among those subjects: chemical engineering has the highest percentage of female students with 46 percent, while mechanical engineering (almost 15 percent) and electrical engineering (15.7 percent) feature the lowest percentage of women studying these subjects.

The subjects of education, social work and nursing show that more than 80 percent of the students are female. This means that in these fields, men are strongly underrepresented. However, there are also subjects that show a gender balance: business studies and political science (both 52.8 percent) as well as economics (48.7 percent) have an almost perfect balance of female and male students.

Figure 4.2: Percentage of female students in U-Multirank subjects 2017/ 2018

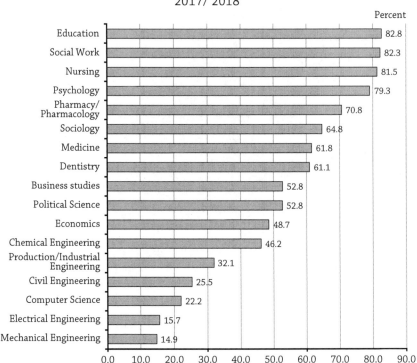

Source: Authors' own depiction based on U-Multirank data from 2017 (average of the years 2013, 2014, 2015) and U-Multirank data from 2018 (average of the years 2014, 2015, 2016).

U-Multirank updates its subject data every three years. This makes possible the analysis of selected subjects such as in business studies, mechanical engineering, electrical engineering and computer science over time. The comparison of the 2014 and 2017 results shows an increase in the percentage of women for all four subjects. Although electrical and mechanical engineering have a very low percentage of female students, there is a tendency for more women to study these engineering subjects.

To ensure the reliability of these findings, we also take into consideration Eurostat data (no date). Although Eurostat's data collection operates on different cycles than U-Multirank's, and even though not all subjects are covered by both data sources, we can still determine and verify general trends in the data. Figure 4.3 shows the percentage of female graduates per subject area according to Eurostat. In general, there are similar tendencies in both datasets: engineering, manufacturing and construction fields have a low percentage of female graduates (2012: 27.2 percent), while the area of education and training shows the highest percentage of women (2012: 80.4 percent). In addition, health and welfare subjects had many women graduating in 2012 (75.8 percent). In U-Multirank, this subject area is covered by social work, medicine, dentistry and pharmacy—the percentage of women in the named fields is above the 50 percent threshold.

Comparing the proportions of female graduates for the years 2007 and 2012 does not reveal explicit changes; some subject areas show a slight increase, while others decrease. There is no clear increase of female graduates in traditionally male-dominated subjects or decrease of female graduates in traditionally female-dominated subjects.

Figure 4.3: Female graduates per field—as percent of all graduates (2007 and 2012)

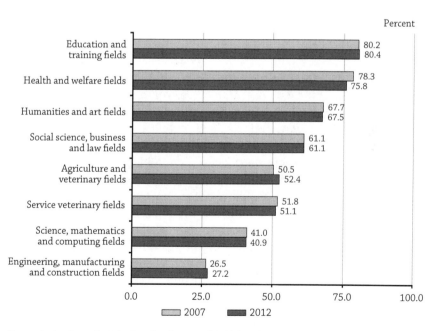

Source: Authors' own depiction based on Eurostat (2018) data from 2007 and 2012. Graduates for ISCED 5 and 6.

Adding further information regarding gender balance at the subject level, U-Multirank developed a new indicator for its 2018 publication. This new indicator gives information on the likelihood of female Bachelor and Master level students earning a PhD degree at a given university, in a particular subject. Rather than simply giving a momentary picture of how many females receive a PhD degree compared to their male counterparts, this allows for a prediction of the academic career chances of women. It does so by taking into consideration the early stages of women's academic careers at Bachelor and Master levels and putting them into relation to the following ones. This makes it possible to reflect on the question of how dedicated a university is to the furtherment of study success of its female students as well as their professional careers. The indicator takes the ratio of female PhD graduates to female students and puts it into relation to that of male PhD graduates to male students. It is assumed that this should be in perfect balance, at 0, and female and male students have the same chances of achieving a PhD degree. If this is not the case, a positive deviation from the perfect balance signifies a positive chance for female students to gain a PhD degree, while a negative deviation from the perfect balance means that female students are less likely to gain a PhD degree in comparison to male students.

For U-Multirank 2018, 383 of the participating departments reported the required data for the calculation of the indicator, gender balance. Below, Table 4.2 shows the average of gender balance by subject. U-Multirank focuses on specific subject areas in three-year cycles. This is due to the unlikelihood of the data changing much within the period of one year. Additionally, the questionnaire used to collect data on students, staff and finances spans a three-year period as well.

For the 2018 edition of U-Multirank, the social sciences as well as health and welfare subjects were focused on, and gender balance values were therefore presented for the nine subjects of dentistry, education, medicine, nursing, pharmacy/pharmacology, political science, psychology, social work and sociology. For all of these nine subjects, the average of the gender balance indicator was negative. This implies that the possibility is higher for men to complete a PhD at the respective department and university than it is for women. It should be mentioned that particularly the subjects of social work, education and nursing—which according to Figure 4.2 above are studied by more women than men, showing a predominance of men in finishing a PhD degree. While still showing negative averages, dentistry, pharmacy/pharmacology and medicine are closer to zero. This means that in the latter subjects, women and men are on a more equal

Table 4.2: Average of gender balance indicator U-Multirank 2018

Subject	Average gender balance indicator	Number of Departments included
Dentistry	–0.3	24
Education	–1.0	45
Medicine	–0.2	79
Nursing	–0.8	28
Pharmacy/ Pharmacology	–0.2	34
Political Science	–0.5	52
Psychology	–0.4	60
Social Work	–1.0	21
Sociology	–0.4	40

Source: Authors' own calculations and depiction based on U-Muiltirank data from 2018.

footing in relation to achieving a PhD degree, yet it is still more likely for men to do so. This result is in line with the previous findings that PhD graduates are more often men than women as shown in Figure 4.1. However, at the same time it is also a surprising finding as the subject groups that are included in the analysis are dominated by female Bachelor graduates as presented in Figure 4.3.

Conclusion

This chapter argues that for most European countries, the distribution of women and men is imbalanced when considering students: women are overrepresented amongst the postgraduates. However, the opposite is true when examining further career steps of women in HE. Taking the differences between subjects into account, women are underrepresented in traditionally male-dominated subject areas, such as engineering, mathematics and computing. The same years examined show that men are also underrepresented in subject areas typically dominated by women, for instance, in education and training, health and welfare, and the social sciences. In doing so, this analysis links its findings to policy suggestions addressing gender imbalances in the HE system.

The analysis and results section of this chapter showed that there are different types of gender imbalances. First, women are overrepresented when we talk about students and graduates (ISCED 6 and ISCED 7). This continues to be true for most of the European countries (Luxembourg, Switzerland and Turkey make the exceptions). Interestingly, western European countries have fewer female graduates than eastern European countries. However, if one takes further career steps into account (PhD graduates, academic staff, and professorships) the gender imbalance changes in the favour of men. Women are dramatically underrepresented at the top of academic positions—namely professorships. Only every fourth professor is female in Europe. Comparing the years 2011 and 2014, the chapter observes in addition to the above that there is no significant change in the percentages of the proportion of women in all categories of academic positions over time. With the exception of ISCED 6 graduates, it seems that the proportion of women increased slightly over the years.

Additionally, the chapter determines a trend of an increasing percentage of women in HE over the years. Nonetheless, there is a higher probability of gaining a PhD degree for male students.

This chapter provides new evidence for such policy-oriented studies in three key regards: first, it casts a wider geographical net and does not exclusively focus on one country or area. In turn, it covers more than 1,600 HEIs across countries. Second, it encompasses data from multiple academic levels, from students to professorships. Thirdly, it does not focus only on one subject area or one aspect of academic life such as bibliometrics or teaching, but instead covers a wide range of both. At the time of writing, gender imbalances in HE persist at all degree and qualification levels. This chapter provides up-to-date evidence for this finding and therefore highlights the need for more research into the reasons for this situation in HE. The evidence confirms there being imbalances in terms of subjects studied and academic positions held by women and men. Therefore, the present chapter's findings have important implications for the further development of academic potential and competition, as a high number of countries examined in this chapter harbour unused intellectual capital. Furthermore, it shows that the balance of genders has not yet been achieved in the HE sector in European countries. It takes a more comprehensive view regarding the countries covered and examines the situation of females in HE at a later point of time. It argues that the situation regarding academic position and subjects is similar in European countries 10 years after the situation of women in Australian HE was analysed by Carrington and Pratt (2003, 6). Our findings also support those of Oppi et al., namely that few women stay in academia after obtaining a PhD degree (2014, 14). In terms of policy recommendations, our findings therefore—still—relate to advice given by UNESCO in 2002 presented in the introduction (p. 107) and requiring implementation by policy makers and HE management and leadership. The goal should be the balance of men and women within academia, no matter what the study subject may be.

References

Carrington, Kerry, and Angela Pratt. 2003. 'How Far Have We Come? Gender Disparities in the Australian Higher Education System'. *Social Policy Group*, June 16, 2003. Accessed July 27, 2018. https://www.researchgate.net/publication/237526022_How_Far_Have_We_Come_Gender_Disparities_in_the_Australian_Higher_Education_System.

Civera, Alice, and Davide Donina. 2017. 'The Italian Higher Education System: Gender Inequality?' Paper presented at the workshop "Gender Equality in the Higher Education System: Comparing European Experiences and Challenges." Milan, November 10.

Cohen, Laurie, and Ellen Hillbom. 2015. 'Review of Gender Disparity at LUSEM'. Accessed July 27, 2018. https://www.lusem.lu.se/media/ehl/omehl/review-of-gender-disparity.pdf.

EIGE. 2018. 'Concepts and Definitions'. Accessed July 27, 2018. http://eige.europa.eu/gender-mainstreaming/concepts-and-definitions.

ETER. 2018. 'Database'. Accessed July 27, 2018. https://www.eter-project.com/#/search.

Eurostat. 2018. 'Database on Equality (age and gender)'. Accessed July 27, 2018. http://ec.europa.eu/eurostat/web/equality/data/database.

Eurostat. 2019. 'Bevölkerung nach Alter und NUTS 3 Regionen [cens_11ag_r3]' [Population by age and NUTS 3 regions]. Accessed January 4, 2019. http://appsso.eurostat.ec.europa.eu/nui/show.do?dataset=cens_11ag_r3&lang=de.

Goodall, Amanda, and Margit Osterloh. 2017. 'Women and Competition: Can Random Selection Break the Deadlock?' Paper presented at the workshop 'Gender Equality in the Higher Education System: Comparing European Experiences and Challenges'. Milan, November 10.

Hillman, Nick, and Nicholas Robinson. 2016. 'Boys to Men: The Underachievement of Young Men in Higher Education—and How to Start Tackling It'. *Higher Education Policy Institute Report* 84: 1–64. Accessed July 27, 2018. https://www.hepi.ac.uk/wp-content/uploads/2016/05/Boys-to-Men.pdf.

Hilton, Douglas. 2015. 'Practical Policies can Combat Gender Inequality'. *Nature*, June 25, 2017. Accessed July 27, 2018. https://www.nature.com/news/practical-policies-can-combat-gender-inequality-1.17856.

Index Mundi. 2018. 'Sex Ratio in the European Union'. Accessed July 27, 2018. https://www.indexmundi.com/european_union/sex_ratio.html.

Larivière, Vincent, Chaoqun Ni, Yves Gingras, Blaise Cronin, and Cassidy Sugimoto. 2013. 'Global Gender Disparities in Science'. *Nature* 504: 211–213. https://www.nature.com/news/bibliometrics-global-gender-disparities-in-science-1.14321.

Lepori, Benedetto, Andrea Bonaccorsi, Alessandro Daraio, Cinzia Daraio, Hebe Gunnes, Elisabeth Hovdhaugen, Michael Ploder, Monica Scannapieco, and Daniel Wagner-Schuster. 2018. *Implementing and Disseminating the European Tertiary Education Register—Handbook for Data Collection*. Brussels: European Commission. Accessed July 27, 2018. https://www.eter-project.com/uploads/assets/pdf/ETERIII_handbook_running.pdf.

OECD. 2017. *The Pursuit of Gender Equality: An Uphill Battle*. Paris: OECD Publishing. http://dx.doi.org/10.1787/9789264281318-en.

Oppi, Chiara, Emidia Vagnoni, Cristina Fioravanti, and Caterina Cavicchi. 2014. 'Gender Diversity and Governance: An Explorative Study of Italian Universities'. Paper presented at the 'International Symposium on Gender Equality in the Academia—Best Practices'. Istanbul, November.

Shepherd, Sue. 2017. 'Why are There so Few Female Leaders in Higher Education: A Case of Structure or Agency?' *Management in Education* 31 (2): 82–87.

U-Multirank. 2018a. 'Compare Universities as a Whole'. Accessed July 27, 2018. https://www.umultirank.org/compare?section=comparePrefs&mode=likewithlike&instutionalField=true&name=null&trackType=compare.

U-Multirank. 2018b. 'Rankings by Subject'. Accessed July 27, 2018. https://www.umultirank.org/compare?section=compareSubject&mode=likewithlike&name=null&trackType=compare.

UNESCO. 2002. *Women and Management in Higher Education: A Good Practice Handbook*. Paris: United Nations Educational, Scientific and Cultural Organization. http://www.unesco.org/education/pdf/singh.pdf.

UNESCO. 2012. *International Standard Classification of Education – ISCED 2011*. Montreal, Quebec: UNESCO Institute for Statistics. https://www.openemis.org/wp-content/uploads/2018/04/unesco-international-standard-classification-education-isced-2011-en.pdf.

Universität Liechtenstein. No year. 'Our Study Programmes'. Accessed January 4, 2019. https://www.uni.li/en/study/our-master-programmes.

van den Brink, Marieke, Yvonne Benschop, and Willy Jansen. 2010. 'Transparency as a Tool for Gender Equality'. *Organization Studies* 31 (12): 1–25.

Winchester, Hilary P.M., and Lynette Browning. 2015. 'Gender equality in Academia: A Critical Reflection'. *Journal of Higher Education Policy and Management*, 37 (3): 269–281.

Rankings, Evaluation
and their Impact on Academia

CHAPTER 5

Do Classifications and Rankings Improve or Damage Institutions?

Victor M. H. Borden, Cynthia Cogswell and Fox Troilo

Institutions of higher education compare themselves against one another. In examining the practices of peers, defining aspirations, and identifying and adopting effective practices, comparison is inescapable. External comparisons, composed through rankings and classifications, often surface resistance and unease. Many academics consider rankings to be misguided, shallow, and misaligned with the true purposes of higher education. The influence of rankings on institutional behaviour is seen as at least a waste of resources and, more perversely, a threat to autonomy and mission-focus.

However, institutional rankings and classifications influence students' enrolment decisions, staff recruiting, alumni giving, and institutional strategy. This paper focuses on how US research universities address, respond to, and manage external rankings and classifications. We explore how the quality of higher education is defined and represented by such external systems as the Carnegie Classification of Institutions of Higher Education, US News and World Report rankings (USNWR), and international 'World-Class University' rankings, and how institutions respond to these classification and ranking systems to negotiate mission-related ideals of quality with these external representations.

Ranking colleges and universities is not a new phenomenon; however, the number of public media and academic centres that provide a ranking system has grown substantially. The USNWR rankings, created in 1983, are the best-known and most influential rankings in the United States, as well as the most widely criticised among institutional and educational researchers. USNWR and leading international rankings (for example, the Times Higher Education World University Rankings and the Shanghai Consultancy's Academic Ranking of World Universities) have shifted the purpose of rankings from their earlier uses in academic and policy research into a consumer product (Hazelkorn and Gibson 2018). Across the more elite HEIs in the United States, the USNWR ranking system dominates campus conversations given its undergraduate focus.

USNWR releases its annual 'Best Colleges' ranking report in the early fall, first to campus senior leadership and then to the public. Their rankings are informed by existing public data and data they collect. The USNWR rankings are most highly related to the quality of entering students and the financial wealth of the institution. More specifically, the measures used in the USNWR ranking include: reputation (based on surveys of senior college officers and high school counsellors); selectivity (entry exam scores and high school grades); graduation and retention rates (including both actual and a performance measure that relates actual to predicted values based on student input); faculty resources (including student/faculty ratio, class size, percent of faculty with a terminal degree, faculty compensation and percent of full-time faculty); alumni donation (percent that donate); and financial resources (spending on instruction and support per student).

The reputation component of the USNWR rankings accounts for 20% of the ranking. However, reputation is highly correlated with other included measures of selectivity and financial wealth (Volkwein and Sweitzer 2006). Similarly, graduation and retention rates are highly correlated with selectivity. Although the USNWR ranking also includes a graduation rate performance measure that accounts for selectivity, it is only weighted 8% compared to 22% for the raw graduation rate and highly correlated one-year retention (persistence) measure. An internal study conducted at one of the author's institutions, using national data, discovered that just three of the measures incorporated in the USNWR rankings—peer assessment score, graduation rate, and expenditures per student—accounted for 98% of the variance in overall score among institutions. This and similar institutional and national studies show clearly that the USNWR ranking is based on reputation, student academic quality, and financial resources.

Graham and Thompson (2001) provide a very clear argument about the pitfalls of USNWR's rankings. They contend that the most glaring omissions from USNWR rankings are measures of student learning and good educational practices. They wrote: 'U.S. News' rankings primarily register a school's wealth, reputation, and the achievement of the high-school students it admits' (para. 13). In response to such claims, USNWR states, '[t]he data U.S. News gathers on colleges—and the rankings of the schools that arise from these data—serve as an objective guide by which students and their parents can compare the academic quality of schools.' (Morse, Brooks, and Mason 2018). Debates on its value notwithstanding, it is clear that the USNWR ranking is related to a specific conception of quality that aligns with the elite purposes of higher education and against wide participation and objectives related to social equity.

The Carnegie Classification of Institutions of Higher Education (CCIHE) was initially developed for use in research and policy development. Because of its origins from a 'trusted source', the Carnegie Classifications are respected and used throughout US higher education for reporting and planning purposes. Responsibility for maintaining and updating the CCIHE was licensed by the Carnegie Foundation for the Advancement of Teaching to the Indiana University Center for Postsecondary Education in 2014. Recognizing expectations and interests for accommodating the more rapid pace of change in higher education, the schedule for updates was reduced from a five-year to a three-year cycle beginning with the 2018 update.

In recent years, several international research rankings have gained traction as potential metrics related to university quality and reputation. Among these, the Academic Ranking of World Universities (ARWU), Times Higher Education World University Rankings, and QS World University Rankings have had the most visibility, although a range of other competing rankings have spread the influence of such rankings around the globe. Although generally carrying more weight outside the United States than within, the world rankings also influence behaviour among the elite research universities within the United States.

The value and impact of university rankings has been debated for years. As is true with almost any attempt to provide simple performance information about complex organisations (universities, hospitals, cities, countries, and so on), the professionals and administrators within those entities decry as inappropriate representing the performance or effectiveness of the institution according to a few simple numbers. At the same time, institutions that receive high, or higher than expected rankings often publicise the ranking proudly.

Among the limitations of rankings, Hazelkorn (2015) cited the lack of pertinent, reliable and directly comparable data, especially across nations and regions. Ioniddis et al. (2007) found little evidence of construct validity among the measures employed in rankings. Despite noted limitations in reliability and validity, Shin and Toutkoushian (2011) describe the array of impacts rankings have on university behaviours, including: shifting the emphasis toward English as a primary language; focusing research and program development toward publications that have greater impact on ranking measures; and influencing recruiting practices, sometimes known as raiding, where institutions vie competitively for 'star' (high producing) faculty.

A comprehensive review of the impact of global research university rankings sponsored by the European University Association (EUA) examined the positive and negative ways that rankings, particularly those that focus on 'world-class research universities', have influenced higher education policy and practices (Rauhvargers 2013). Among the negative influences, the report notes the monolithic view of quality that these rankings promote, the limited number of institutions considered by these rankings, the subjective selection of weights, the lack of reliability of reputation measures, lack of transparency, and the perverse impacts that these measures can have on university performance. Despite these drawbacks, the EUA report notes several positive impacts, including: focusing increased attention on the importance of higher education for global competitiveness among nations; fostering greater accountability and increased pressure to improve management practices; and the indication that there is little evidence that rankings bias or otherwise impact consumer choice.

How do universities manage these rankings and classifications? Who at the institution is involved and how do the rankings inform decision making? Also do these external systems result in institutional staff paying too much attention to issues like student selectivity and scientific research and less to student learning and scholarship in the humanities and other less 'prolific' but equally important disciplinary endeavours?

Using an intrinsic case study approach, below are descriptions of how two institutions and a higher education research and consulting organisation address these questions. The institution cases describe the internal, 'lived experience' of classifications and rankings, including how they are managed. The research and consulting organisation case provides a cross-institutional perspective that describes common themes among institutions seeking to improve their ranking or classification. Additionally, the cases note the types of research and analysis that staff conduct to replicate the Carnegie Classification and USNWR methodologies to inform campus discussions and actions.

Before presenting the cases, it is important to consider the use of the term 'selectivity' in the US context. In some countries and contexts, the term is used to describe how institutions seek to serve national objectives related to widening participation or addressing participation gaps by gender, social class, or ethnic origin. Other times, it may refer the ratio of enrolment demand to available spaces. This latter conception is a component of the term's use in the US context (percent of applicants admitted). Additionally, the US context for this term connotes the academic quality of students admitted to the institution and is thus related to exclusive or elite, rather than inclusive practices. This last aspect of the term's use is critical to the current analysis. Attention paid to improving rankings and prestige has been cited as a pressure that results in colleges and universities becoming more exclusive and abandoning or at least paying less attention to important societal goals for diversity and inclusion (Espeland and Sauder 2008, Kuh and Pascarella 2004, Pusser and Marginson 2013).

HEI Experience 1: Dartmouth College

Dartmouth College (Dartmouth) is a 4-year, private, Ivy League institution, located in Hanover, New Hampshire, enrolling approximately 6500 students, two-thirds of whom are traditional-aged undergraduates residing on-campus with the remaining students enrolled in one of the four graduate schools. The Ivy League includes nine well-renowned institutions that share a rich and lengthy heritage. Having Ivy League status but with a smaller-than-Ivy League enrolment, institutional leadership and staff are attuned to how decisions could impact rankings and classifications. Dartmouth competes and compares with the Ivy League institutions that generally have between 5000 and 10,000 undergraduates (with one at about 15,000), but which also have much larger graduate programs, ranging in size from 3000 to 23,000.

The impact of rankings and classifications generally revolves around comparisons of benchmarking data, including the various measures upon which rankings are based. Like many HEIs in the United States, Dartmouth College's Office of Institutional Research (OIR) mission is to provide timely and accurate analytical services and information, to internal and external constituents, for executive decision making and policy development. This includes data collection and management, analysis, and reporting. The OIR staff are central to campus discussions and debates about Dartmouth College's ranking and classification. The remainder of this section relates the experience as viewed by OIR staff.

Conversations with faculty about rankings and classifications are organic. Faculty cite a shift in the Carnegie Classification that occurred in 2015 in writing about the future of STEM (Science, Technology, Engineering and Mathematics) initiatives on campus (Dartmouth College 2016). Faculty salary data, one of the measures employed in the USNWR rankings, is used by faculty in dashboards and regular discussions on teaching, learning, and faculty retention.

The Admissions Office continuously monitors the rankings. Because one of the measures that was traditionally used in the USNWR is the percent of applicants admitted, the office had a recent goal of increasing the number of applications, which it met. Unfortunately, in the most recent version of the rankings (https://www.usnews.com/best-colleges, accessed December 21, 2018) the admissions rate was dropped as a ranking measure from the 'Best College' calculations.

Despite its size, with rigorous research and a large footprint that includes a medical school, Dartmouth has most often been classified in the highest level research category of the Carnegie Classifications, colloquially known as 'R1'. However, Dartmouth dropped into the second category in the 2015 update, which became the headline for an article on the classification update in the nationally visible *Washington Post* newspaper (Anderson 2016). In the latest 2018 update, Dartmouth shifted back into the R1 category. The Office of Institutional Research is responsible for submitting required information for rankings and classification and is a key leader in interpreting the results. The impact of the rankings and classifications on Dartmouth College are generally felt first and foremost within OIR, which must focus considerable time and resources on addressing Dartmouth's place within these external systems.

Over the last few years, OIR has replicated the USNWR rankings via a Visual Basic for Applications (VBA) model in Microsoft Excel. Using a statistical model to predict the overall USNWR scores for national universities, a calculator predicts how the overall USNWR score and rank would change depending on the values of rankings criteria. The predictive model is very accurate (R^2=.998) because the ranking system is formulaic. The interactive calculator allows users to manipulate scores on all criteria to see how predicted, overall score, and rank changes. The calculator uses coefficients from the regression model to produce a predicted overall score. It also generates predicted rankings using a lookup table that matches overall scores to the corresponding 5-year average ranks.

Generally, the calculator is used internally to highlight criteria under Dartmouth's direct control, such as student selectivity metrics and faculty and financial resources. The calculator was also leveraged in discussions regarding Dartmouth's 2015 status change within CCHIE's Basic Classification schema, as noted above. With Dartmouth's drop from R1 to R2 status making national news, campus leaders requested OIR staff to conduct research to determine why this occurred. In order to understand this shift, OIR directed its full attention to replicating the results.

The determination of R1 status within the CCIHE is based on a 'research activity index' that employs both per-capita measures and aggregate measures of research activity. The measures are as follows: research & development (R&D) expenditures in science and engineering (S&E); R&D expenditures in non-science and engineering fields (Non-S&E); S&E research staff; doctorates conferred in humanities fields, in social science fields, in STEM fields, and in other fields. Aggregate values of all these measures are used to calculate an aggregate index while a second per-capita index is determined based on per-capita values for R&D expenditures in science and engineering; R&D expenditures in non-science and engineering fields; S&E research staff. It should be noted, given its small size, Dartmouth's R1 classification is dependent on the per-capita metrics.

OIR downloaded the CCIHE data and produced interactive reports, including 'What-if' scenarios, to assist senior leadership in assessing how Dartmouth compared to its peers and what it would take to return to R1 status in the next CCIHE update. In total, nine scenarios were created by adjusting the various aggregate and per-capita measures; however, given the small size of graduate programs, only scenarios with adjustments in R&D expenditures (S&E and Non-S&E), research staff, and doctoral degrees in Social Sciences and STEM were further examined.

The what-if scenarios were used with the new Vice Provost for Research who wanted to more closely examine the research and development (R&D) expenditure data. A group of administrators from across campus discussed and debated the data and its impact on a federally-mandated submission to the National Science Foundation, the government agency that tracks research nationally. There were concerns that Dartmouth may not have been 'counting' expenditure data to the extent possible on the Higher Education Research and Development Survey (HERD) which is the data source for the CCHIE's research & development (R&D) expenditure metrics. In this instance the focus is on accounting and reporting practices rather than actual levels of spending.

Other campus leaders reviewed the financial data related to academic expenditure employed in the USNWR rankings that are submitted through mandated reports to the National Center for Education Statistics. Using the USNWR VBA calculator described earlier, OIR staff determined how drops in some categories of expenditure would negatively impact the USNWR ranking. This understanding provided senior administrators with information on the consequences of spending decisions. In particular, it created negative consequences for defunding academic operations and, in particular, instruction and student support.

In addition to these intensive and time-consuming efforts among OIR staff and senior leadership, others on campus regularly discuss the rankings, including academic Deans, academic staff, and administrative staff. In contrast to the types of discussions and activities noted above, these broader campus discussions are more casual and most often relate to ensuring a low student to faculty ratio, small class sizes, and resources directed toward academic and research operations, as consonant with Dartmouth College's image as a small liberal arts undergraduate college that has intensive research-oriented graduate programs.

HEI Experience 2: Indiana University

Indiana University (IU) is a large, multi-campus, public, university enrolling 45,000 students at its residential 'flagship' campus, and 30,000 at its urban-based campus that includes large health programs. Because of its nature as a large, multi-campus institution, the institution has long-grappled with how its organisational structure cannot be well-accommodated in rankings that apply to each individual campus. The flagship campus, Bloomington (IUB), and the urban research campus, Indiana University Purdue University Indianapolis (IUPUI), include programs that span both campuses and, in several cases, are state-wide programs. Central to this analysis, the IU School of Medicine (IUSoM) is headquartered in Indianapolis but reports to the University President (who is based at the Bloomington campus) and not the IUPUI or IUB chief campus officer.

Indiana University is one of the charter public universities of the Association of American Universities (AAU), a consortium of 60 US and 2 Canadian universities considered to represent the most elite North American research universities. When it entered the AAU in 1909, IU was a single university that included the traditional Bloomington campus, with health programs in Indianapolis. The IUB/IUSoM configuration is still considered to be the AAU member, even though most of the IUSoM data have traditionally been included in state and federal reports as part of the IUPUI campus. In fact, the University Graduate School and the IU Research Administration divisions have University-wide portfolios.

The complicated configuration of IU is not uncommon among large, state-wide public universities, many of which organise their health centres into separate systems with multiple campuses (such as in Texas, Louisiana, and most recently Tennessee). Moreover, since international research university rankings employ mostly public data sources and themselves 'construct' the institutions as they deem appropriate, there is often a mis-alignment between how these rankings represent institutions and how the institutions are actually organised. For the past several years, IU leadership has been communicating with international ranking administrators, most notably the Shanghai Consultancy, purveyors of the Academic Ranking of World Universities, to represent the institution's research and bibliometric measures appropriately.

The most pressing issues for IU as related to undergraduate-focused rankings, especially the 'Best Colleges' rankings of USNWR, reflect other areas of frustration for IU's public representation within rankings. In this case, the issue pertains more to the focus of the USNWR rankings on student selectivity, resources, and reputation.

Public research universities generally have much larger undergraduate than graduate student populations. This reflects these institutions' roles in serving state objectives of educating and retaining, within the state, student talent. In comparison, private research universities, especially those high within the research rankings, generally enrol larger numbers of graduate students than undergraduates, for which they are highly selective and, given their high costs, also attract larger proportions of affluent students and smaller proportions of low income students (e.g., those eligible for the federal Pell Grant that assists low-income students).

IU and other members of the Big 10 athletic conference (which includes 13 flagship public universities and one private university) compete with each other both on and off the field for prestige. Even as IU took steps to become increasingly selective, the other Big 10 campuses did the same. Some, like the University of Michigan, were historically highly selective, while others, like the University of Minnesota and Ohio State University, transformed themselves from historically wide access institutions, to currently highly selective. As noted earlier, concerns with prestige and reputation, magnified by the popular rankings, have led most US public research universities to become increasingly selective and less inclusive.

This situation affects campus discourse among the leadership and faculty in several notable ways. The deans of the IUB schools and college cannot understand why their graduate programs are generally highly ranked, including a number of Top 10 programs in the USNWR 'Best Graduate Schools' Rankings, while the overall 'Best College' ranking is perceived as much lower (dropping to 90th place from 76 between 2016 and 2017, despite the overall indicators not changing much).

The President of IU is increasingly frustrated about how IU ranks internationally, especially since the rankings are so inconsistent (101–150 in ARWU, having fallen out of the Top 100 a few years ago: 117 in Times Higher Ed, up from 150 in 2017 and 201–250 in 2016; 323 in QS Top Universities). The Chancellor of the IUPUI campus, administrative leadership, and campus academic staff are consistently frustrated by how they are represented, especially if the IUSoM is not attributed to their campus, where it physically resides along with health schools in Nursing, Public Health, Dentistry, and Health and Rehabilitative Sciences, which are attributed to their campus.

Even with the Medical School, IUPUI has been classified in the second highest research activity category ('R2') of the Carnegie Classifications. Recent efforts to recognise the IUSoM reporting line to the University President, who is also the chief executive for the Bloomington Campus, has resulted in some IUSoM measures being reported with the Bloomington campus, most notably the annual research expenditures. This shift of reporting makes it less likely that IUPUI will be classified as an 'R1' institution.

As a result of these circumstances, both IUB and IUPUI have been working diligently to optimise their representation within both the undergraduate USNWR rankings and the international research rankings. The most appropriate activities that actually focus on expanding research output are understandably longer-term strategies, for which the seeds are just being planted. Chief among these are the IU Grand Challenges initiative, which includes allocating several hundred million dollars to identifying a few focused interdisciplinary efforts to build research and impact capacities around 'big problems'. The institution has thus far identified three such challenges: opioid addiction; environmental change; and precision health. The institution has further provided investment support in a series of 'Emerging Areas of Research' to engage faculty in a diverse array of programs.

More mundanely, staff from the institutional research office and related analytic areas continue to analyse IU campus measures and reporting practices to understand how to be better reflected in the rankings while maintaining commitment to honest and transparent reporting. Perhaps one of the best examples of this, albeit one that is already longstanding, is how students' entering test scores are represented. Following a practice that is common among competing institutions, the institution counts the highest Mathematics and highest verbal score for SAT tests among those who submit multiple SAT (Indiana is an SAT state and students often take the test several times to improve their scores); as well as the highest ACT composite among students who submit such scores. If a student submits both SAT and ACT scores, the highest among those is considered as part of the institution's overall statistics.

In addition, each campus is working rigorously on improving retention and graduation rates. Most recently, IUB has been employing learning and other student analytics to increase each student's likelihood of persisting to graduation in four years. Although students can take longer to graduate without penalty, public policy interest in efficient use of resources have made 'on-time' (four-year) graduation a priority. This activity also includes nuanced tweaking of the institution's admissions policies and practices, such as giving more consideration to the rigour of a student's high school curriculum, to improve both selectivity and student diversity, through strategic use of scholarship funds and programmatic support efforts.

As part of its efforts to shape the enrolment profile and meet institutional goals to both increase the quality and diversity of entering students, the Bloomington enrolment management division distributes institutional scholarship monies using advanced analytic techniques. Although these techniques include student financial need, they also include measures of student merit. These practices, although common especially among 'flagship' public research universities, have been criticised for detracting from meeting state and federal goals for widening participation and closing performance gaps (Goldrik-Rab, Harris and Trostel 2009; Heller 2006).

In summary, the visibility and external impact of the USNWR rankings, the CCIHE, and several international rankings have forced the institution to consider how its organisational structure promotes or facilitates campus rankings and classifications. These efforts range from very positive, mission critical activities related to enhancing research and the quality of undergraduate and graduate programs to more mundane activities that require time and attention from centralised administrative staff. At its most perverse, this has led to changes in organisational structures that are made to improve rankings regardless of their disruptiveness, costs, and impacts on program quality.

Across-HEI Experience: Hanover Research

Opinions on rankings vary widely both within the academic community and among consumers (students and other collaborating partners) and other constituents. While countless debates have been held and articles written regarding their merit, fairness, and value (with likely many more to come), there is little disagreement that an institution benefits when holding a higher rank on any particular scheme. Stated differently, there appears to be no harm, and surely some good in enjoying a high placement. For this reason, institutions around the globe evaluate and implement strategies to influence their position. This view, although considered demeaning by academics, is a pragmatic reality for senior leadership. As a result, senior leaders develop formal or informal strategic plans to boost their position in rankings and the CCIHE. The third and final point of view included in this analysis is from an individual who works for a national research consulting group that has been frequently engaged by HEIs seeking to improve their position within rankings and classifications.

The first step in creating and enacting a strategic plan to increase rankings placement is to assess relative positioning compared to other institutions. This provides an understanding of where the institution is over- and under-performing on each metric used to establish rank, and thus signalling specific areas for positive improvement, as well as the magnitude of the potential opportunity. One way to perform this assessment is through rankings reconstructions. As noted through the Dartmouth experience, it is possible to recreate the USWNR ranking methodology and thus build simulation tools to understand how hypothetical variations in metrics would ultimately influence position, all other elements held equal. Understanding strengths and weaknesses in the context of the ranking indicators is critical to influencing change.

While each ranking has its own associated methodology, at their core all rankings consist of objective metrics, subjective metrics, or some combination of both, categorised with weights assigned to each score. The subjective metrics typically relate to reputation and brand awareness, and in many instances, are among the most heavily weighted variable(s). For example, for USNWR's Best Global Universities rankings, two of the top three indicators are 'Global research reputation' and 'Regional research reputation', each weighted at 12.5% of the total. The institutional values come from the approximately 30,000 responses to a survey of academics conducted by Clarivate Analytics (https://clarivate.com/). The objective metrics include quantifiable opinion-free variables such as number of citations recorded in the past year, the distribution of entry exam scores of students, and the average class size.

The type of metric an institution wants to work on improving determines the strategy and approach. With objective metrics, a path forward is a little better defined than with subjective variables. For example, a U.S.-based business school performed a USNWR rankings reconstruction for full-time MBA programs and discovered that they were underperforming across several factors including: employment rate at graduation, employment rate three months after graduation, average undergraduate grade-point average (GPA), and average entry test (GMAT) score. For the first two metrics, the business school immediately allocated financial and human resources to their career centre both to improve placement rates and to track student outcomes. In order to improve their student-centred metrics, the institution first used a rankings simulation tool to establish target average values for the next cohort. Next, they developed a predictive model to ascertain the probability of a student enrolling given their characteristics (including GMAT score and undergraduate GPA) combined with certain financial aid values. This allowed the business school to strategically award scholarships at optimal levels to the students they strongly desired, while at the same time not over-paying for them.

After implementing these data-driven strategies, this particular institution jumped 18 positions in the next annual publication of USNWR. Many other institutions experienced a similar boon, leveraging the same analytical methodology—Georgia State University College of Law, a public law school located in Atlanta, Georgia improved their rank from 64 to 56; the University of Missouri's Trulaske College of Business, improved from 79 to 59; and University of Texas Arlington, an 'R1' university, improved the ranking of the graduate engineering program using a strategic data analysis to first move into the top 100, and again in a subsequent cycle to improve from 94 to 82.

Subjective metrics are more challenging to manipulate because the institution has less direct control over them. There are ways, however, to influence elements like reputation starting with an understanding of externally perceived strengths and weaknesses as they relate to brand recognition and assessment. A common way to perform this is through primary research. By independently surveying peers, the very ones who participate in ranking surveys that determine reputation-based scores, institutions can receive first-hand knowledge of how well-known they are as well as how 'the voters' perceive specific attributes. This can allow an institution to begin rebranding or marketing to address specific systemic issues or use the information at a micro-level to begin building partnerships that could positively influence future rankings using the 'one voter at a time' strategy.

Given that institutional reputation derives from the perceptions of students, peer institutions, industry members, and the local community, the micro-level strategy primarily involves the creation and cultivation of various kinds of partnerships with each of these groups. In terms of higher education partnerships, institutions may partner with individual institutions or academic consortia in a variety of ways, including sharing or integrating curriculum offerings. Partnership models include cross-registration, shared departments, joint or sequential degrees, credit recognition, student exchange, shared faculty, invitational speaker series, and curriculum licensing/franchising. This often leads to direct collaboration which will raise and positively influence brand awareness but could also have a halo effect. Research output, especially if completed jointly, is often an objective metric considered in rankings. For example, the University of Exeter uses the signing of memorandums of understanding, such as one with Peking University supporting research and student exchange, to create publicity for its international efforts. Seeking partnership with more highly ranked institutions has become a fairly common strategy that may not only help the seeking institution but further enhance the reputation of the leading institutions.

On the macro-level, institutions can engage in various forms of marketing to increase brand awareness. A common strategy is to dedicate a significant amount of messaging, across a variety of platforms, highlighting research. Furthermore, focusing on one particular area or topic of research rather than several may prove advantageous—depth may resonate more than breadth among peers as voters associate an institution with something specific. Relatedly, highlighting the achievements of faculty and making them accessible for interviews or guest lectures can also help raise institutional awareness positively.

Another strategy in which institutions engage to assist global reputation is to build awareness and partnerships through students; this can have a domino effect. For example, internationally well-known institutions will often create resources for groups of international students to attract them to study-abroad programs or next-level academic degrees that are all country-specific. This means offering resources such as websites and access to academic counsellors in native languages. For example, the University of Reading developed an in-depth guide which touches on many efforts that Reading is making to connect with China and Chinese students. The guide provides information on multiple partnerships between Reading and Chinese institutions, work the University is doing in China, including crop research and archaeology, and the staff that work in the region. It also provides more student-specific information including alumni information and profiles, student profiles, and groups available to students. International institutions often become aware of these kinds of activities which can result in positive brand awareness for the host institution.

Institutions can also leverage secondary research to make informed decisions regarding strategic actions. The University of Georgia (UGA), for example, had the goal in 2013 of becoming a premiere destination for online learning. To achieve this, they sought to expand and optimise their program portfolio of online offerings. To evaluate which opportunities would be most viable, UGA engaged in market research, using a variety of metrics to assess the potential magnitude of success for various programs of interest across three basic dimensions: student demand, as measured by historical degree completions; labour market demand as assessed through employment statistics by industry and an evaluation of specific current job openings; and the competitive landscape to both assess current levels of saturation as well as to develop positioning strategy through differentiation.

Through these market assessments, UGA was able to successfully launch several online programs, bringing their total up to 29 by 2016, with new offerings including an M.Ed in Human Resources and Organisational Development, and an M.Ed in Adult Education among others. The expansion of its online portfolio correlated with significant jumps in their USNWR rankings positions between 2015 and 2016—UGA went from 90 to five in the category of 'Best Online Bachelor's Programs' and from 22 to three in the category of 'Best Online Graduate Education Programs'.

Reflection and Conclusion

Classifications and rankings attempt to distil the complicated scope and work of higher education into simple numbers. Notwithstanding perverse influence, rankings capture attention of students, stakeholders, and the public. This chapter has detailed how two institutions manage rankings and classification. In addition, the across-institution section described steps other institutions have taken to better understand and to influence positively their ranking.

As noted in the introduction of this chapter, the academic literature on rankings is highly critical of the use of applying subjective and somewhat arbitrary weights to simple metrics as reflective of the quality of very complex organisations that, in effect, are actually a variety of 'businesses' that share a common parent brand. This chapter sought to shed light on how institutions manage, cope, and respond to these external assessments. The lived, campus reality of these assessment systems is supported by increasingly complex institutional research and numerable campus conversations about what the rankings actually measure. As Hazelkorn and Gibson (2018, 238) have noted, rankings and classifications have 'succeeded in taking the relatively mundane function of data collection and analysis out of the back office, and placing it at the centre of strategic decision-making and performance measurement'.

Perhaps the most warranted criticism of rankings is their focus on the elite goals of higher education to the detriment of widening participation goals that many states and nations seek to address. The cases in this chapter describe two institutions that feel pressure to maintain and even enhance the exclusivity of their admissions in order to be ranked highly in the most influential US undergraduate-focused rankings, the USNWR Best Colleges. We also cite above the impact this pressure has on the use of institutional resources to attract high academic quality students through merit-based aid, to the possible detriment of meeting the financial need of students from less affluent backgrounds. While acknowledging this criticism, it is also important to note that the pressure for these actions comes not only from rankings. A highly selective private institution like Dartmouth, is compared to its highly selective peers across a range of media, including consumer-oriented college guides that pre-date the rankings. For public institutions, like Indiana University, state and national policy has contributed to the ability-based stratification of institutions. The US federal government has taken the primary responsibility for meeting student financial need, with some supplements from state governments. This leaves the institution open to use its own funds for broader discretionary purposes, including improving the quality profile of incoming students. A significant number of state governments have developed policy that channels top academic students to the higher cost programs in the more selective flagship institutions and less academically prepared students to less costly regional four-year institutions, as well as the large two-year Community College sector in the United States.

Rankings and classifications lead institutions to consider minimalistic, external representations of their characteristics and performance as defined by media groups and academic research centres. Because of their appeal and visibility, institutions that seek to manage their image pay close attention and apply considerable resources to give their image a positive impact, despite the well-known limitations of these representational systems. While often a 'thorn in the side', institutions most often respond in ways intended to enhance their educational and research quality. Surely, there are HEIs that waste valuable time and effort by gaming such measures, which often results in embarrassing exposure and has a negative impact on image. Some institutions may indeed make changes for the sake of rankings that do not serve mission-related purposes. However, the cases in this chapter based on the experiences of the authors, describe how the institutions they work at and have consulted with generally try to 'look their best' and enhance their image through efforts to improve their most mission-critical activities of teaching, research and service.

References

Anderson, Nick. 2016. 'In New Sorting of Colleges, Dartmouth Falls Out of an Exclusive Group'. *Washington Post,* February 4, 2016. Accessed December 21, 2018. https://www.washingtonpost.com/news/grade-point/wp/2016/02/04/in-new-sorting-of-colleges-dartmouth-falls-out-of-an-exclusive-group/.

Dartmouth College. 2016. 'Dartmouth Science Strategy Report: Executive Summary'. December 21, 2016. Retrieved December 21, 2018 from https://www.dartmouth.edu/~provost/sciencestrategy/science_strategy_executive_summary.pdf.

Espeland, Wendy, and Michael Sauder. 2008. 'Rankings and Diversity'. *Southern California Review of Law & Social Justice* 18: 587–608.

Goldrick-Rab, Sara, Douglas N. Harris, and Philip A. Trostel. 2009. 'Why Financial Aid Matters (or Does Not) for College Success: Toward a New Interdisciplinary Perspective'. In *Higher Education: Handbook of Theory and Research,* edited by John C. Smart, 1–45. Dordrecht: Springer.

Graham, Amy, and Nicholas Thompson. 2001. 'Broken Ranks'. *Washington Monthly* 33 (9): 9–13.

Hazelkorn, Ellen. 2016. *Rankings and the Reshaping of Higher Education: The Battle for World-Class Excellence* (2nd ed.). New York: Palgrave Macmillan.

Hazelkorn, Ellen, and Andrew Gibson. 2018. 'The Impact and Influence of Rankings on the Quality, Performance and Accountability Agenda'. In *Research Handbook on Quality, Performance and Accountability in Higher Education,* edited by Ellen Hazelkorn, Hamish Coates, and Alexander McCormick, 232–248. Cheltenham, UK: Edward Elgar.

Heller, Donald E. 2006. 'Merit Aid and College Access'. Symposium on the consequences of merit-based student aid. Madison, WI: University of Wisconsin-Madison, Wisconsin Center for the Advancement of Postsecondary Education.

Ioannidis, John P.A., Nikolaos A. Patsopoulos, Fotini K. Kavvoura, Athina Tatsioni, Evangelos Evangelou, Ioanna Kouri, Despina G. Contopoulos-Ioannidis, and George Liberopoulos. 2017. 'International Ranking Systems for Universities and Institutions: A Critical Appraisal'. *BMC Medicine* 5 (1): 1–9.

Kuh, George D., and Ernest T. Pascarella. 2004. 'What Does Institutional Selectivity Tell Us About Educational Quality?' *Change: The Magazine of Higher Learning* 36 (5): 52–59.

Morse, Robert, Eric Brooks, and Matt Mason. 2018. 'Frequently Asked Questions: 2019 Best Colleges Rankings'. U.S. News & World Report, September 9, 2018. Retrieved December 21, 2018 from https://www.usnews.com/education/best-colleges/articles/rankings-faq.

Pusser, Brian, and Simon Marginson. 2013. 'University Rankings in Critical Perspective'. *The Journal of Higher Education* 84 (4): 544–568.

Rauhvargers, Andrejs. 2013. 'Global University Rankings and their Impact: Report II'. Brussels: European University Association. Accessed December 21, 2018 from https://ki.se/sites/default/files/eua_global_university_rankings_and_their_impact_report_ii.pdf.

Shin, Jung Cheol, and Robert K. Toutkoushian. 2011. 'The Past, Present, and Future of University Rankings'. In *University Rankings: Theoretical Basis, Methodol-*

ogy and Impacts on Global Higher Education, edited by Jung Cheol Shin, Robert K. Toutkoushian, and Ulrich. Teichler, 1–16. Dordrecht: Springer.

Volkwein, J. Fredericks, and Kyle V. Sweitzer. 2006. 'Institutional Prestige and Reputation Among Research Universities and Liberal Arts Colleges'. *Research in Higher Education* 47 (2): 129–148.

CHAPTER 6

National Evaluation Systems and Universities' Strategic Capacities: Case Studies among European Universities

Laura Behrmann and Thorben Sembritzki

Introduction

By the end of the 1980s, the research focus on higher education (HE) and research governance had shifted towards the complex interplay of different actors, strategies, instruments and mechanisms (Wittek 2007). This shift was intensified by national HE policies that gave universities an increased autonomy. Nevertheless, they remain embedded in national governance systems that are constituted by rather indirect modern forms of governance ('steering from a distance'; de Boer, Leisyte and Enders 2006), a development that naturally differs from country to country in its details. Against this background, evaluation of research has become an increasingly important policy practice. Fuelled by demands for greater accountability and the rise of international competition, different National Evaluation Systems (NES) have been implemented (de Boer, Enders and Schimank 2007). They involve different actors (state, academic or independent) and are organised in processes with different degrees of formalisation. Their results have to serve both state and universities; evaluation can be used for disclosure and assessment of performance as well as for developmental purposes.

In this chapter we offer a comparative framework of three NES—the British Research Excellence Framework (REF), the French *Haut conseil d'évaluation de la recherche et de l'enseignement supérieur* (HCERES; 'High Commission for Evaluation of Research and Higher Education'), and the German North Rhine-Westphalian (NRW) *Leistungsorientierte Mittelvergabe* (LOM—which loosely translates as 'performance based funding'); we compare them empirically in order to analyse the impact of NES as an instrument for universities' governance and their intra-organisational coordination. We ask: to what extent do NES inform, support and influence the strategic capacity of universities? What impact do evaluation systems, their procedures and outcomes have on organisational governance?

Universities' Actorhood within the Context of Evaluation

Various studies have considered the interaction between state and research organisations by looking at different elements of national HE systems (de Boer, Enders and Schimank 2007; Dawson, van Steen and van der Meulen 2009; Dobbins and Knill 2014). With a few exceptions, this obsession of HE scholars with the macro-level has led to neglecting the study of universities as governance actors. After the 'organisational turn' in HE it has become more reasonable to view it as '…an integrated, goal-oriented entity that is deliberately choosing its own actions and that can thus be held responsible for what it does' (Krücken and Meier 2006, 241; for a closer look at universities' actorhood in the governance of sciences and research; see also Whitley 2012 and Thoenig and Paradeise 2018).

Prior research has shown repeatedly that the self-governance of academic institutions, with its actions and practices, depends on the institution's (inter)national position and recognition—based on the importance attached to status-related dimensions like excellence (expert evaluation) and reputation (social evaluation) (e.g., Paradeise and Thoenig 2013). Organisations negotiate their goals and orientations within multiple 'fields', for example of the regional or state variety (Hüther and Krücken 2016). Within this framework we consider universities as actors of research governance. As Paradeise and Thoenig (2013) have found, evaluation is a key instrument for the governance of science and universities. Results are used as an input, justification or basis for strategy building (Musselin 2017; Gläser et al. 2010; Geuna and Martin 2003; Rossi, Lipsey and Freeman 2004). Especially elite universities tend to show robust, high strategic capacities; they pay attention to the impact of competitive dynamics, to international and societal contexts and to empowerment of management and academic staff. 'Strategies are run continuously' (Thoenig and Paradeise 2018, 60); they are not just written down in mission statements or programmatic lines, they also encourage the participation of management and staff in the strategizing processes. From this perspective on organisations in contemporary sociology, we analyse and compare the universities' handling of the evaluation processes (and results) and their contribution to a strategic capacity—e.g., in the sense of organisational learning, forming a research strategy and the 'becoming' of an organisation.

National Evaluation Systems in UK, Germany and France

Evaluations are systematic investigations of the utility and value of an object. With regard to research, evaluations can be focused on organisational dimensions, like research units or entire institutions, research projects or publications. They offer criteria for 'excellence' and major orientations for higher education institutions (HEI), like priority devoted to publications or a common goal for organisational development. State-implemented NES are intended to pursue three purposes, but not necessarily all of them at once: (1) to inform universities and stakeholders about the quality of research, (2) to provide incentives or recommendations for improving research, and (3) to support research by redistributing resources. We present three different NES, namely from France, the UK and Germany/NRW. Our findings for Germany are limited to NRW, as HE policies in Germany are in the responsibility of the 16 federal states, and there is no centralised system of evaluation. We have chosen NRW because it is not only the biggest German federal state (measured by population), but also constitutes the densest university landscape in Europe (with regard to the number of students and universities).

In Germany/NRW and the UK, universities cope with long-standing and established NES: the German LOM has been in existence since 1999, and the British Research Assessment Exercise (RAE) (predecessor of the REF) since 1986. In the UK, the core element of the REF—peer-review of publications—has remained the same over time; however, since the early introduction—and after every iteration of the RAE and REF—there have been passionate, extensive discussions in the academic community about this way of evaluating research. These have resulted in (minor) changes to the evaluation's methodology, like the introduction of additional case studies or emphasis on impact. In NRW, the implementation of the LOM has been relatively smooth, but currently the functionality and effectiveness of the LOM as an evaluation system is viewed critically within the academic community and the evaluated institutions. In contrast to NRW and UK, France has been a late starter in the introduction of competitive governance instruments; the first NES was not established until 2007. There are several reasons for this late development: on the one hand, research has only recently become a central task of the universities; on the other hand, competition is deemed as contradictory to the French ideal of 'Egalité'. Accordingly, differentiation and stratification have long been rejected to a considerable extent. However, the relatively low positions of French universities in the 2003 Academic Ranking of World Universities ('Shanghai-

Ranking')—with only two French universities among the top 100 universities, in comparison to nine from the UK and five from Germany—have accelerated a transformation of its academic system and the introduction of a NES.

Table 6.1: Comparison of NES

	France (HCERES)	UK (REF)	NRW (LOM)
Implementation	Introduced in 2007	Introduced in 1986 as RAE (REF since 2014)	Introduced in 1999
Executed by	HCERES (AERES until 2014) as independent agency	HEFCE (since 2018 by Research England)	Federal Ministry
Inclusion of Academic Peers	Yes	Yes	No
Timeframe	Quinquennial periods (different group of universities every year)	Every 6–7 years (parallel for all universities)	Every year (parallel for all universities)
Continuity	Regular changes in proceedings and topics	Slight changes of criteria over time	No crucial changes
Evaluation Object	University as a whole as well as individual units: position and strategy of the organisation (governance, research activities, education and internationality)	Units of Assessment (UOA) inside of each university: quality of research (publications, societal impact and research environment)	University as a whole: Performance (third party funding, teaching, gender equality)
Evaluation Methods	Ex-ante and ex-post – Panels and site visits – Peer review, self-report and panel reports	Ex-ante: – Process of expert/ peer-review by panels for each UOA – Quality-profile for each submission (from 4* to 1*)	Ex-ante: – Submission and registration of performance key figures from each university

	France (HCERES)	UK (REF)	NRW (LOM)
Results	Final report, open access	Ranking between institutions and UOA, open access	Results do not get published
Impact	Informs the Development Contract (COP); quality assurance for organisational development	Basis for the allocation of parts of basic funding between universities as well as for an (informal) distribution of reputation (via ranking)	Basis for the allocation of parts of the basic funding between universities

The French NES is executed by HCERES (formerly named AERES, *'Agence d'Evaluation de la recherche et de l'enseignement supérieur'*). Its introduction is linked to merger processes of French HEIs since 2007 which aim to reduce institutional complexity. The main purpose of the NES is to support organisational development (Musselin 2017) in the sense of research activities and international visibility. The evaluation process differs from our other cases. It is based on a combination of qualitative (descriptive and contextualising) methods like self-evaluation reports, site visits of a committee, and expert panels with peer reviews. As there is no standard-protocol with distinct criteria as in the REF or the LOM, the evaluation just needs to follow topics like research activities and environment, visibility and recognition of research, teaching and the academic agenda (HCERES 2016). However, evaluation is based on case specific topics like the university's self-imposed goals and development priorities; it is open to integrating singularities and peculiarities of each university. The public presentation of the results is a descriptive report including recommendations for the future development of the university. The French NES is linked to the management of universities more directly than REF or LOM are, as the results are meant to serve as a knowledge base for further management decisions (Musselin 2017). Universities are not obliged to act in accordance with the evaluation results and recommendations. There is no comparison to other universities. Evaluation only informs the development contracts between the state and each university. The evaluation periods (a five-year-cycle starting every year for a different group of universities) are synchronised with the development contracts which define the subsequent organisational goals.

In contrast to the French evaluation, the REF and LOM do not just assess research (in a broader sense); their results are directly linked to performance-based funding. Despite this common goal, they use different approaches.

The REF is the UK's system for assessing the quality of research in its HEI. REF procedures are at present controlled by Research England (until 2018 by the arms-length government body HEFCE), with the goal of increasing selectivity in the allocation of public resources (Geuna and Piolatto 2015). The REF functions as a quality-related (QR) performance-based funding measure that allocates funds to individual universities. This QR-funding represents about 20 percent of the overall research income from all sources for British public HEIs (de Boer et al. 2015, 112). Based on peer review, but with a fixed set of assessment criteria, the REF evaluates research outputs (normally publications) from eligible researchers, the research environment offered by the Units of Assessment (UOA), and the societal impact of the UOAs (up to 36 UOAs in one university). For the latter, as part of the assessment process, each UOA has to submit case studies demonstrating the impact of their research on wider society. The evaluation is carried out by academic experts that are organised in disciplinary panels. The REF turns the manifestations of qualitative evaluation objects (publications, impact and environment) into standardised, quantitative indicators. By doing so the REF results offer an ordinally-scaled ranking between each UOA—from 1* (recognised nationally) to 4* (world-leading). This ranking, on the one hand, serves as a basis for the allocation of QR-funding between the universities. On the other hand, the ranking offers a unit of quality measurement that can be used to compare UOAs within as well as between universities. Altogether, the REF uses a qualitative approach, but the final outcome is quantitative.

In NRW the Ministry for Culture and Science uses the LOM to allocate part of the basic funding (20%) to individual universities. The assessment is not based on the quality of research, as in the UK, but instead uses quantitative performance-related indicators with a specific focus: besides research success (45% of the LOM; measured by the amount of third party funding) there are accompanying awards for teaching (another 45%; measured by the number of graduates), and the final 10% for gender equality among professors (de Boer et al. 2015, 10).[1] The LOM uses quantitative data; it is an indicator-based system which, unlike the REF, is character-

---

[1] In the analysis of the LOM's implications for the universities' strategic capacities (see section 5), we are excluding the indicators for teaching and gender equality; the same goes for the UK, where the REF is accompanied by the Teaching Excellence and Student Outcomes Framework (TEF), which, unlike the LOM,

ised by the absence of peer judgements. But, like the REF, it is built as an incentive for market-like competition and redistribution of funds: the Ministry compares the results of the evaluated universities and divides out the evaluation-related funds between them. As the LOM results do not get published, the universities are not able to compare each other's results directly, but they are able to use their results for intra-organisational purposes.

Besides serving as a performance based funding measure, there is another common denominator for the REF and the LOM: unlike the French case-specific NES, the REF and the LOM apply the same country-specific dimensions for assessment to every unit—in NRW the universities are evaluated as a whole, while in the UK there are many units (UOA) in one university. Thus, both NES are creating a strong and common framework for each university. Across these three approaches, organisation is addressed differently: in the UK as a sum of individual units, in NRW as a single unit and in France—additionally—as a whole. In section 5 below we will lay out which differences have an impact on the universities' strategic capacities. Section 4 will discuss the approach to the research.

SAMPLING AND METHODS

Along this contrastive spectrum of evaluation instruments, we compare the universities' strategic capacities with regard to their NES in France, the UK and Germany/NRW[2] (Glaser and Strauss 1967). We have chosen universities that are 'combining a rather high level of international prestige and [...] excellence' (Thoenig and Paradeise 2016, 305); they usually demonstrate a well-developed strategic capacity (Thoenig and Paradeise 2018). According to the Times Higher Education Ranking 2017 and the CWTS-Leiden Ranking 2017 all institutions in our sample belong to a broader group of research-strong universities (top 10 on a national level). For the analysis[3] we have conducted comparative case studies across these univer-

---

does not count the number of graduates, but works as an assessment of the quality of undergraduate teaching.

[2] In addition to NRW we have analysed the governance of research in other German federal states, where there are no comparable evaluation systems in place; this is why we only present one German case.

[3] Our research is part of the project 'Governance and performance of research – An international comparison of scientific systems and their organisations', which has been carried out at the German Centre for Higher Education Research and

sities (Creswell et al. 2007). Our dataset consists of 20 expert interviews (Meuser and Nagel 2009) with Presidents, Vice-Presidents, Academic Registrars, Deans and Heads of Departments (HODs) from seven universities, and eight interviews with representatives of the Ministries and agencies (such as HCERES and the former HEFCE).

Table 6.2: Sample for case studies

	Pseudonyms for Cases	Number of Interviews
Germany (NRW)	University A	n=4
France	University B	n=3
	University C	n=2
	University D	n=2
UK (England)	University E	n=4
	University F	n=3
	University G	n=2
Total	**7 Universities**	**N=20**

The interviews were transcribed in the original language[4] and anonymised. We have analysed them combining inductive and deductive coding (Schreier 2012). Obviously, the small number of cases cannot cover the logical combinations of possible outcomes and explanatory factors, but they indicate interesting comparative evidence.

Evaluations and Organisational Governance: Empirical Findings from Case Studies

FRANCE: 'THE GENTLE METHOD'

The interview partners point out that universities have to cope with a lot of new tasks and requirements such as mergers of research organisations and universities, the growing importance of research or a demographic gap in

---

Science Studies (DZHW) and funded by the German Federal Ministry of Education and Research.

[4] We have translated the French and German interview passages into English.

the staff. In this transformation process, evaluation reports are welcomed as handy instruments used especially by Management. The mostly positive perception of the evaluation is attributed to its procedures: self-reports alongside certain topics and panel visits enhance the organisation's self-reflection, as they take into account the particularities of its 'Gestalt':

> We appreciate the evaluation because it does not exclusively concentrate on performance [...], it also looks at organisational efficiency and quality. (University C: Dean)

Evaluation reports of HCERES offer recommendations for future development processes, which on the one hand are very general, for example attending to internationality and excellence, and on the other hand are case-specific, for example clarifying the competence between two units of research to avoid duplication. Results serve as information and are used as authority and justification for management decisions.

> Evaluations are very important for a lab director because the evaluation is able to point out things that you may already have in mind, but that you are not able to state. (University D: Member of the Board of Directors)

The report empowers the position of University Management, for example the Deans and Lab Directors. At the same time the absence of specific performance indicators as in the REF or LOM encourages the intra-organisational dialogue and reflection on quality, efficiency and goal setting.

> I think it's a good thing that units are evaluated, because it forces units to look at whether they have met the goals they gave themselves and to develop new goals. (University C: Vice-President)

Although the French NES does not gear all activities towards performance indicators, the topics and the results create an overall orientation that supports political goals, for example, competition, internationality and a differentiation of the research landscape.

As research is of growing interest, university management aims to support research activities and to improve research conditions. Interviewees report on processes of reorganisation: one university has established a Research Department that supports research proposals and English publications. International visibility of research is emphasised via NES as being of increasing importance; this in return leads universities to build strategies in order to obtain more international research projects and to produce more international publications. For strengthening research new structures like research clusters or special bodies for strategy setting have been introduced:

> And this [Cluster Board] is where we will discuss strategies and responses to proposals. For some proposals there is a need for coordination at the level of units [e.g., Research Clusters]. Quite often the evaluation falls back on us. [...] It is really a work of consultation and expertise, [...] it has influence, and so it becomes a strategic starting point for us. (University B: Research Cluster Leader)

Our interviewees lack the potential pressure of an external sanction to justify their actions; accordingly, the evaluation is considered as a weak instrument. The evaluation is not directly connected to sanction instruments or incentives. From this point of view the openness and particularities of the NES report are viewed rather critically:

> Sometimes the HCERES reports are attenuated. They are quite codified and politically correct. [...] They may be too gentle. (University C: Vice-President)

Written words evoke a higher need for interpretation than indicator-based outcomes like in the REF or the LOM; clear facts, tangible judgements to produce pressure on decision making are missing. However, there is another problem associated with that: French evaluation does not help to identify excellence at a glance.

> But for our University [and the evaluation report], the challenge arises because all our units are good to very good. [...] And so although everything is very good, one must be able to see those who are excellent. (University C: Vice-President)

From this point of view the evaluation does not provide clear information about quality differences, as the REF does; strategising and decision making remains difficult. This perspective is comprehensible given the French historical background that universities are exempt from state steering—university management is not used to this style of decision-making in terms of organisational development. The question is how will they make use of the evaluation in future years? Will they get used to this autonomy or are they expecting a new steering instrument which might be a more standardised evaluation like the REF. Other deficits of the evaluation are mentioned in the interviews as well. Our interview partners complain about the great effort and the magnitude of resources that it demands— scarce resources that are lacking elsewhere.

As the evaluation and the development contracts are organised quinquennially, the university does not have to cope with continuous requirements. The evaluation presents itself as a singular event that has not been internalised by the management processes as has happened for the REF or the LOM. The HCERES is perceived as an external intervention that is repeated every five years, but with changing topics. So far, unlike the REF or LOM, it is far from being self-sustaining.

Moreover, interviewees state that 'personal relationships' (University C: Vice-President) with the state (contacts between members of the Ministry and universities, so-called old boy networks) remain the most important factor for informing strategy building. In consequence, when it comes to staff involvement, dialogues and strategy setting it is rather a question of individual network positions than of the quality of performance (see also Friedberg and Musselin 1993).

The evaluation offers some guidance on the extensive transformation processes of HE in France, but it is insufficient to cover the complexity of the organisation in an even more complex system. Evaluation in France clearly supports the emergence of organisational actorhood in the sense of formulating objectives and goals, reflecting on decisions and their implications, fostering competitive dynamics and developing mainstream orientations like strengthening research, but it does not compensate for the reduced state-steering. Whether evaluations are perceived as helpful for increasing strategic capacity depends on the creativity and courageousness of actors in the universities.

UK: 'WE ARE COMPLETELY AUTONOMOUS'

UK universities claim to be 'completely autonomous' (University F: President) in how they decide to govern their own research efforts. Nonetheless, the REF's strong focus on research quality and research impact is described as a priority shift to which they needed to adjust:

> It structures everything we do on the research side. So when we appoint
> people we look at what contribution they'll make to the REF, […] when

people are thinking about what they have to do to manage their own time, they're focused very much on what they need to do for the REF. Departments in constructing their strategy will be thinking about how to get the most out of the REF. (University E: Faculty Chair)

The integration of the REF cycle into the university governance of research is defined as a process that has to be aligned with the universities' research strategies. The main purpose of these research strategies is to commit the researchers to the overall goal of research excellence and, at the same time, to communicate that the university is willing to support their efforts:

> Part of our strategy is an explicit statement of research expectations, and this is perhaps a good example of how policy was developed in this University. [...] To support research performance the University will provide A, B, C, D and in turn we expect you to behave A, B, C, D. [...] it also gives a clear steer and this was a bit that was most controversial in at least some [Departments] that in a REF cycle of five or six years you would be expected to produce four items or equivalent of three star or four star quality. (University E: Vice-President for Research)

The universities have adapted to the REF process by creating an internal control mechanism that gets 'peer-review managed' (University E: Vice-President for Research) through the Departments or Faculties. It underlies the REF's logic of producing high quality publications, but at the same time offers informed insights for administrators and researchers involved:

> So there's a lot of planning a long time in advance been going on for a couple of years and part of that we'd be doing irrespective of the REF: Monitoring our performance individually and collectively and that would be assessing research outputs, assessing research grant income, and assessing impact and citations with the key measures. That is done anyway on an annual performance review for the whole university and it's built up from individual [...] Faculties to senior level. (University E: President)

On the one hand, an annual performance review—which can be found in a similar way in each of the universities—is used to accompany and prepare for the REF, and on the other hand the results are communicated across the different university levels in order to adjust research and publication strategies in accordance with the REF:

And actually part of that sphere was to deliberately pull back from high volume low quality outputs. [...] the key steer there in terms of quality is to aim for prestigious high quality work. (University E: Vice-President for Research)

The universities are faced with a demanding pressure that stems directly from the REF. Therefore, Deans and HODs delegate this pressure to the UOA and their researchers. As they are the ones that decide which publications will be chosen for the REF-submission they use the incentive of competition around reputation that comes with representing the UOA and contributing to a best-possible evaluation result. 'To succeed in this endeavour, universities and their departments must increase their competitiveness by recruiting researchers with a particularly wide record of third-party funds and publications' (Münch and Schäfer 2013, 61). In order to achieve both, obtaining and attracting them, UOA and universities need to prove their institutional excellence in the REF because its 'outcomes will feed into a department's reputation' (University E: Faculty Chair). This creates a Matthew-effect: universities and their UOAs that have achieved a certain level of excellence in the REF use the outcome to improve their reputation; this in return, increases their strategic capacities to aspire towards even higher excellence. On the downside, universities and UOAs with a 'bad' or worsening REF outcome may experience an immediate decrease of their capacities.

The ranking informs the organisation and its members to what extent the UOAs have achieved a certain degree of excellence (in the sense of the ranking). Subsequently, these results are used as a basis for further consultations between University Leadership, Faculties and Departments on how to make use of the REF results—which remain quite abstract in the sense that they are not delivered as qualitative judgements (despite being based on peer-review), but instead only allow for a standardised and highly aggregated comparison of different units. While in France the descriptive evaluation results are very open in order to invoke further interpretations, the scope for interpretation of the REF's results is limited by its form as an ordinally-scaled ranking:

And there are rankings that are published on everything imaginable: for comparing universities as a whole, for comparing disciplines, [...] and everybody uses the best ones. So you can say: 'Well this unit we were topping by all measures, this one we didn't do very well in'. And then there would be a major review that would follow on why we didn't do

very well: 'Was it the submission or is it just that we're not very good?'
(University E: President)

Although the results are intended as elements of an unmistakable ranking, the universities have to find their own way to handle them. For a contextualising interpretation they have to rely on their own control mechanism—the annual performance review, which provides the necessary
context information for all researchers and their Departments on how
they may improve. The adaptation of the annual performance review to
the REF demonstrates the strength and effectiveness of the REF's impact.
The 'long period of preparation for the REF' (University G: HOD) has
been aligned with the agenda set by the university, moving the coordination from state control to institutional control: the REF functions not
only as a NES, but also as an instrument for an organisationally controlled
evaluation.

The emergence of internal control mechanisms can be interpreted
as sustained organisational attention to the evaluation of research. Their
complementarity to the REF has, in turn, increased the relevance and
omnipresence of the REF. So, although the universities claim to be totally
autonomous in their decisions and actions, when it comes to governing
their own research efforts, their strategic capacity is clearly framed by the
REF's logic of accountability and competition, which has been deeply
internalised within the organisation and its members.

GERMANY/NRW: 'ACTUALLY, IT DOES NOT MATTER'

Both performance-based funding systems, the REF and the LOM, provide
incentives in the form of funding grants which are signalled through market-like outcomes (de Boer et al. 2015): the better a university performs
with regard to the measurement indicators, the more money it receives.
One might conclude that both NES serve as governance instruments in
order to sustain a hierarchical micromanagement of universities. But this
assumption neglects the fact that the evaluations in both countries, although their frameworks are defined by politics, determine neither how
the universities are supposed to handle the outcome nor the funding that
is attached to it.

The intra-organisational allocation remains in the hands of the universities, as in the NRW university: on the one hand, some academic autonomy still remains; on the other hand, the formalised procedures that define
how the LOM requirements need to be implemented affect the University
Board and the Deans who need to agree on how the funds will be allocated

to and within the Faculties; their professors have the ultimate freedom to decide what the LOM funds will get spent on:

> The professors have to decide for themselves what they are doing. That is not pre-determined by the university; for example, you may spend only 60 percent for research, only 40 percent for teaching. You can spend everything on teaching, or everything for research. (University A: Academic Registrar)

The internal allocation of the LOM funds does not fully match the model at the federal state level:

> We steer slightly differently. [...] we [the Board] have an agreement with the Faculties in the funding of the university that says they will get such a budget in the next few years, regardless of the LOM developments. We as a central body absorb the fluctuations. (University A: Academic Registrar)

As a consequence, the intra-organisational arrangements for the allocation of LOM funds are basically disabling the intended effect of the LOM to foster competition inside and between universities, and to award those that succeed. For the internal allocation model little attention is paid to competitive dynamics between the Faculties. Instead high attention is paid to resources for implementing the overall research strategy—this is the common goal of both the University Board and the Deans. The LOM's relative failure to incentivise research performance and the passivity of University Board and Deans at promoting competition can be explained by the interviewees; they state that the LOM gives incentives for what the researchers are supposed to do anyway—to attract external funding in order to be able to conduct further research:

> The LOM has no direct impact on research, but rather an indirect one. That we simply have to see that our third-party funding is correspondingly good. But you do not have that alone in your hand. It depends actually on the professors and their activity. [...] But, as I said, when it comes to third party funding, I see little need for action [from Faculties or University Board] because the external funding is quite big. (University A: Dean)

In addition to that the behaviour of researchers is perceived as barely susceptible to influence. Altogether, the organisation does not adapt to the LOM's objectives of incentivising research efforts in order to improve the university's LOM results:

> Yes, let's say, actually it does not matter. The result of the LOM pleases us. [...] But we do not orient the direction of research to the LOM. Instead, the LOM is the result of our research, of all our activities here. Not just research, but also our teaching activities. And strategically, we're not looking at how we'd do better in the LOM if we drive Strategy A or B. We do not care, but we align our strategy with how we believe we are most successful. (University A: Academic Registrar)

Despite these restrictions, both institutional (with regard to the LOM that does not provide a comparable ranking) and organisational (with regard to the high autonomy of professors in the university), the LOM does expand the organisational strategic capacities in the sense that its results can get used by the University Board as a justification for management decisions, if deemed necessary—like redistributing a professorship that is up for reappointment to another Department, or providing equipment or personnel that is needed to ensure the ability to act in new research areas. The LOM supports further processes of self-evaluation and organisational learning as well as a coherent development of the organisation's units, but only by providing basic information. It is mostly the outcome (in the form of funding) rather than the result of the LOM that empowers organisational actions in NRW—while it is both, results and outcome, in the UK, and results only in France.

IMPACT OF NES ON ORGANISATIONAL STRATEGIC CAPACITIES

In our case studies we have identified different NES components with an impact on the organisational 'strategic capacity' (see Thoenig and Paradeise 2018, 61).

Table 6.3: Impact of NES on organisational strategic capacities

	France (HCERES)	UK (REF)	NRW (LOM)
Resource allocation via NES	Not at all	Adaptation of REF model	Own allocation model
Structural changes	Yes	No	No
Installation of main value orientation	Yes, on research	Yes, on publications	No
Timeframe	Temporal distance	Omnipresent	Present

	France (HCERES)	UK (REF)	NRW (LOM)
Attention to competitive dynamics	Between research institutions	Very high: competition between UOAs and universities	Not at all
Empowerment of management	Information, reflection and justification	Information and justification	Primarily on resource allocation
Empowerment of academic staff	Strong involvement (networks)	Depending on results (stratification)	No
Assurance for decision-making	No	Yes	Yes
Objectives and goals for strategising	Yes	No	No
Action mode	Negotiation and influence	Comparison and observation	Observation
Strategic capacity	**High impact, but no clear goal orientation for actions**	**High impact with clear goal orientation for actions**	**Low impact, but clear goal orientation for actions**

The resources that are allocated via NES are either redistributed via adaptation of the NES model (UK) or by implementing a proprietary model (NRW). Structural changes are only initiated in the French cases, which can be traced to the purpose of the French evaluation to support organisational development.

The character of NES supports the organisational value orientation. In the UK all researchers are committed to paying attention to the REF criteria in their daily work; the evaluation with a focus on high quality publications has become omnipresent: 'The reactivity of rankings will then result in research being only carried out in such a way as to conform with indicators of relevance to resources' (Münch and Schäfer 2013, 60). This is not the case for the LOM that does not provide a visible ranking that can be attributed to researcher's efforts; accordingly—and although it is a performance-based funding system—it fails to create a compliance between researchers and LOM in the sense of an intrinsic motivation. In France the criteria increase the importance of research activities, but as criteria are still changing, and as the universities are concerned with the evaluation only periodically at long intervals the impact is low.

The nature of the results and how they are presented (numbers vs written report) is affecting the attention paid to competition. In the UK we observed a very high emphasis on competitive dynamics. Stratification is a topic between organisations in a national and international context. French evaluation pays little attention to competition but has evoked a special path of tying HEI to a nation-state framework.

Evaluations empower management; it becomes sensitised to research activities and can also exploit evaluation results for justifying decisions. In the French cases we observe more dialogue and reflection than in the UK cases, but due to the long-term implementation of the REF, university management in the UK case has achieved a higher level of professionalism than in France. Empowerment of management in the UK becomes linked to striving for excellence, while in France this is happening through the involvement of individuals in political networks. In the case of NRW the empowerment of management is limited to the justification of management decisions.

Building on these observations we can explain the interplay of assurance for decision-making and goal setting within the organisations: universities in the UK and NRW know what they have to do for a better result in the next evaluation—or to be excellent regardless of the evaluation (as in NRW). In France the report contains recommendations that address processes, but objectives and goals are not as distinct and clear as in the REF. The REF implements an external goal orientation; universities in the UK are used to their actorhood and know how to exploit the REF for their strategy building—but always in accordance with the REF. The French NES leaves it to the universities to decide the extent to which they follow up on the recommendations. As they are not familiar with this kind of actorhood, some universities follow the recommendations; others ignore or even reject them.

Finally, we can identify NES-specific organisational action modes for our cases: in the UK cases we have a high level of (intra-)organisational observation and comparison, while in the French cases mutual negotiating and influencing is of higher importance. We can sum up that NES serve organisational strategy building in different ways: in the UK cases organisational actorhood has adapted to the REF's goals and uses them to expand HEIs' strategic capacity, in France organisational actorhood and strategic capacity is an effect of the organisational evaluation, while in NRW the impact is low—despite a clear goal orientation.

Conclusion and Discussion

Our comparative qualitative case studies provide a number of findings that hold significance. At a general level, the study explains how each NES has an impact on universities' strategy capacities. The empirically observed action modes—observing (and comparing) versus negotiating and influencing—illustrate the effect on intra-organisational governance.

Although our analyses are based on top performing research universities we would like to point out some findings regarding HE systems: in France the empowerment of organisational actors through evaluations could open up further opportunities for diverse organisational developments that are not limited to pre-determined goals, like achieving a certain kind of 'excellence'; at the same time, the lack of a clear goal orientation could also hamper decision-making processes in organisations. In the UK the room for organisational manoeuvres depends strongly on the placement in the REF ranking; for universities that strive for 'excellence' achieving a good REF outcome has become a means to an end. In NRW the LOM outcome has very little impact on the university's governance and its strategic capacities, but it might have for other NRW universities that are not as successful in attracting external funding, but want to expand their research efforts; they, accordingly, depend on a good (and improving) outcome in the LOM and the additional funding that is attached.

For our findings it is important to keep in mind that the national context has to be included as an explanatory factor: universities' actorhood depends on different stages of societal transformation. But as other authors already noted—being sensitive to a specific historical and cultural development is a challenge for the methodology of international comparison.

In this chapter we have looked at organisational capacities and capabilities influenced by NES. However, our findings also show tendencies for different effects on individual researchers; for further research it might be interesting to include their perspective and to analyse the effects of NES on their orientations and actions.

References

Creswell, John W., William E. Hanson, Vicki L. Plano Clark, and Alejandro Morales. 2007. 'Qualitative Research Designs: Selection and Implementation'. *The Counseling Psychologist* 35 (2): 236–264. Accessed November 02, 2018. doi: 10.1177/0011000006287390.

Dawson, James, Jan Steen, and Barend van der Meulen. 2009. *Science Systems Compared: A First Description of Governance Innovations in Six Science Systems.* Den Haag: Rathenau Instituut.

de Boer, Harry, Ben Jongbloed, Paul Benneworth, Leon Cremonini, Renze Kolster, Andrea Kottmann, Katharina Lemmens-Krug, and Hans Vossensteyn. 2015. *Performance-based Funding and Performance Agreements in Fourteen Higher Educations Systems.* Enschede: CHEPS.

de Boer, Harry, Jürgen Enders, and Uwe Schimank. 2007. 'On the Way towards New Public Management? The Governance of University Systems in England, the Netherlands, Austria, and Germany'. In *Theory of the Firm: Governance, Residual Claims and Organizational Forms (Preface and Introduction)*, edited by Michael J. Jensen, 137–152. Dordrecht: Springer.

de Boer, Harry, Liudvika Leisyte, and Jürgen Enders. 2006. 'The Netherlands – Steering from a Distance'. In *Reforming University Governance – Changing Conditions for Research in Four European Countries*, edited by Barbara M. Kehm and Ute Lanzendorf, 59–98. Bonn: Lemmens.

Dobbins, Michael, and Christoph Knill. 2014. *Higher Education Governance and Policy Change in Western Europe. International Challenges to Historical Institutions.* Basingstoke: Palgrave Macmillan.

Friedberg, Erhard, and Christine Musselin. 1993. *L'Etat face aux universités en France et en Allemagne.* Paris: Anthropos.

Geuna, Aldo, and Ben Martin. 2003. 'University Research Evaluation and Funding. An International Comparison'. *Minerva* 41:277–304. Accessed November 02, 2018. doi: https://doi.org/10.1023/B:MINE.0000005155.70870.bd.

Geuna, Aldo, and Matteo Piolatto. 2015. *Research Assessment in the UK and Italy: Costly and Difficult, but Probably Worth (at Least for a While).* Brighton: Science Policy Research Unit.

Glaser, Barney G., and Anselm L. Strauss. 1967. *The Discovery of Grounded Theory: Strategies for Qualitative Research.* Chicago: Aldine.

Gläser, Jochen, Stefan Lange, Grit Laudel, and Uwe Schimank. 2010. 'Informed Authority? The Limited Use of Research Evaluation Systems for Managerial Control in Universities'. In *Reconfiguring Knowledge Production: Changing Authority Relationships in the Sciences and Their Consequences for Intellectual Innovation*, edited by Richard Whitley, Jochen Gläser, and Lars Engwall, 149–183. Oxford: Oxford University Press.10.1007/s10734-015-9974-7.

HCERES Évaluation des unités de recherche. 2016. Référentiel d'évaluation des unités de recherche. *Haut Conseil de l'évaluation de la recherche et de l'enseignement supérieur.*

Hüther, Otto, and Georg Krücken. 2016. 'Nested Organisational Fields: Isomorphism and Differentiation among European Universities'. In *Research in the Sociology of Organisations*, edited by Elizabeth Popp Berman and Catherine Paradeise, 53–83. Bingley: Emerald Group Publishing Limited.

Krücken, Georg, and Frank Meier. 2006. 'Turning the University into an Organizational Actor'. In *Globalization and Organization*, edited by Gili Drori, John Meyer and Hokyu Hwang, 241–257. Oxford: Oxford University Press.

Meuser, Michael, and Ulrike Nagel. 2009. 'The Expert Interview and Changes in Knowledge Production'. In *Interviewing Experts*, edited by Alexander Bogner, Beate Littig, and Wolfgang Menz, 17–42. Basingstoke: Palgrave Macmillan.

Münch, Richard, and Len Ole Schäfer. 2014. 'Rankings, Diversity and the Power of Renewal in Science. A Comparison between Germany, the UK and the US'. In *European Journal of Education*, 49 (1): 60–76. Accessed January 21, 2019. doi: 10.1111/ejed.12065.

Musselin, Christine. 2017. *La grande course des universités*. Paris: Presses de la Sciences Po.

Paradeise, Catherine, and Jean-Claude Thoenig. 2013. 'Academic Institutions in Search of Quality: Local Orders and Global Standards'. *SAGE journals* 34 (2): 189–218. Accessed October 26, 2018. doi: https://doi.org/10.1177/0170840612473550.

Paradeise, Catherine, Emanuela Reale, Ivar Bleiklie, and Ewan Ferlie. 2009. *University Governance. Western European Comparative Perspective*. Dordrecht: Springer.

Rossi, Peter H., Mark W. Lipsey, and Howard E. Freeman. 2004. *Evaluation: A Systematic Approach*. Thousand Oaks, London, New Delhi: Sage publications.

Schreier, Margrit 2012. *Qualitative Content Analysis in Practice*. Los Angeles, London, New Delhi, Singapore, Washington DC: Sage publications.

Thoenig, Jean-Claude, and Catherine Paradeise. 2016. 'Strategic Capacity and Organisational Capabilities: A Challenge for Universities'. *Minerva* 54: 293–324. Accessed November 02, 2018. doi: 10.1007/s11024-016-9297-6.

Thoenig, Jean-Claude, and Catherine Paradeise. 2018. 'Higher Education Institutions as Strategic Actors'. *European Review* 26: 57–69. Accessed November 02, 2018. doi: 10.1017/S1062798717000540.

Whitley, Richard. 2012. 'Transforming Universities. National Conditions of Their Varied Organisational Actorhood'. *Minerva* 50 (4): 493–510. doi:10.1007/s11024-012-9215-5.

Wittek, Rafael. 2007. 'Governance from a Sociological Perspective'. In *New Forms of Governance in Research Organizations. Disciplinary Approaches, Interfaces and Integration*, edited by Dorothea Jansen, 71–98. Dordrecht: Springer.

Student Experience and the 'Three Cs'

Recruiting and Managing Students

CHAPTER 7

Searching for the Perfect Match: Evaluation of Personal Statements Using a Multi-method Approach

Julia Zeeh, Karl Ledermüller and Michaela Kobler-Weiß

Introduction und Background to the Study

In European higher education, two major trends can be observed: growth in student numbers and increased student mobility. These changes have triggered an intensified competition among Higher Education Institutions (HEIs) with the attraction and recruitment of the best applicants becoming increasingly important.

In such a competitive HEI setting, it is crucial for universities to identify prospective students who are meeting their requirements. Thus, in the drive to attract the top students, universities have generated a broad set of admission procedures. University admissions can take numerous forms and there are different approaches in different countries. In the UK, for instance, prior educational attainment is critical for admission to the majority of HEIs. Interviews are also a common type of entry assessment. In other cases, universities rely on written entry exams while others prefer a combination of different assessment types. In Austria, there is an increasing reliance on written entry tests. While it is generally assumed that these tests must fulfil certain quality standards, other assessment techniques have not been subject to thorough evaluation. We would thus like to address this gap, at least partially, by evaluating the content of personal statements. Such an approach could enrich the academic discourse on the validity and effectiveness of admission procedures.

In the present chapter we suggest a new approach for evaluating personal statements as one kind of entry assessment. By means of empirical research methods, we aim to show how a multi-method approach can help HEIs to evaluate personal statements and to find their 'ideal student fit' with regard to signals, social dimension and study success.

Theoretical Background

STUDY SUCCESS, DROPOUT AND PRESELECTION

The intensified competition among HEIs has led to a situation in which they are increasingly under pressure to create effective learning environments in order to achieve good learning outcomes and keep dropout rates low. There is abundant empirical literature on study success. Numerous studies show that it is affected by a multitude of variables which can be grouped into three main categories:

(1) Personal factors, for example cognitive capacity and psychological factors such as study motivation (compare, for instance, Blüthmann et al. 2011; Heublein et al. 2003 and 2009; Kolland 2011; Schiefele et al. 2007)

(2) Curriculum structure and academic support, for example study support, social orientation (see Heublein et al. 2009; Kolland 2011) and finally

(3) External factors, for example including employment and social class (see, for instance, Bargel and Bargel 2010; Geißler 2006; Heublein et al. 2003 and 2009; Pechar and Wroblewski 1998; Schiefele et al. 2007; Unger et al. 2015; ESU 2008).

More recently, there has been substantive research on how motivational factors influence successful learning (Linnenbrink and Pintrich 2002, 313; Helmke and Weinert 1997, 11). These studies show that different types of motivation can have either a positive or a negative impact on study success (Clark et al. 2014; Eccles and Wigfield 2002). Most studies differentiate between extrinsic and intrinsic motivation. Extrinsic motivation refers to situations where external pressure makes a person undertake a particular action. Intrinsic motivation, on the other hand, means that an action is triggered by a person's genuine interest (Aronson et al. 2004). With regard to study success, intrinsic motivation is superior to its extrinsic counterpart. In general, it is assumed that students who are driven by intrinsic motivation deal with course topics more intensively and more comprehensively, and thus achieve better learning results (Schlag 2004; Prenzel 1996).

However, there is consensus that learning effectiveness is determined not only by psychosocial factors (e.g., study motivation) but also by sociodemographic factors such as social background (Blüthmann et al. 2011; McKenzie and Schweitzer 2001; Schiefele et al. 2007; Bargel and Bargel 2010; Geißler 2006; Pechar and Wroblewski 1998; Unger et al. 2015; ESU 2008). Limited access to social, cultural and economic capital as well as habitus discrepancies (mismatch between school and university habitus) may lead to a reduced likelihood of successful study completion (Nairz-Wirth et al. 2017). Moreover, socio-economic background clearly affects the motivation to study: students from lower social classes tend to choose their studies based on anticipated financial benefits and seldom based on the promise of cultural education (Bargel and Bargel 2010, 11–12).

PERSONAL STATEMENTS AND SIGNALS

Personal statements belong to the same classification as letters of recommendation and previous work experience, namely non-cognitive selection tools. In an HEI setting, their primary purpose is to provide applicants with means of expressing their interest in a particular study program (de Visser et al. 2017; Fastre et al. 2008). Universities, on the other hand, can use personal statements to find out to what extent the prospective students' expectations actually correspond to what a certain degree program has to offer (Reumer and van der Wende 2010).

In general, personal statements not only contain pure motivation to study at a specific HEI but also signals intended to convince the representatives of HEIs that they are an ideal fit. The statements in application letters can thus be defined as 'managing HEIs' expectations' meaning that students tell HEIs what they assume the institutions want to hear. That is, they anticipate what students think the HEI's academic recruitment and selection teams would like to read; and this substantially affects the expectations communicated in their personal statement.

Spence (1973) argues that recruiting decisions in companies can be, from a decision-theory point of view, classified as decisions under uncertain conditions with incomplete information. This argument is also valid for HEI student recruiting decisions. Signals, especially when the prerequisites for being able to send them are costly (e.g., obtaining an elite school graduation certificate or cultivating certain leisure activities that express a particular motivation) support recruitment officers in their decisions. We assume that applicants use personal statements to send signals to HEIs that express their actual, as well as the supposedly desired motivation, that is, what students think the HEIs representatives would *like* them to say.

Taking into account this potential social desirability bias, the present chapter will treat the statements expressed in students' application letters as 'signals'.

RESEARCH QUESTIONS

In our analysis of personal statements, we assume that applicants send signals to an HEI in order to express their (socially desirable) motivation for taking up studies at this particular institution. Analysing signals enables HEIs not only to learn more about prospective students' anticipations of expectations but also to investigate the link between signals and student performance as well as effects relating to social class.

The present study will address the following research questions:

What are (the most frequent) words or rather signals[1] applicants use in their personal statements?
Considering the competitive HEI setting and the drive to attract the top students, universities would be well advised to learn more about prospective students' personal reasons to study at a specific HEI. Although there has been substantive research on how motivational factors can influence study success (Linnenbrink and Pintrich 2002, 313), the statements in students' application letters have not yet been analysed from this perspective. The focus of this research thus addresses the question of how specific statements relate to study success.

Which of those signals leads to positive academic performance?
Given the tough competition among HEIs, universities could try to strengthen their international positioning by addressing and selecting students whose signals are in accordance with the universities' strategic orientation. HEIs with an international focus, for instance, will look for students cultivating an equally global mind-set while those particularly strong on research are more likely to attract students aiming to pursue a research career. Conversely, the analysis of frequently stated signals could in turn influence and shape marketing strategies and courses as well as curricula development.

---

[1] For our definition of 'signals' see p. 133.

What is the relationship between signals, study success and social class?

Finally, another useful analysis criterion is the social dimension of higher education as its enhancement is one of the targets of the European Higher Education Area (EHEA). In the London Communiqué (2007), members of the EHEA have agreed, inter alia, to ensure that the cohort diversity of the total population should be reflected at all levels of higher education— starting with the date of admission (London 2007, 5).

Thus, HEIs could substantially benefit from considering the social dimension in the evaluation of their assessment techniques. When analysing the impact of different signals on study success, it is crucial to consider what impact the students' social status can have on their reasons to study at a specific HEI. Therefore, this paper will try to investigate the complex interrelation between signals, study success and social class.[2]

Approach

DEFINITIONS

In order to answer the identified research questions, 16,600 personal statements were examined; these were submitted between the academic year 2013/14 and 2016/17 as part of the application process for the bachelor's program 'Business, Economics and Social Sciences' at the Vienna University of Business and Economics (WU). The submission of personal statements was the second step in the application process. First, prospective students had to complete an online registration form and secondly, they had to submit their personal statement using a free text box on the application form. The analysis was conducted by means of the open-source statistical environment R (R Core Team 2018) and several packages (tm (2018), wordcloud (2018), stringr (2018), SnowballC (2014), qpcR (2018), cluster (2018), fpc (2018), lattice (2018), tibble (2018), dplyr (2018), tidytext (2018), tidyr (2018).

Study success was measured through ECTS credits awarded to the student. As part of the entrance exam for the academic year 2016/17, a questionnaire with sociodemographic questions for evaluation purposes was distributed. Therefore, all analysis related to social background is based on this data set (n=2,918). Social class was measured by means of an index taking the level of education and professional status of the appli-

---

[2] These questions are further discussed in: Zeeh, Ledermüller, Kobler-Weiß, 2018.

cants' parents into account (Unger et al. 2015). For analysis, students were grouped in four different social classes: Upper, upper middle, middle and lower social class.

METHOD

To ensure a high level of usability and applicability of the results, a three-stage multi-method approach, combining quantitative and qualitative methods, was applied to investigate the interrelation between different signals, social class and study success.

In the first stage, text-mining techniques were used to help discover patterns in the data and identify differences in signals between the different social strata. We followed the 'bag-of-words' model that ignores the order of keywords, phrases or other text elements in a document and focuses on frequency of domain specific anchor phrases (after tokenization) in the elements of our corpus. Classic text mining procedures were applied to build document-term matrixes for further analysis (Feinerer and Hornik 2018).

However, classical text-mining techniques based on the bag-of-words model do not shed light on context-related issues. As word order within a sentence is ignored and words are counted by frequency in a document of a corpus, a deeper understanding of the text is difficult to achieve. Therefore, we decided to use qualitative inductive content analysis to elaborate a set (and structure) of domain-specific signal words in order to get a more detailed and differentiated picture of the signals sent by students. In a multi-stage approach, about 1,000 randomly selected personal statements were coded using the Mayring (2010) approach, whereby the most frequent generalisations were aggregated to categories. By systematically extracting categories, 51 signals were found and integrated in the complete corpus by means of the anchor phrases extracted by qualitative text analysis. We used clustering methods to analyse the similarities of signal words. Consequently, a total of 51 signals was reduced to 35 unique signals.

By means of the anchor phrases, a multivariate linear model was created based on the document-term matrix with meta-information. In this step, qualitative and quantitative approaches were used jointly: anchor phrases were assigned to key categories and the relation between these categories (i.e., different types of signals), study success (measured through ECTS credits during the first study semester) and social class was examined.

Results

MOST FREQUENT SIGNALS

This section examines the most frequent signals applicants have stated in their personal statements. In order to gain a rough insight into the data, we applied text-mining techniques without string manipulation. Figure 7.1 shows the 100 most frequent words (without stop words).

Figure 7.1. Most frequent words

Figure 7.1 shows that applicants frequently mention interest in the subject (e.g., 'business administration') respectively in economy ('economy') or education per se ('education'). In addition, internationality is emphasised ('international', 'English', 'languages'). Finally, school education appears to be another important signal ('school', 'high school').

However, the bag-of-words model only allows for superficial interpretation. A qualitative inductive content analysis enables a more detailed and differentiated picture. Figure 7.2 shows the reduction from 51 to 35 final signals.

Figure 7.2 Reduction to 35 signals

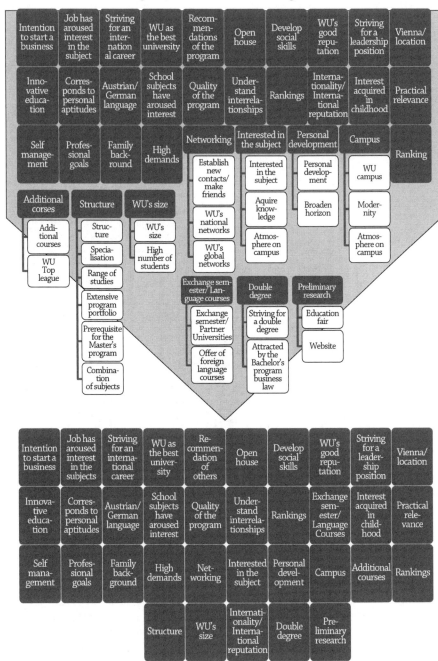

Figure 7.3 shows the most frequent signals expressed in personal statements that were submitted between study year 2013/14 and 2016/17. As Figure 7.1 indicates, the most frequent signal is interest in the subject, often aroused through school subjects. Another important signal is professional goals. Furthermore, applicants often mention recommendations by friends or relatives as well as the opportunity to do an exchange semester or attend language courses.

The following statement expresses 'interest in the subject' and 'professional goals' as well as 'striving for an international career':

The reason why I want to study economics is that I have a strong interest in the complex business world and am looking for a future profession that I can pursue in many places around the world.

Figure 7.3. Most frequent signals

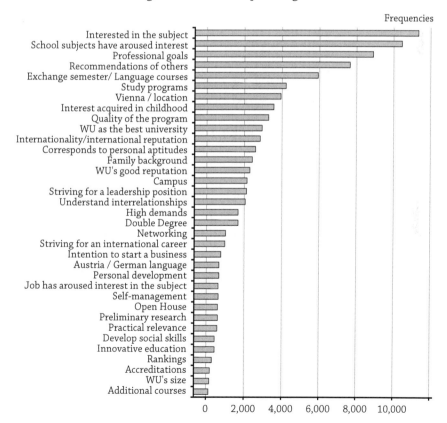

SIGNALS AND STUDY SUCCESS

This section will consider which signals lead to better academic results. Therefore, we carried out a statistical estimation, multivariate linear model, to examine the relationship between ECTS credits as independent variables and 35 different signals as dependent variables. Figure 7.4 shows that there are significant positive correlations between study success (operationalised through ECTS credits) and the following signals:

- Understand social and economic interrelations (Estimate = 8.74 | p=0.00)
- Information gathered in advance (Estimate = 3.07 | p=0.02)
- WU's size (Estimate = 2.21 | p=0.00)
- Quality of the program (Estimate = 2.17 | p=0.02)
- Innovative education (Estimate = 2.1 | p=0.00)
- Vienna/Location (Estimate = 1.62 | p=0.00)
- Campus (Estimate = 1.37 | p=0.00)
- Intention to start a business (Estimate = 1.24 | p=0.03)
- Interest acquired in childhood (Estimate = 1.05 | p=0.00)
- Develop social skills (Estimate = 0.68 | p=0.04)
- Interest in the subject (Estimate = 0.68 | p=0.00)

In addition, there is a significant negative correlation between study success and recommendations of others (Estimate = -0.89 | p=0.02).

Condensing the results, the desire to understand social and economic interrelations has the greatest impact on student success. What is more, one of our key findings is that prior research about the university and course program also has a positive impact on student success.

Figure 7.4 Linear model study success and signals

Coefficients:	Estimate Std.	Error	t value	Pr(>|t|)
(Intercept)	1.617e+01	9.592e-01	16.863	<2e-16***
mydat$Accreditations	4.205e-01	4.456e-01	0.944	0.345407
mydat$Demands	1.559e-00	3.279e-01	4.755	2.00e-06***
mydat$Exchange_semester	−5.414e-01	3.627e-01	−1.493	0.135594
mydat$Professional_goals	−2.244e-01	3.599e-01	−0.623	0.533037

Coefficients:	Estimate Std.	Error	t value	Pr(>|t|)
mydat$Best_university	7.357e-01	4.582e-01	1.606	0.10S365
mydat$Double_degree	−4.199e-01	3.261e-01	−1.288	0.197863
mydat$Recommendations	−8.918e-01	3.918e-01	−2.276	0.022869*
mydat$Family_background	−1.053e-01	4.070e-01	−0.259	0.795764
mydat$Leadership_position	−4.611e-01	1.306e-00	−0.353	0.724149
mydat$WU_size	2.219e-00	3.959e-01	5.604	2.14e-08***
mydat$Good_reputation	6.317e-01	8.308e-01	0.760	0.447045
mydat$Innovative_education	2.097e+00	6.780e-01	3.093	0.001986**
mydat$Job_interest	3.099e-01	3.435e-01	0.902	0.367026
mydat$Childhood_interest	1.045e-00	3.777e-01	2.767	0.005671**
mydat$Aptitudes	9.321e-01	5.571e-01	1.673	0.094312.
mydat$Networking	−8.726e-01	6.665e-01	−1.309	0.190471
mydat$Austria_German	−7.459e-01	6.718e-01	−1.110	0.266867
mydat$Personal_development	−5.962e-01	7.125e-01	−1.258	0.208455
mydat$Practical_relevance	4.944e-01	3.496e-01	1.414	0.157295
mydat$Quality	2.171e+00	9.522e-01	2.280	0.022609*
mydat$Rankings	1.632e-01	7.075e-01	0.231	0.817571
mydat$information_gathered	3.073e+00	4.790e-01	6.415	1.46e-10***
mydat$School_interest	−1.067e-01	6.779e-01	−0.157	0.874973
mydat$Self_managament	2,014e-01	8.207e-01	0.245	0.806187
mydat$Social_skills	6.864e-01	3.274e-01	2.096	0.036076*
mydat$Study_program	6.930e-01	7.515e-01	0.922	0.356440
mydat$Interest_subject	3.442e-00	7.028e-01	4.898	9.81e-07***
mydat$Open_house	1.449e-01	6.264e-01	0.231	0.817050
mydat$Start_business	1.239e+00	5.713e-01	2.169	0.030114*
mydat$International_career	−5.6S3e-01	3.309e-01	−1.717	0.085918.

Coefficients:	Estimate Std.	Error	t value	Pr(>|t|)
mydat$Vienna/location	1.617e-00	3.825e-01	4.229	2.36e-05***
mydat$Internationality	6.437e-01	4.135e-01	1.557	0.119515
mydat$Campus	1.368e+00	4.135e-01	3.310	0.000937***
mydat$Interrelationships	8.740e-00	1.523e+00	5.740	9.69e-09***
mydat$Additional_courses	–3.501e-08	4.340e-08	-0.807	0.419918

*Signif.codes: 0 '***' 0.001 '**' 0.01 '*' 0.05 '.' 0.1 ' ' 1*
Residual standard error: 16.89 on 11866 degrees of freedom
Multiple R-squared: 0.02398, Adjusted R-squared: 0.0211
F-statistic: 8.328 on 35 and 11866 DF: p-value: < 2.2e-16

SOCIAL CLASS

This section examines the relationship between signals, study success and social class, based on the personal statements submitted for the term 2016/17.

Figure 7.5 Comparison wordcloud of social strata and most frequent words

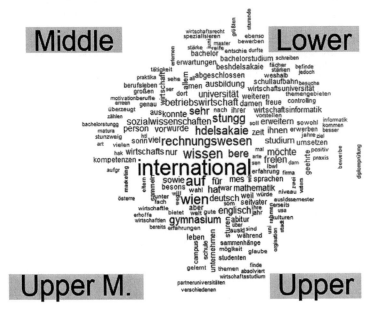

Figure 7.5 shows that words like 'international', 'Vienna' and 'academic secondary school' often occur in letters of applicants from higher social classes. There are only a few differences between the middle and the middle upper class; middle class applicants often mention the Bachelor's Program 'Business, Economics and Social Sciences', in their personal statements. On the contrary, applicants of the lower social classes more frequently mention 'secondary vocational high school', 'accounting' and 'knowledge'. Overall, the general differences identified between social classes in relation to signals in the statements of support were negligible.

Table 7.1 Most frequent signals and social strata

	Upper class	Upper middle class	Middle class	Lower class
Interested in the subject	11.34	12.16	12.78	12.59
School subjects have aroused interest	10.74	11.29	11.9	11.76
Professional goals	8.46	9.66	10.56	10.26
Recommendations of others	7.72	8.61	8.84	9.51
Exchange semester / Language courses	6.73	5.55	5.36	4.09
Study programs	4.87	5.09	5.11	6.17
Vienna / location	4.61	4.53	3.77	3.84
Interest acquired in childhood	3.81	3.79	3.14	3.84
Campus	3.66	3.07	3.44	3.17
Quality of the program	3.49	3.5	3.77	4.09
Corresponds to personal aptitudes	3.42	4.11	4.53	4.09
Intemationality/Intemational reputation	3.37	2.56	1.76	1.75
Family background	3.23	2.63	1.22	0.92
WU as the best university	2.9	3.09	2.85	3.42
WU's good reputation	2.64	2.75	2.39	2.75
Double Degree	2.32	2.07	1.84	2.34

	Upper class	Upper middle class	Middle class	Lower class
Striving for a leadership position	2.21	2	2.14	1.83
Understand interrelationships	2.12	1.65	1.51	1.17
High demands	1.5	2.07	2.22	1.92
Networking	1.26	1.04	1.01	0.75
Open House	1.15	0.8	1.26	1.08
Job has aroused interest for the subject	1.14	0.95	0.84	1
Striving for an international career	0.95	1.02	1.01	0.5
Self-management	0.93	0.9	1.01	0.92
Austria / German language	0.83	0.66	0.67	0.5
Intention to start a business	0.64	1.1	0.88	1.08
Personal development	0.63	0.71	0.75	0.67
Rankings	0.6	0.25	0.29	0.17
Information gathered in advance	0.59	0.61	0.67	0.75
Innovative education	0.58	0.37	0.63	0.42
Practical relevance	0.51	0.63	0.96	1.75
Develop social skills	0.44	0.31	0.46	0.17
WU's size	0.29	0.25	0.21	0.42
Additional courses	0.17	0.08	0.17	0.17
Accreditations	0.15	0.1	0.04	0.17

In order to better illustrate the differences between different social classes, relative frequencies were calculated. As shown in Figure 7.6, applicants from upper class use 'rankings', 'family background' and 'international prestige' disproportionately often and conversely, 'practical relevance' and the 'intention to start a business' disproportionately infrequently. Applicants from upper middle class mention 'family background' as well but also the 'intention to start a business' and 'striving for an international career'. Furthermore, they refer to 'additional courses' and 'practical relevance' only occasionally. Signals that are often mentioned in personal statements from middle class applicants are the 'development of social skills' and the 'innovative education at WU' while signals that are seldom mentioned are 'accreditation', 'family background' and the 'size of WU'. Almost half of the statements relating to the practical relevance of the program can be found in personal statements from applicants belonging to lower social classes. Other frequent signals in these strata are 'accreditation' and 'size of WU'. It is notable that there are many signals rarely mentioned by applicants belonging to lower social classes, such as 'family background', 'development of social skills', 'rankings' and 'striving for an international career'.

Figure 7.6. Signals and social strata

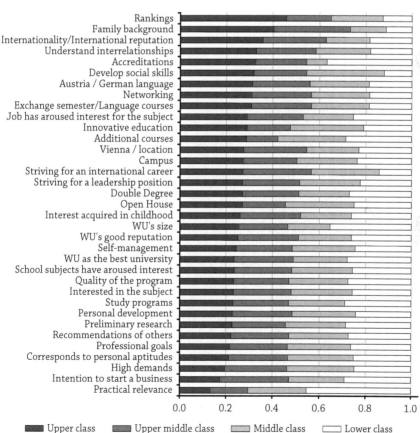

These findings appear to be consistent with theories that emphasise the central role of security motives for lower classes: when choosing their studies, they prefer shorter, more structured and application-oriented programs. Due to lower financial capacity and security, prospective students from lower social classes can be economically constrained and are thus often unable to consider internationality or HEIs with high tuition fees (Bargel and Bargel 2010, 10).

However, the analysis of variance shows significant differences for the following signals:

- Exchange semester/ Language courses (p=0.00)
- Professional goals (p=0.00)
- Understand social and economic interrelations (p=0.00)
- Vienna/Location (p=0.00)
- International prestige (p=0.00)
- Family background (p=0.00)
- Practical relevance (p=0.00)
- Rankings (p=0.00)
- Interest in the subject (p=0.01)
- Starting a business (p=0.04)
- Campus (p=0.04)
- Recommendations (p=0.04)

Combining the results of this and the previous sections shows that there are some signals that have a positive effect on study success and are often mentioned by applicants from upper social classes, such as the desire to understand social and economic interrelations. On the other hand, there are also signals with a positive effect on study success that are more often found in personal statements from applicants belonging to lower social classes, for instance 'information gathered in advance' and 'size of WU'. This leads to the assumption that study success is affected, among other factors, by both the social class and the associated different kinds of signals. This hypothesis is also supported by the results of the analysis of variance between study success and social class. Although students from upper and upper middle class have a higher study performance than students from middle or lower class, the difference is not significant (see Figure 7.7). This result aligns with earlier findings regarding study performance at WU (Dünser and Zeeh 2015) which show that student performance is significantly lower if students work more than 10 hours/week and/or struggle with the reconciliation of work and studies. This is particularly relevant as jobs taken up by lower class students are often characterised by long working hours and inflexible time schedules.

Figure 7.7 Study success and social strata

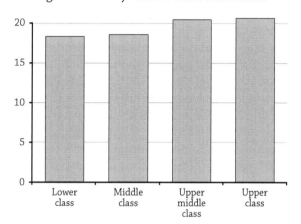

Reflections and Conclusion

The paper shows that a strong signal for student success is the desire to learn more about complex economic relationships. Additionally, being informed about the curriculum is also a strong predictor of academic success. In cases where the personal statement referred to signals relating to recommendations to study at a particular HEI, this kind of extrinsic motivation was found to be weakly negatively correlated with academic success. By contrast, signals that indicate intrinsic motivation are highly positively related to study success.

Findings regarding the most frequent signals could play a role in discussions about opinions and expectations of prospective students; this could have a potential impact on curricular developments. Furthermore, these signals are also relevant when it comes to designing the marketing activities of a Higher Education Institution. However, there is another important dimension to this: socio-economic status. In order to ensure cohort diversity, HEIs would be well-advised to take a closer look at the signals frequently sent by applicants from lower social classes. Our results indicate that the reasons for deciding to take up studies differ between students from different social strata. Therefore, HEIs developing their communication strategy on the basis of this knowledge would most likely be more successful in attracting students from more diverse social backgrounds. Finally, our findings indicate that personal statements should not be relied upon in isolation on when it comes to student recruitment decisions. The regression model analysing the impact of the signals on study success has very little prognostic validity. The primary reason is that what students state in their motivation letters should be interpreted as 'signals', that is a reflection of what students *assume* the HEI wants to hear, rather than of their real personal motivation. What is more, we have found that social strata and cultural social desirability as well as other variables, such as gender, actually do have an impact on the signals sent in personal statements. Student rankings solely based on personal statements would most probably lead to a social strata and gender bias; however, given selectors' awareness of the signals in such statements, they can be used to ensure that HEIs recruit students from across the range of social classes.

References

Bargel, Holger, and Tino Bargel. 2010. *Ungleichheiten und Benachteiligungen im Hochschulsystem aufgrund der sozialen Herkunft der Studierenden.* Arbeitspapier. Düsseldorf: Demokratische und Soziale Hochschule. No.2, Hans-Böckler-Stiftung.

Blüthmann, Irmela, Felicitas Thiel, and Christine Wolfgramm. 2011. *Abbruchtendenzen in den Bachelorstudiengängen. Individuelle Schwierigkeiten oder Studienbedingungen?* Die hochschule 1/2011.

Clark, Margaret, Steven Middleton, Daniel Nguyen, and Lauren Zwick. 2014. 'Mediating Relationships between Academic Motivation, Academic Integration and Academic Performance'. *Learning and Individual Differences* 33: 30–38.

De Vissier, Marieke, Cornelia Fluit, Janke Cohen-Schotanus, and Roland Laan. 2017. 'The Effects of a Non-cognitive Versus Cognitive Admission Procedure within Cohorts in one Medical School'. *Advances in Health Sciences Education* 23 (1): 187–200.

Dünser, Lukas, and Julia Zeeh. 2015. 'Evaluierung der Studien(in)aktivität'. In *Eine Frage der Wirksamkeit? Qualitätsmanagement als Impulsgeber für Veränderungen an Hochschulen,* edited by Oliver Vettori, Gudrun Salmhofer, Lukas Mitterauer, and Karl Ledermüller, 221-238. Bielefeld: UVW UniversitätsVerlagWebler.

Eccles, Jacquelynne, and Allen Wigfield. 2002. 'Motivational Beliefs, Values, and Goals'. *Annual Review of Psychology* 53 (1): 109–132.

Eppler, Marion, and Beverly Harju. 1997. 'Achievement Motivation Goals in Relation to Academic Performance in Traditional and Nontraditional College Students'. *Research in Higher Education* 38 (5): 557–573

European Students' Union—ESU. 2008. *Equality Handbook.* Brussels.

Fastre, Greet, Wim H. Gijselaers, and Mien Segers. 2008. 'Selection to Ensure Study Success: Looking for Multiple Criteria in the Case of a European Master of Science Program in Business'. *Journal of Education for Business* 84 (1): 47–54.

Geißler, Rainer. 2006. 'Bildungschancen und soziale Herkunft'. *Archiv für Wissenschaft und Praxis der sozialen Arbeit* 4: 34–49.

Feinerer, Ingo, and Kurt Hornik. 2018. *tm: Text Mining Package.* R package version 0.7-4. https://CRAN.R-project.org/package=tm

Heublein, Ulrich, Heike Spangenberg, and Dieter Sommer. 2003. *Ursachen des Studienabbruchs Analyse 2002.* HIS: Projektbericht.

Heublein, Ulrich, Christopher Hutzsch, Jochen Schreiber, Dieter Sommer, and Georg Besuch. 2009. *Ursachen des Studienabbruchs in Bachelor- und in herkömmlichen Studiengängen. Ergebnisse einer bundesweiten Befragung von Exmatrikulierten des Studienjahres 2007/08.* HIS: Projektbericht.

Helmke, Andreas, and Franz Weinert. 1997. 'Bedingungsfaktoren schulischer Leistung'. In *Psychologie des Unterrichts und der Schule*, edited by Weinert, Franz, 71–176. Göttingen: Hogrefe.

Kolland, Franz. 2011. *Studienabbruch: Zwischen Kontinuität und Krise. Eine empirische Untersuchung an Österreichs Universitäten.* Vienna: Braumüller.

Ledermüller, Karl, and Julia Zeeh. 2017. *Getting Out of the Maze! Designing Successful Learning Environments while Navigating with Big Data. A Structural Equation Model Based Institutional Approach to Predict Study Success.* Paper presented in track 4 at the EAIR 39th Annual Forum in Porto, Portugal.

London Communiqué. 2007. *Towards the European Higher Education Area: Responding to Challenges in a Globalised world.* https://www.edu.ro/sites/default/files/u39/Londra%202007.pdf.

Mayring, Philipp. 2010. *Qualitative Inhaltsanalyse: Grundlagen und Techniken (Neuausgabe).* Weinheim: Beltz.

McKenzie, Kirsten, and Robert Schweitzer. 2001. 'Who Succeeds at University? Factors Predicting Academic Performance in First Year Australian University Students'. *Higher Education Research & Development* 20 (1): 21–33.

OECD. 2014. *Education at a Glance 2014: OECD Indicators.* OECD Publishing.

Nairz-Wirth, Erna, and Klaus Feldmann. 2015. *Dropping out of University. Obstacles to Overcome for Non-traditional Students.* Paper presented in track 3 at the EAIR 37th Annual Forum in Krems, Austria.

Nairz-Wirth, Erna, Feldmann, Klaus, and Judith Spiegl. 2017. 'Habitus Conflicts and Experiences of Symbolic Violence as Obstacles for Non-traditional Students'. *European Educational Research Journal* 16 (1): 12–29.

Pechar, Hans, and Angela Wroblewski. 1998. *Non-traditional-Students in Österreich. Studienbedingungen bei Nebenerwerbstätigkeit, verspätetem Übertritt und alternativem Hochschulzugang.* Ungedr. Endbericht. http://www.equi.at/dateien/non-traditional_students.pdf

Prenzel, Manfred. 1996. 'Bedingungen für selbstbestimmt motiviertes und interessiertes Lernen im Studium'. In: *Lehr- und Lernprobleme im Studium. Bedingungen und Veränderungsmöglichkeiten*, by Lompscher, Joachim and Heinz Mandl, 11–22. Bern: Hans Huber.

R Core Team. 2018. *R: A Language and Environment for Statistical Computing.* R Foundation for Statistical Computing. Vienna, Austria (2018). https://www.R-project.org.

Reumer, Christoffel, and Marijk van der Wende. 2010. *Excellence and Diversity: The Emergence of Selective Admission Policies in Dutch Higher Education. A Case Study on Amsterdam University College.* https://escholarship.org/uc/item/4502w5pj.

Robbins, Steven B., Kristy Lauver, Huy Le, Daniel Davis, Ronelle Langley, and Aaron Carlstrom. 2004. 'Do Psychosocial and Study Skill Factors Predict College Outcomes? A Metaanalysis'. *Psychological Bulletin* 130: 261–288. http://dx.doi.org/10.1037/0033-2909.130.2.261

Schlag, Bernhard. 2004. *Lern- und Leistungsmotivation.* 2., überarbeitete Auflage, Wiesbaden: VS Verlag für Sozialwissenschaften.

Schiefele, Ulrich, Andreas Krapp, and Adolf Winteler. 1992. 'Interest as a Predictor of Academic Achievement: A Meta-analysis of Research'. In *The Role of Interest in Learning and Development,* edited by Renninger KA, S. Hidi, and A. Krapp, 183–212. Hillsdale, NJ: Lawrence Elbaum Associates.

Schiefele, Ulrich, Lilian Streblow, and Julia Brinkmann. 2007. 'Aussteigen oder Durchhalten. Was unterscheidet Studienabbrecher von anderen Studierenden'. *Zeitschrift für Entwicklungspsychologie und Pädagogische Psychologie* 39 (3): 127–140.

Unger, Martin. 2015. *Studierende-Sozialerhebung 2015. Bericht zur sozialen Lage der Studierenden.* vol 2: Studierende. Projektbericht.

Wild, Elke, Manfred Hofer, and Reinhard Pekrun. 2006. 'Psychologie des Lernens'. In *Pädagogische Psychologie* 5, vollständig überarbeitete Auflage, edited by Andreas Krapp and Bernd Weidenmann, 203–268. Weinheim: Beltz.

Zeeh, Julia, Karl Ledermüller, and Michaela Kobler-Weiß. 2018. 'Evaluierung von Motivationsschreiben als Instrument in universitären Aufnahmeverfahren'. *Zeitschrift für Hochschulentwicklung* 13 (4): 227–250.

CHAPTER 8

'Learning to Fly': Higher Education Students' and Institutional Leaders' Perceptions of the Relevance of Institutional Support Mechanisms in their Integration Process

Maria José Sá, Teresa Carvalho
and Maria de Lourdes Machado-Taylor[1]

Introduction

Studies of student achievement in higher education have been undertaken since the 1960s. Most studies highlight the broad range of factors that influence students' academic performance, persistence and dropout (Spady 1971; Tinto 1993). More recently, however, the focus of the research has been on strategies aimed at increasing students' success (Baer and Duin 2014). According to the literature, institutional factors play a significant role in students' performance and persistence, also impacting on dropout (Swail, Redd and Perna 2003). These factors relate to the institution's ability to support students academically and socially during their academic studies. While this support is very important throughout the whole higher education process, it is particularly crucial at the beginning of the students' academic experience. Student persistence is related to course content and teaching, as well as to student support mechanisms including mentoring, counselling and vocational guidance (Mbuva 2011; Swail et al. 2003; Young-Jones et al. 2013). Tinto and Pusser (2006) identify three main types of student support: 1. academic support, in the form of development courses, supplementary education and study groups; 2. social support, through counselling and mentoring programs; and 3. financial support, in

───────────────

[1] The authors wish to thank FCT (Foundation for Science and Technology) and ESF (European Social Fund), within the scope of the Third Community Support Framework, for the financial support granted to this research.

the form of scholarships and loans. Academic, social and economic sup-port provided to students is critical in their educational path and, hence, in their persistence, academic performance and success (Tinto 2011, 2012a). Moreover, higher education institutions (HEIs) are already starting to acknowledge that, besides providing their students with theoretical and practical knowledge, they need to prepare their students with competen-cies that will help them in integrating and operating in the labour market once they graduate and start a job (Thune and Støren 2015; Pavlin 2014). Therefore, HEIs should develop strategies to support student integration and socialisation especially during their first year, so as to support students in an environment that is unknown to them (Attinasi 1989) and continue that process throughout the students' educational path and insertion into the labour world.

This chapter analyses the influence ascribed both by students and institutional leaders to support mechanisms that promote integration and academic success. An exploration of the theoretical underpinnings is pre-sented, followed by the methodology used in the study, the main find-ings and their discussion. The chapter closes with some conclusions and recommendations.

Previous Research

When students enrol in higher education, they bring along a set of indi-vidual *traits*, that is, intrinsic features that characterise and influence their attitudes towards learning (Tinto 1993). How these traits align with the characteristics of the HEI influences the level of student interaction and in-tegration in the institutional environment (Terenzini and Pascarella 1980; Tinto 1993). This notion of *trait* somehow finds a parallel with the concept of *grit* put forward by Duckworth, Peterson, Matthews and Kelly (2007) and Duckworth and Quinn (2009). The authors define grit as 'persever-ance and passion for long-term goals' (Duckworth et al. 2007, 1087). This concept entails behaviours of embracing challenges, striving to attain goals and resilience in face of hardships and even failure. According to the au-thors, grit is central in attaining high performance and results, regardless of the arena in which the individual is operating (Duckworth et al. 2007). Karlsen and Pritchard (2017) add another interesting dimension that has similarities with the concept of *grit*. This concept, called *sisu*, is '[…] derived from Finnish and well-known to Nordic people as the ability to endure pain and adversity. It is seen as strength of will, determination and the capacity to act rationally in the face of hardship. It is not short-lived bravery: rather it is an inner ability to sustain an action against the odds. As such it resembles the perseverance and coping ability of psychological resilience' (p. 3). As a student from a polytechnic institute that participated in the present study puts it, '*I set my teaching goal one step at a time, one training programme at a time; I finished the 12th grade* [compulsory education in Portugal], *the vocational training programme, I will get, if everything goes well, the Bachelor's degree, I already have the papers ready to enrol in the Master's degree, so one step at a time*'. Another concept that might be associated with student *traits* is the one offered by Carol Dweck in her 2006 acclaimed work *Mindset: The New Psychology of Success*, where she uses the terms *fixed mindset* and *growth mindset* to refer to the beliefs that commonly underlie learning and intelligence. According to the author, people with a fixed mindset believe that intelligence is static and thus tend to avoid challenges, give up easily and regard effort as being useless, whereas people with a growth mindset believe that intelligence can be developed and hence tend to embrace challenges, show attitudes of resilience and perseverance and perceive effort as the path toward achievement and success. In the academic arena, Dweck's (2006) theory advocates that if students believe that they can be brighter, they dedicate extra time and effort to their work, which leads to enhanced performance and, consequently, to higher achievement. This growth mindset is present, for example, in the following stance of a university student who participated in the present study: '*I think that when you embark on a new adventure, you have everything to succeed, you just have to want, just have the willpower. [...] there were grades that showed me that I can do this [...] and that when I conclude the degree, I can have the traits that companies are looking for. I always have that hope, and I keep working for it, to be good at what I am studying, at what I am doing*'.

Furthermore, Bliss and Sandifor (2004) argue that higher education students are influenced by two types of culture: the student culture, which includes the students' traits, values, and beliefs; and the institutional culture, which is composed of the features, beliefs and values conveyed and shared by the institution. The balance between these two cultural universes determines the degree of student integration, interaction, commitment and success.

Swail et al. presented, in 2003, the Geometric Model of Student Persistence and Success. This model describes how the relationship between cognitive, social and institutional factors influences student development and persistence. The model emphasises the importance of institutional factors which are related to the institution's ability to support students academically and socially during their academic studies. It stresses the importance of university support mechanisms. These mechanisms include mentoring, tutoring, counselling, vocational guidance and financial support. These academic services provide student support that extends beyond the classroom and describes how the HEI considers its role in supporting its students (Swail et al. 2003).

Swail and co-authors (ibid.) contend that this model facilitates a discussion of the dynamics between the cognitive, social and institutional factors that characterise the students' experience in higher education. The term *balance* is used to identify students who persist in their education. That is, the student needs to find a balance between the forces exerted by cognitive, social and institutional factors in order to secure development, persistence and success in higher education. Without balance, there is a potential risk of decreasing social integration which leads to a greater chance of the student dropping out of the higher education system. It is this fundamental but, at the same time, precarious balance between student resources (what they bring to the institution) and institutional resources (what the institution offers students) that will determine students' social and academic integration. The more positive this balance, the greater the likelihood that they will persist and succeed (Swail et al. 2003, 44, 62, 80, 87).

Tinto (2012b) advocates that HEIs need to intensify efforts to develop a coherent and integrated framework of support that enhances student success. The author presents an integrated strategy to promote higher education student success. Measures included in this strategy are: (i) the integration of students in the institutional environment; (ii) the alignment between the academic support and the first year of the study programmes; (iv) the assurance that counselling is provided to all students; and (v) the systematic and permanent alignment between students' experiences from the moment they enrol in the HEI until they conclude their programmes.

Student monitoring is vital for the process of continuous improvement of the institution. It allows students' progress to be measured and their needs to be anticipated. Monitoring also allows an HEI to assess the impact of the interventions and retention strategies (Swail et al. 2003). In fact, the more information the institution accrues on the student's needs, the better prepared it will be to design and implement programs and services that meet these needs. Thus, the likelihood of students improving their performance and achieving success is higher in academic institutions that promote follow-up and provide feedback regarding their performance (Tinto and Pusser 2006).

Higher education students' success is, therefore, determined not only by their personal and social traits but also, and largely, by the experiences that are made available to them by the HEI, especially in their first year. Hence, the promotion of academic success also involves an institutional analysis that focuses, among other critical aspects, on deep knowledge and understanding of the factors underlying students' success, both in academic and in personal terms (Ferreira, Almeida and Soares 2001).

The present chapter seeks to answer the following research question: Are institutional support mechanisms perceived by students and institutional leaders as relevant for students' integration process?

Methodology

The methodology chosen is qualitative in nature, given that the main purpose of the study is to grasp the importance ascribed by both students and institutional leaders from four Portuguese HEIs to the services provided by the institutions to support academic performance and overall experience. The HEIs are the University of Minho, the University of Porto, the Polytechnic Institute of Cávado and Ave and the Polytechnic Institute of Porto. Hence, and on the basis of what is advocated in the literature, qualitative methods are more suited to grasp and interpret meanings, which, in this case, are associated with student and institutional perceptions of the support mechanisms provided by the HEIs (Denzin and Lincoln 1994, 2011; Merriam 2009; Savenye and Robinson 1996; Willig 2001).

SAMPLE

58 individual interviews were carried out, 40 with students and 18 with senior academics from four Portuguese HEIs, two universities and two polytechnic institutes, all from the public subsystem. The sample selection was intended to be representative of institutional structures and delivery. The student sample comprised 40 individuals, 21 (52.5%) of whom were undergraduate students and 19 (47.5%) of whom were postgraduate students. 19 students were male and 21 were female students. Staff interviews were conducted with senior academics responsible for decision making at the institutional level, as well as with Vice/Pro-Rectors and Vice-Presidents. All staff interviewed dealt with issues relating to quality, training, education, organisation and academic activities. Furthermore, the Student's Ombudsman, students' representatives on the Pedagogical

Council and presidents of Students' Unions were also included in the staff sample.

DATA COLLECTION METHODS AND DATA ANALYSIS

The data collection instruments used in the study were threefold: (1) semi-structured interview with students; (2) semi-structured interview with institutional leaders; and (3) document analysis. Three related methods were used to enable data triangulation to secure greater confidence, credibility and validity in the research outcomes (Fielding 2012; Ghrayeb, Damodaran and Vohra 2011). Textual data were evaluated using content analysis. This approach, which uses content coding, reduces the high volume text into content categories (Bardin 1977; Krippendorff 2004; Mayring 2014). The interview was identified as the unit of analysis, in line with Graneheim and Lundman (2004), and data were coded by paragraph and sentence, as proposed by Strauss and Corbin (1998).

Results and Discussion

STUDENT SUPPORT MECHANISMS

As previously stated, the aspects related to student support mechanisms can take three main forms: (1) academic support, in the form of development courses, supplementary education and study groups; (2) social support, through counselling and mentoring programs; and (3) financial support, through scholarships and loans, among others (Tinto and Pusser 2006). In addition to these three types of support, emphasised as important contributions to the promotion of student wellbeing, the analysis of the narratives allowed the identification of a fourth type of support, related to employment. All HEIs involved in the investigation were concerned to provide their students with useful tools and skills in order to secure graduate employment. Furthermore, it is becoming increasingly common for HEIs to monitor the integration of their graduates into the labour market. This is the main finding of the study and reveals that HEIs are, indeed, gaining awareness of the importance of providing their students with transversal competencies that are critical for future graduates to successfully operate in the labour market (Thune and Støren 2015; Pavlin 2014). The subsections that follow present the institutional leaders' and students' perceptions regarding each of the distinct types of support, also complemented by the institutional vision resulting from document analysis.

Academic support

One mechanism identified by all the senior academics interviewed was the importance of an effective operational structure in the delivery of academic programmes. The role of the programme director was identified as critical for successful student support. A university leader reported that, in his institution, it is mandatory to have '[...] *a structure that is composed, first, of a programme director, followed by a monitoring committee composed of the programme director and representatives of the programmes' various year cohorts, and then an academic committee, which monitors performance problems or excessive failure rates in certain courses*' (university leader). It was stated that the functioning of this structure '*is effective, because the students of the programmes themselves are, in a way, the first to warn when something is going wrong; it is a very effective component of proximity*' (university leader).

The relationship between the programme director and the students was also highlighted as being critical for integration. The intensity of these dynamics is, naturally, affected by the personality of each programme director, but, in any case, this structure '*establishes an experience of closeness between the programme director and the student, and the possibility of monitoring and counselling is very positive*' (university leader). Furthermore, the support from teachers other than the programme directors, both inside and outside the classroom, is also perceived by students as important. A Bachelor's student comments that '*I get along very well with present and past teachers of mine, and I know that if I need anything these people are available to help me, even if they are no longer my teachers; anything I need, they are there to help me*' (polytechnic institute student).

Other students' monitoring and support actions include '*tutorial activities in certain academic areas where there are particularly high failure rates*' (university leader). Institutional leaders identify the importance of monitoring support to ensure that effective '*action, follow-up and feedback plans are proposed to solve some unsatisfactory situations that may occur*' (university leader). Other student mechanisms identified by leaders include peer tutoring programs, particularly for first-year students. Freshers need additional support in their interaction with the institutional environment, in comparison with their colleagues who have been in the institution for a longer period and who, consequently, have already undergone this socialisation process (Young-Jones et al. 2013). Students who are the first in their family to enrol in higher education benefit from this approach. As a Bachelor's student states, '*I had the support of mentoring, which is a service organised by teachers who supervise and then there are students who volunteer as tutors that help* [...] *It went so well that I later signed up to be a tutor too*' (university student). A colleague also refers to this support as being central to students' integration: '*there is a mentoring system that welcomes the new students and gives them closer support*' (university student). The analysis of institutional documents also confirms this preoccupation with the students' academic support, namely through the existence of an office for learning and teaching support and the overall enhancement of structures to support the HEI's academic activity (University of Porto 2010). The Statutes of the other universities clearly replicate this concern in supporting its students in academic terms, as one of its services provides '*pedagogical and administrative support for students and for teaching projects*' (University of Minho 2017, 20779).

Social support

Interviews with institutional leaders highlighted the strong concern for the students' wellbeing. Support Services provide a range of services, including medical support. Social support is aligned with the student needs, with some HEIs providing specific support for international students. In one interview the Vice-Rector of the University of Minho referred to the existence of an international relations service which was '*very important for students who go to study abroad under international exchange programmes and for incoming students who come to study in Portuguese universities under international exchange programmes*' (university leader). Specific support is also provided for disabled students with the provision of an inclusion office and special conditions, and this is acknowledged by students: '*In terms of accessibility, I think it is good, for example, for people with reduced mobility*' (university student). As stated in the Statutes of the University of Minho (2017), its services entail '*support for students with disabilities*' (p. 20779), this being one of its cross-cutting measures targeting the inclusion of disabled students (University of Minho 2010). It is also stated in the Statutes of this University (University of Minho 2017) that the university is responsible for '*granting aid to students within the context of social support*' (p. 20770). This same responsibility is stated in the Statutes of the University of Porto (2009). Moreover, according to the Quality Plan of the University of Minho (2010), medical support is provided to all members of the academic community, in addition to preventive and screening actions. Overall, students have a positive perception regarding social support provided by their HEI, stating that '*in terms of social support, we are well equipped*' (polytechnic institute student) and '*Concerning social support, I am pleased*' (university student).

Financial support

Financial support was discussed in many of the senior academic interviews. One university leader commented that there is the '*need to promote other systems of social support to students who are experiencing serious difficulties in pursuing their higher education studies*' (university leader). This HEI, similarly to other institutions, has '[...] *an emergency social fund, which consists of a non-refundable cash benefit, intended to cover specific situations arising from contingencies that may arise and that cannot be solved within the normal scope of social action*' (university leader). The Quality Plan of the Polytechnic Institute of Porto (2017, 24) states that the institution's Social Services have the purpose of '*guaranteeing conditions of equity in the access to higher education, in the face of situations of economic need of the respective household, ensuring the best conditions for a successful school attendance, through the provision of direct and indirect support*'.

This form of support is perceived by students as very important and it even prevents some students with financial difficulties from dropping out: '*We are going through a period of economic hardship, and the Social Services Office is always very supportive, concerned about the students who cannot afford the expenses here; they help a lot with the meals, with reprographics, sometimes even with tuition fees: we have an emergency fund in the institution for these situations*' (polytechnic institute student).

Employability support

Vocational guidance was seen by all university leaders as critical to supporting students to ensure employment success. This was seen in a range of structures, including student support offices, '*employment offices or vocational guidance offices*' (polytechnic institute leader), which address, '*among other things, student employment contracts*' (university leader), as well as the '*students' office [...] that carries out many activities throughout the year, such as courses on how to prepare a CV, how to respond to an interview, etc.*' (polytechnic institute leader). Additionally, there are many activities throughout the year, such as courses on how to behave in an employment interview, study techniques, relaxation techniques and stress management. Furthermore, at a time when self-employment is an increasing trend, HEIs foster abilities in their students, seeking the '*enhancement of university action in the field of business incubation and entrepreneurship, through the implementation of effective measures to support student entrepreneurship, especially amongst postgraduate students*' (University of Minho 2009, 14). Bearing in mind the relevance of preparing their students for the labour market, HEIs strive to '*develop transferable competencies, namely: instrumental, with special relevance to the communication and time management skills; interpersonal skills, with emphasis on the capacity to work in interdisciplinary teams and in multicultural contexts; systems, with emphasis on creativity and spirit of initiative*' (University of Minho 2009, 7). Likewise, the Statutes of the University of Porto (2009, 19106) state that one of its main duties as an educational institution is the '*training in a global, cultural, scientific, technical, artistic, civic and ethical sense—within the framework of diversified teaching and learning processes, aiming at the development of specific and transferable skills and competencies and the diffusion of knowledge*'. This HEI, in its Activity Plan for 2017, stated that one of its central axes for that year was to '*value education and training in an integral and transformative sense, ensuring quality standards at all levels of education [...] aiming at attaining high levels of employability and impact on society*' (University of Porto 2016, 22). Furthermore, the Statutes of the Polytechnic Institute of Cávado and Ave (2014) state that the institutional mission entails, among others, the provision of '*areas of expertise for engaging in professional activities at the national and international levels, promoting mobility and employability*' (p. 27882) of its students. The Polytechnic Institute of Porto (2017, 24) has an Office of Academic and Professional Integration which '*is a specialised and personalised service area, whose services support students in defining and pursuing their academic goals, overcoming personal difficulties, identifying and responding to a diversity of personal development opportunities, facilitating the transition process and integration into the labour market*'.

In general, students are satisfied with their preparation for the labour market. A university student states that '*in terms of theoretical and practical preparation, no place prepares us like this one, because we have the best teachers in the area*'. This positive view is corroborated by a polytechnic institute student, who claims that hers is '*a welcoming institution, an institution that enables me to accrue knowledge, because I think that this is important in terms of graduating and not going out in the dark to the labour market, because I think it is important for a person to understand what happens outside, and this institution, in my opinion, is exceptional, because it provides training in terms of lectures, seminars, etc., which I think is good*'. However, some students complain of a deficient practical dimension in their study programmes, and there are those who even state that '*It is very difficult for the university to prepare us concretely for professional life*' (university student). Yet, most students interviewed perceive that their study programmes have '*a very strong component, not a direct link, but a preparation for responding to the labour market, that is, there is a way for us to learn how to do things*' (polytechnic institute student).

In addition to monitoring student progress during their academic course, all HEIs in the investigation sought to monitor and support student integration in the labour market following successful completion of their academic studies. In some of the HEIs studied specific projects had been initiated to follow up students *'from the moment they complete their training, through a project developed by the institution'* (university leader). One project allows students to express their perceptions regarding their first contact with the labour market. This is valuable information from the institutional point of view, in order to obtain information that allows the HEI *'to perceive where it should go in the restructuring of its educational offer, in new approaches'* (university leader). This monitoring of the graduates' insertion in the labour market is explicitly mentioned in the Quality Manual of the Polytechnic Institute of Porto (2017, 24–25), which states that *'it is particularly relevant to do the monitoring of the transition of graduates to the labour market in order to take a closer look at the professional situation, to adapt the training obtained to the requirements of the labour world and to promote lifelong learning'*.

In addition to the recent graduates, HEIs also collected information on public and private organisations that employ their graduates, to accrue knowledge about the different forms of student integration in the labour market, for example, through an employment and entrepreneurship office. These offices carry out studies on the issues connected to employability. In the context of these studies, the recent graduates are asked about their professional status, namely *'whether they are already employed, how long it took for them to get a job, and whether they are working in their educational field'* (polytechnic institute leader). With the data collected and analysed, HEIs obtain indicators to measure the employability index, the degree of satisfaction with the academic training and the verification of training needs. This issue takes on particular relevance if we consider that, according to the study developed by Sarrico et al. (2013), only 48% of the graduates from university Bachelor's programmes get a job in activity sectors that are related to the area of their study programme, though the average is substantially higher for students in the polytechnic subsector (57%).

This concern with issues related to employability, namely through the existence of offices that support the professional integration of new graduates and the monitoring of their professional career after they conclude their training in the institution, is clearly visible in most Portuguese HEIs. In fact, according to a study developed by Cardoso et al. (2012), 78.5% of the 367 websites of the Portuguese HEIs analysed in their study provide information on the topics related to employability and entrepreneurship, with 64% providing information directly related to their professional integration support offices and entrepreneurship support offices. The analysis of institutional documents reveals this concern with monitoring the insertion of graduates into the labour market, inasmuch as one HEI has in place an Observatory, whose purpose is to design '*data collection instruments on the relevance and adequacy of the educational offer, the formative efficiency, the employability, and the professional path and performance of our graduates*' (University of Minho 2010, 19).

Conclusion

A positive experience is paramount for student persistence, performance, satisfaction and success in Higher Education. A negative experience results in perceptions of difficulty, frustration and feelings of chaos. In addition, a negative experience can prevent students from making the most of their academic environment and limit their engagement with the social services provided by the institution. Studies in this field show that the services that the HEI provides its students play an important role in building a positive experience for students (Ciobanu 2013). Furthermore, a good academic and social integration plays a central role in students' satisfaction and commitment to the HEI. In these times of changing dynamics in higher education, it is no longer enough to attract students; HEIs must have in place strategies for their students to integrate, retain, satisfy and graduate with success. Moreover, it is critical that these strategies are extended to the provision of tools that prepare students for the labour market and, additionally, also monitor their first professional experiences. HEIs are gaining an increasing awareness of the relevance of these monitoring actions, especially as they enable them to assess the post-graduation success of their students, but these actions also help HEIs to improve and tailor their educational offer to the needs of both their graduates and the labour market.

Pascarella and Terenzini (2005) argue that if student involvement and commitment is a key aspect in ensuring interventions are effective, then HEIs should focus their attention on the ways and mechanisms that can be used to keep their students engaged and committed. According to the authors, this is possible through the inclusion of activities at the academic, social and extracurricular levels that can foster this involvement and commitment to students' personal goals and to the HEI as a whole.

In terms of student support mechanisms, results of this study show that mentoring, counselling and vocational guidance processes, which are documented in the literature as affecting the performance and permanence of students in higher education (Mbuva 2011; Young-Jones et al. 2013), are provided by the HEIs studied. This research supports findings identified in the literature that student support takes four main forms: (i) academic support (e.g., development courses, supplementary education and study groups); (ii) social support (e.g., counselling and mentoring programs); (iii) financial support (e.g., scholarships and loans); and (iv) provision of tools and skills in job search and/or job creation, and follow-up of the process of integration of their graduates in the labour market.

The HEIs studied all have services that offer pastoral, financial, educational and employment support. This investigation has identified that besides monitoring students throughout their academic path, HEIs also monitor and support student integration in the labour market, via, for example, employability and entrepreneurial offices, which is the main and most relevant finding of the study. HEIs have several projects to monitor students from the moment they conclude their training and enter the labour market to the time they are capable of finding their way around on their own. Indeed, all the measures, offices and overall employability support that the four HEIs that participated in this study have in force may be seen as an indicator of their awareness that it is no longer sufficient to prepare their students in terms of theoretical and practical knowledge, no matter how high-quality standards they may have in this respect. Today, more than ever before, HEIs need to provide students with an all-encompassing training, via, for instance, '[…] *the provision of courses and teaching and evaluation methods that promote a diversified training in terms of scientific and personal competencies and cooperative and transdisciplinary work*' (University of Porto 2016, 29). The main goal of this diversified training is to equip HEI students with tools and skills that will allow them more successfully to search for a job and integrate into the labour market (Thune and Støren 2015; Pavlin 2014).

In summary, results from this research study provide a positive answer to the research question that steered this chapter, inasmuch as institutional support mechanisms are perceived by students and institutional leaders as relevant for students' integration process. Indeed, results show that, in addition to the more traditional support services that focus on academic, social and financial support, HEIs are increasingly aware of the need to provide support for their graduates' integration into the workplace. This is carried out by including in the course syllabuses content and action to meet the new labour market needs and enhance transferable competencies that will be highly helpful for the future professionals; and additionally, by monitoring graduate insertion in the professional arena. Furthermore, the comparison of both student and staff views on HEI support reveal that the perceptions of both groups of institutional actors are well attuned. Indeed, HEIs seek to offer their student population a wide range of efficient mechanisms to ease their integration and experience throughout their educational pathway. In turn, students feel that they are supported and cared for by their HEIs. This is certainly a very relevant result for institutions which strive to attract, satisfy, retain and, ultimately, provide their students with a very positive academic experience and also with the tools that will help them be successful once they leave the higher education and enter the labour market.

References

Attinasi, Louis C. 1989. 'Getting in: Mexican Americans' Perceptions of University Attendance and the Implications for Freshman Year Persistence'. *The Journal of Higher Education* 60 (3): 247–277.

Baer, Linda, and Ann Hill Duin. 2014. 'Retain your Students! The Analytics, Policies and Politics of Reinvention Strategies'. *Planning for Higher Education Journal* 42 (3): 1–12.

Bardin, Laurence. 1977. *Análise de Conteúdo* [Content analysis]. Lisbon: Edições.

Bliss, Leonard B., and Janice R. Sandiford. 2004. 'Linking Study Behaviors and Student Culture to Academic Success among Hispanic Students'. *Community College Journal of Research and Practice* 28 (3): 281–295.

Cardoso, José Luís, Vítor Escária, Vítor Sérgio Ferreira, Paulo Madruga, Alevandra Raimundo, and Marta Pedro Varanda. 2012. *Empregabilidade e Ensino Superior em Portugal* [Employability and higher education in Portugal]. Lisbon: A3ES – Agency for Assessment and Accreditation of Higher Education.

Ciobanu, Alina. 2013. 'The Role of Student Services in the Improving of Student Experience in Higher Education'. *Procedia – Social and Behavioral Sciences* 92: 169–173.

Denzin, Norman K., and Yvonna S. Lincoln, eds. 1994. *Handbook of Qualitative Research*. Thousand Oaks, CA: Sage.

Denzin, Norman K., and Yvonna S. Lincoln. 2011. *The Handbook of Qualitative Research*, 4th ed. Thousand Oaks, CA: Sage.

Duckworth, Angela L., Christopher Peterson, Michael D. Matthews, and Dennis R. Kelly. 2007. 'Grit: Perseverance and Passion for Long-Term Goals'. *Journal of Personality and Social Psychology* 92 (6): 1087–1101.

Duckworth, Angela L., and Patrick D. Quinn. 2009. 'Development and Validation of the Short Grit Scale (Grit-S)'. *Journal of Personality Assessment* 91 (2): 166–174.

Dweck, Carol S. 2006. *Mindset: The New Psychology of Success*. New York: Ballantine Books.

Ferreira, Joaquim Armando, Leandro S. Almeida, and Ana Paula Soares. 2001. 'Adaptação Académica em Estudantes do 1.º Ano: Diferenças de Género, Situação de Estudante e Curso' [Academic adaptation in 1st year students: gender differences, student situation and programme]. *Psico-USF* 6 (1): 1–10.

Fielding, Nigel G. 2012. 'Triangulation and Mixed Methods Designs: Data Integration with New Research Technologies'. *Journal of Mixed Methods Research* 6 (2): 124–136.

Ghrayeb, Omar, Purushhothaman Damodaran, and Promod Vohra. 2011. 'Art of Triangulation: An Effective Assessment Validation Strategy'. *Global Journal of Engineering Education* 13 (3): 96–101.

Graneheim, Ulla Hallgren, and Berit Lundman. 2004. 'Qualitative Content Analysis in Nursing Research: Concepts, Procedures and Measures to Achieve Trustworthiness'. *Nurse Education Today* 24 (2): 105–112.

Karlsen, Jan Erik, and Rosalind M. O. Pritchard. 2013. 'Resilience – The Ability to Adapt'. In *Resilient Universities: Confronting Changes in a Challenging World*, edited by J. E. Karlsen, and Rosalind M. O. Pritchard, 1–15. Oxford and New York: Peter Lang.

Krippendorff, Klaus. 2004. *Content Analysis. An Introduction to its Methodology*, 2nd ed. Thousand Oaks, California: Sage.

Mayring, Philipp. 2014. *Qualitative Content Analysis: Theoretical Foundation, Basic Procedures and Software Solution*. Klagenfurt: GESIS.

Mbuva, James M. 2011. 'An Examination of Student Retention and Student Success in High School, College, and University'. *Journal of Higher Education Theory and Practice* 11 (4): 92–101.

Merriam, Sharan B. 2009. *Qualitative Research. A Guide to Design and Implementation*. San Francisco: Jossey-Brass.

Pascarella, Ernest T., and Patrick T. Terenzini. 2005. *How College Affects Students. Vol. 2. A Third Decade of Research*. San Francisco: Jossey-Bass.

Pavlin, Samo. 2014. 'The role of higher education in supporting graduates' early labour market careers'. *International Journal of Manpower* 35 (4): 576–590.

Polytechnic Institute of Cávado and Ave. 2014. 'Estatutos do Instituto Politécnico do Cávado e do Ave' [Statutes of the Polytechnic Institute of Cávado and Ave]. *Official Gazette of Portugal* II (214). Available at https://ipca.pt/ipca/apresentacao/o-ipca/estatutos/. Accessed on January 12, 2019.

Polytechnic Institute of Porto. 2009. 'Estatutos do Instituto Politécnico do Porto' [Statutes of the Polytechnic Institute of Porto). *Official Gazette of Portugal* II (22). Available at https://sigarra.up.pt/up/pt/legislacao_geral.ver_legislacao?p_nr=3208. Accessed on January 11, 2019.

Polytechnic Institute of Porto. 2017. *Manual de Qualidade* [Quality manual]. Available at https://www.ipp.pt/apresentacao/qualidade. Accessed on January 11, 2019.

Sarrico, Cláudia S., Maria João Rosa, Pedro Nuno Teixeira, Isabel Machado, and Ricardo Biscaia. 2013. *A Eficiência Formativa e a Empregabilidade no Ensino Superior* [Educational efficiency and employability in higher education]. Lisbon: A3ES – Agency for Assessment and Accreditation of Higher Education.

Savenye, Wilhelmina C., and Rhonda S. Robinson. 1996. 'Qualitative Research Issues and Methods: An Introduction for Educational Technologists'. In *Handbook of Research for Educational Communications and Technology*, edited by J.M. Spector, M.D. Merrill, J. Elen, and M.J. Bishop, 1171–1195. Bloomington: AECT.

Spady, William G. 1971. 'Dropouts from Higher Education: Toward an Empirical Model'. *Interchange* 2 (3): 38–62.

Strauss, Anselm L., and Juliet M. Corbin. 1998. *Basics of Qualitative Research: Grounded Theory Procedures and Techniques*, 2nd ed. Newbury Park, CA: Sage.

Swail, Watson Scott, Kenneth E. Redd, and Laura W. Perna. 2003. *Retaining Minority Students in Higher Education. A Framework for Success*. San Francisco, California: Wiley.

Terenzini, Patrick T., and Ernest T. Pascarella 1980. 'Towards the Validation of Tinto's Model of College Student Attrition: A Review of Recent Studies'. *Research in Higher Education* 12 (3): 271–282.

Tinto, Vincent. 1993. *Leaving College: Rethinking the Causes and Cures of Student Attrition*, 2nd ed. Chicago: The University of Chicago Press.

Tinto, Vincent. 2011. *Taking Student Success Seriously in the College Classroom*. Syracuse: Syracuse University.

Tinto, Vincent. 2012a. 'Enhancing Student Success: Taking the Classroom Success Seriously'. *The International Journal of the First Year in Higher Education* 3 (1): 1–8.

Tinto, Vincent. 2012b. *Completing College: Rethinking Institutional Action*. Chicago: The University of Chicago Press.

Tinto, Vincent, and Brian Pusser. 2006. *Moving from Theory to Action: Building a Model of Institutional Action for Student Success*. Washington, DC: National Postsecondary Education Cooperative (NPEC).

Thune, Taran, and Støren, Liv Anne. 2015. 'Study and Labour Market Effects of Graduate Students' Interaction with work Organisations During Education— A Cohort Study'. *Education + Training* 57 (7): 702–722.

University of Minho. 2009. *Programa de Acção para o Quadriénio 2009-2013* [Action program for the 2009-2013 four-year period]. Available at https://www.uminho.pt/PT/uminho/Informacao-Institucional/Paginas/Planos-e-Relatorios.aspx. Accessed on January 12, 2019.

University of Minho. 2010. *Plano da Qualidade* [Quality plan]. Available at https://www.uminho.pt/PT/uminho/Qualidade/SIGAQ-UM/Paginas/O-Plano-da-Qualidade.aspx. Accessed on January 12, 2019.

University of Minho. 2017. 'Estatutos da Universidade do Minho' [Statutes of the University of Minho]. *Official Gazette of Portugal* II (183). Available at https://www.uminho.pt/EN/uminho/institutional-information/Pages/Statutes.aspx. Accessed on January 12, 2019.

University of Porto. 2009. 'Estatutos da Universidade do Porto' [Statutes of the University of Porto]. *Official Gazette of Portugal* II (93). Available at https://sigarra.up.pt/up/pt/legislacao_geral.ver_legislacao?p_nr=3208. Accessed on January 11, 2019.

University of Porto. 2016. *2017 Plano de Atividades* [2017 Activity plan]. Available at https://sigarra.up.pt/up/pt/web_base.gera_pagina?p_pagina=brochuras-e-relatorios. Accessed on January 11, 2019.

Willig, Carla. 2001. *Introducing Qualitative Research in Psychology. Adventures in Theory and Method*. Philadelphia: Open University Press.

Young-Jones, Adena D., Tracie D. Burt, Stephanie Dixon, and Melissa J. Hawthorne. 2013. 'Academic Advising: Does it Really Impact Student Success?' *Quality Assurance in Education* 21 (1): 7–19.

*Internationalisation
and the Student*

CHAPTER 9

The Perceived Impact of Intercultural Awareness on Peer Interaction: Study of a UK University

Ming Cheng, Olalekan Adeban Adekola, Gayle Pringle Barnes and Linghui Tian

Introduction

The development of intercultural awareness is a major factor that motivates many international students to study abroad (Altbach and Knight 2007), but the level of intercultural awareness on many international campuses appears generally low (Hayward 2000; Soria and Troisi, 2014). For example, Volet and Ang (2012) report that there is lack of interaction between local students and international students from Asian backgrounds. Chinese students are stereotyped as passive learners whose learning is characterised as rote, silent and passive (Turner 2006). This indicates a need to prepare students to appreciate each other's different culture and learning approaches, especially when there is an increasing number of Chinese students studying in the UK, which has provided universities with opportunities as well as challenges in developing students' intercultural awareness (Iannelli and Huang 2014; Zheng 2014). This paper therefore investigates the impact of intercultural awareness on Master's students' experience of peer interaction. Chinese students and their non-Chinese peers at a British university are selected for the study in order to explore and compare whether their peer interaction is affected by their understandings of different cultures and different approaches to learning.

Impact of Internationalisation

Raising students' intercultural awareness is linked with the far-reaching implications of internationalisation for the higher education sector, which involves student mobility, academic cooperation and academic knowledge transfer (Teichler 2015). Students with different cultural identities and worldviews are brought together to operate and interact in the same environment, which inevitably leads to cultural diversity in the learning context (Guo and Chase 2011; Volet and Ang 2012). They need to demonstrate abilities to cope with diverse and complex situations in a multicultural environment, in particular with people who have different values, beliefs and cultural backgrounds (Adler and Gundersen 2008). Chinese students, for example, face differences in communication and learning between their first culture and the host culture (Holmes, 2004). Learning in a culturally diverse setting could sometimes expose them to a hostile educational environment, where misunderstanding, racial tension and stereotyping may adversely influence their academic achievement and psychological health (Ancis et al. 2000).

Differences between educational systems could also affect student learning and performance, and there is evidence that home students perform significantly better than international students (Kelly and Moogan, 2012). Likewise, Lee and Rice (2007) highlighted that international students (mainly Asian students) can face discrimination as a result of stereotypes when studying abroad. Rice et al. (2016) argued that international students who felt disrespected were more likely to be stressed than domestic students. This suggests that studying in a culturally diverse environment places demands on all students to cope with cross-cultural complexities, uncertainties, misunderstandings and conflicts between students' choices of belonging to different cultural groups (Eisenberg et al. 2013).

Call for Intercultural Awareness

There are increasing calls for intercultural awareness in higher education (Sarath 2005; Trius and Shyryaeva 2013), with a general agreement on the need to include an intercultural dimension in university strategies and internationalisation practices (Crichton and Scarino 2011; Deardorff 2006). Intercultural awareness has become a designated key outcome of an internationalised curriculum (Leask 2009). However, the development of intercultural awareness is limited in undergraduate and postgraduate programmes (Gannon 2008), and efforts to assess the development of student intercultural awareness have been anecdotal (Black and Duhon 2006). Moreover, the implementation of effective strategies to achieve intercultural awareness has not been sufficiently well executed in many English-speaking universities (Tian and Lowe 2009).

Recent studies in the USA and UK indicate that stereotyped understandings of Chinese students persist (Huang 2008; Ruble and Zhang

2013), and that Chinese students generally prefer to interact with their fellow Chinese rather than peers from other cultural backgrounds (Xiao and Petraki 2007). According to Kimmel and Volet (2012), this is because students' attitudes towards intercultural interactions can be affected by the quality of their experiences with peers when studying abroad. Chinese students tend to rely on their circle of Chinese friends when it is difficult for them to make friends with students from non-Chinese backgrounds (Briguglio and Smith 2012; Mikal et al. 2015).

This paper echoes the view by Korzilius et al. (2007) and Longo (2009) that intercultural awareness is important to successful learning and that students need to become aware of not only their own culture (cultural awareness), but also of other people's cultures (intercultural awareness). Using the model of intercultural awareness proposed by Baker (2011) as a framework, this paper explores how Chinese Master's students interact with their non-Chinese peers in the classroom; and whether peer interaction has been affected by students' understandings of different cultures and approaches to learning. Intercultural awareness here refers to the knowledge, skills and attitudes needed to communicate in diverse cultural contexts.

Baker's (2011) model incorporates three levels of development, moving from basic cultural awareness to advanced cultural awareness and finally to intercultural awareness. Level 1, basic cultural awareness, involves a conscious understanding of one's own culture and how it influences behaviour, beliefs, values, and communication. There is awareness that other cultures may be different, but this awareness may not include any specific systematic knowledge of other cultures. This is combined with an ability to articulate one's own cultural perspective and to make general comparisons between one's own culture and that of 'others'. Level 2, advanced cultural awareness, involves more complex understanding of cultures. There is an awareness of cultures as fluid, dynamic and relative, combined with specific knowledge of (an)other culture(s). Level 3 is intercultural awareness which moves beyond viewing cultures as bounded entities and demonstrates the ability to mediate and negotiate between different cultural frames of reference.

Using Baker's (2011) model as a conceptual and practical basis to understand intercultural awareness, this study will interpret individual student experiences, with the consideration that intercultural awareness may not develop sequentially. Chinese Master's students and their peers in a British university are selected for study because they have only one year to acclimatise to a new culture and educational objectives and because there is an increasing number of Chinese students studying in the UK and their experience of acculturation remains to be fully understood (Wu & Hammond 2011).

Methodology

This research involved semi-structured interviews with 33 Chinese Master's students and 16 peers from non-Chinese backgrounds at a British university. These participants were recruited via invitation sent by their Schools. This university is selected as an in-depth case for study (Yin 2014). It is an ancient university, ranked as one of the top 200 universities, according to Times Higher Education World University Rankings; well respected for both teaching and research activities, and has a large number of Chinese students on campus. The student interviewees were from engineering and business studies, because these are popular subject areas among Chinese students (HEFCE 2014). A theoretical sampling approach (Punch 2013) was used to select these interviewees. Gender, age, and cultural background were considered. The majority of these participants were in their early 20s. The non-Chinese peers were mainly from Asia, EU, and the UK.

Research ethics approval was sought and granted before the data collection. Informed consent was given to audio-record each interview; transcripts were shared and approved by the interviewees upon their request to ensure that the interviewees were satisfied with them. NVivo software and thematic analysis (Boyatzis 1998) were applied to the interview data, in order to ensure that they were analysed in a rigorous and transparent manner (Creswell 2013).

This project explored two research questions that are identified from the existing research in the field:

- How do Master's students experience intercultural peer interaction at British universities?
- How have Master's students' experiences of interaction been affected by their intercultural awareness?

Findings

The research indicated that peers thought there were three main areas in which Chinese students responded in different ways from them. The differences highlighted were in the areas of interpretations of learning, responses to group work and responses to social interaction. In each area, student interviews highlighted the resilience of stereotyping, fears of discrimination, and tensions between the different groups of students.

INTERPRETATIONS OF APPROACHES TO LEARNING

The first theme emerging from the interviews is that Chinese students have a different approach to learning. Chinese students were commonly described by their peers as being quiet in the classroom, and less likely to participate in classroom discussions. The main explanation given for this by interviewees, both Chinese and their peers, was that the quieter behaviour was due to cultural influence. This demonstrates the basic cultural awareness of students as described by Baker (2011, 203). For example, a Chinese student in engineering studies explained that this is because Chinese students preferred to keep a low profile within their group:

> If I'm in a group where there are lots of Chinese students, I sometimes feel that I should be quiet, because I don't want to stand out. It's also part of a culture thing. (Chinese 7)

Another student from Kazakhstan also related this behaviour to culture, including political influences:

> I think it's perhaps the socialist revolution. I know that because my country was a former socialist country. You are not allowed to be outstanding, to be different, and you should do exactly the same as everyone else, you know. It was the ideology in our country during the socialist time, and maybe this is part of the culture of China now. (Peer 1)

These statements illustrate interviewees' recognition of cultural influences on their own and others' behaviour and making comparisons between cultures. There is also evidence in the comment from Peer 1 of Baker's second level of intercultural awareness, that is, advanced cultural awareness, as the comment emphasises that cultural norms can change over time and in different situations. However, interviewees in general interpreted Chinese students' quiet behaviour in different ways. A few of the peer interviewees described Chinese students as 'passive learners', citing a lack of contribution to classroom discussion. For example, one peer interviewee thought that: 'more than 60% are passive learners. They are waiting for teachers or colleagues to tell them what to do' (Peer 5).

While this statement demonstrates a stereotypical association of Chinese students with passive learning, it also points to some awareness of the complexity of cultures, as the interviewee notes that not all Chinese students will behave in a particular way. Overall, the proportion of interviewees associating quiet behaviour with passive learning is small. The rest of the interviewees, especially those from Asia, point out that Chinese students engage in active learning through other means, such as independent study, and through discussing work with academic staff or friends in private or via email. As one Chinese student suggests:

> Chinese students are quiet in the classroom. It doesn't mean they don't think. Maybe they just don't speak out. After the class when they need to write assignments, they will search for materials. They will read it and maybe write down their views. I don't think if you are silent in the classroom you are a passive learner. (Chinese 2)

Similarly, a peer interviewee notes:

> They are not so aggressive (vocal) during the discussion as I am, but talking with them individually, they have passion. They desire to do something, and I can feel that. (Peer 10)

The concept of basic cultural awareness, involving recognition of 'the role culturally based contexts play in any interpretation of meaning' (Baker 2011, 203) is demonstrated in these comments. There is an awareness of the relative nature of cultural norms, as participants become aware that active learning might be realised in different ways, going beyond classroom interaction. This suggests an advanced cultural awareness that cultural understandings can be fluid, and open to change.

Student interviewees also reflected on the impact of culture on interaction between lecturers and students in the classroom. Different views emerged regarding appropriate ways for students to ask lecturers questions. It was suggested that Chinese students are not interactive during class because they do not participate actively in asking questions of lecturers. One Chinese student associates this behavioural norm with Chinese culture:

> Lots of Chinese friends have questions to ask during the class, but they don't want to initiate the question, because it's not polite to raise questions with the teacher during his speaking, but foreigner classmates just raise their hands and ask directly. (Chinese 20)

However, a peer interviewee questions the efficacy of this approach, demonstrating a different understanding of appropriate behaviour when asking questions:

> Some Chinese students always pose questions to teachers during the break. It is better to ask questions during the lecture because it's much easier to discuss in the class than after that. (Peer 12)

Both these comments demonstrate a basic cultural awareness, focusing on the way that different cultures can have different values and lead to different behaviours. There is no direct evidence in these comments of 'intercultural awareness', or 'a capacity to negotiate and mediate' between different cultural practices (Baker 2011, 203). The comments recognise the cultural factors involved, but do not attempt to resolve the differences in approach.

INTERCULTURAL AWARENESS IN GROUP WORK

The second area in which interviewees observed differences in cultural understandings and practices was group work and this sometimes led to tensions within the group. Peer interviewees tended to report that Chinese students appeared reluctant to take leadership within a group. For example, one interviewee stated:

> Chinese never take initiatives, and they never express their opinions first. I had to ask 'what's your opinion' to see what they have in their mind. (Peer 8)

However, some Chinese participants felt that this perceived lack of initiative was caused largely by Chinese students' lack of confidence in their English language skills. Here is such a view from an engineering student:

> It depends on which topic we are talking about. If we talk with foreigners, sometimes we don't want to show our English is so poor. It's hard for us to explain points. (Chinese 8)

These comments indicate different understandings of the reasons behind an apparent reluctance to assume leadership. The latter comment in particular suggests the second level of intercultural awareness, representing an 'awareness of individuals as members of cultural groups *and* many other social groups' (Baker 2011, 203). The behaviour of students who prefer not to act as leaders in group work may be influenced not only by culture, but also by English language barriers which makes them lack confidence in discussions. There are also comments which recognise a more fluid understanding of cultural behaviours. For example, a peer interviewee reports on how one individual may demonstrate different behaviours in different group work situations:

> Chinese are not always quiet, when you have a group of five people, and four people are from different nations…, and one Chinese. This [Chinese] person starts to communicate brilliantly, and he speaks with everyone. But when you add another Chinese, it's like creating a group of Chinese; they start to be quiet (Peer 9).

This comment describes a situation where certain behaviours are associated with one cultural group. It also suggests a more fluid interpretation of culture in which individuals move between different cultural norms.

Despite the advanced cultural awareness demonstrated by interviewees' statements, group work was identified as problematic by half of the interviewees. One concern is that Chinese students spoke together in Chinese, in the presence of other students who were not Chinese-speakers:

> Chinese always speak Chinese. Sometimes we don't understand what they say. … We need to speak English together when we do group work (Peer 13).

While some Chinese interviewees agreed that this did not benefit group work, others reasoned that this was due to lack of confidence in discussing ideas in English, and that the majority of students were Chinese in their class.

Different approaches to group roles emerged. One Chinese student described a negative experience of working with one group member who was from the EU:

> That boy is really self-important. Because we are one group, our result should be discussed and should combine each student's point, not only his. He just did the presentation himself. I don't think it's fair and I was angry. I think the tutor couldn't just ignore it. The tutor should point it out and tell him it's not good. (Chinese 18)

A peer interviewee also reported hearing discriminatory statements directed towards Chinese students:

I don't want to name [them or] reveal their nationality. They say they don't like Chinese, and they don't want to be in this group with Chinese students. (Peer 1)

The tensions described above suggest that group work could be a key area for interventions to develop and increase intercultural awareness among students from different cultural backgrounds.

SOCIAL INTERACTION

The third view that underpins the interviews is that the cultural values and behaviour of the Chinese students has an impact on social interaction. One common observation from Chinese students themselves is the tendency for them to remain in national groups rather than forming potentially intercultural environments:

I think it's difficult for the Chinese to make deep, good friends with the local people. I think most of the locals stay within their national group. (Chinese 31)

A foreign friend asked me why Chinese people always stay in a group, and I explained perhaps it's the only secure way to say that I have friends. I said: 'If you say you want to get in or on? On communicates better with us, I will be super happy'. (Chinese 3)

These comments suggest that despite a desire from both Chinese students and their peers for more intercultural interaction, barriers emerged. A key concern of Chinese interviewees was that although they could start a conversation with local students, it was challenging to develop strong connections. For example, a student explained this as being due to different cultural behaviours:

[A non-Chinese friend] said, how can I get access to you guys? I said, that could be a problem, because our culture is pretty different. If they want to make friends, they always go to the house party or local pub for drinks. But we don't, we just have dinner, or go shopping with other people. (Chinese 3)

Cultural preferences around socialising are seen as absolute in this comment, which suggests that non-Chinese students might be unwilling to join in activities such as dinners or shopping trips. Nonetheless, this comment suggests that two students from different cultural backgrounds try explicitly to 'negotiate and mediate' between different cultural practices (Baker, 2011, 203). This attempt at mediation is not successful, in the sense that the two students do not appear to find ways to overcome the barriers and identify a mutually comfortable environment for socialising. Their attempts to explain and negotiate these boundaries suggest a 'work-in-progress' form of intercultural awareness.

Other interviewees referred to the challenges caused by different specific cultural understandings of socialising, particularly around attitudes to drinking alcohol:

> I cannot drink alcohol. Like this kind of social activity that university organised, people will drink a lot of alcohol. Whatever you want to drink, you have to drink wine. I will feel embarrassed, so I do not want to go there. (Chinese 17)

However, peer interviewees, especially home students and those from the EU, found it difficult to understand why Chinese students did not like parties and drinking, as they believed that these were important for making friends. These different thoughts about socialising appear to be a significant barrier for Chinese students to establishing friendship with their peers. This indicates that universities need to increase opportunities to develop intercultural awareness among students in order to improve their learning and cultural experiences.

These interviews highlight the challenges of and barriers to going beyond the first level of basic cultural awareness, recognising the multiple factors that impacted on Chinese students' opportunities to make friends from different countries. One factor is that there was simply a lack of opportunities for Chinese students to meet and socialise with peers from different countries on campus, due to the large numbers of Chinese students in the classes. Another barrier was the intensive nature of a one-year Master's course:

> I am lacking opportunities to meet people, because I'm the kind of person who does not like to talk to others. And because the course is pretty heavy, I seldom have time to go to the pub.... I think it's just lack of opportunity to make friends. (Chinese 30)

For this interviewee, it is practical rather than cultural factors which create barriers. Another interviewee also refers to personal rather than cultural reasons:

> The biggest problem is myself. I'm not confident enough during my first few months in the UK, chatting in English. Last time when I was chatting with friends, some of my friends mentioned that I cared too much about other people's image of China, or the image of Chinese people in other's minds. (Chinese 23)

These comments highlight the importance of individual traits (wanting 'to go to the pub', lack of confidence in 'chatting in English', for example) rather than broader cultural differences. They demonstrate 'awareness of multiple voices or perspectives within any cultural grouping' associated with the advanced cultural awareness proposed by Baker (2011, 203).

Discussion and Conclusion

Most interviewees' accounts of their own experience and culture-related behaviours, together with their awareness of other cultures, are a strong indication of basic and advanced cultural awareness. For example, they expressed an awareness of 'individuals as members of cultural groups *and* many other social groups' (Baker 2011, 203) and they reflected on the different factors, such as class size, confidence in speaking English, and cultural preferences, which could affect behaviour in the classroom.

However, the findings suggest that student interviewees encounter considerable barriers when attempting 'to mediate and negotiate between cultural frames of reference and communication modes' (Baker 2011, 205). Despite widespread awareness that cultural influences can lead to different learning behaviours, these differences remained as points of tension. This is evidenced by some learning behaviours of Chinese students, such as silence in the classroom and asking tutors questions after class, being perceived as inappropriate by their peers, especially home students and those from the EU.

Tensions were also reported in group work. Peer interviewees perceived Chinese students as unwilling to take leadership, while Chinese students explained that they lacked confidence in stating their arguments clearly due to language barriers. According to Hwang (2012), the reason could be that Chinese students are afraid of 'losing face', so they adopt a defence mechanism and choose to remain silent rather than voice their opinions. In addition, the large proportion of Chinese students in the class limited their opportunities to improve their English language abilities, which as a result affected their confidence in taking leadership in group work.

Intercultural interaction outside of studies also proved challenging. Most non-Chinese students understood that Chinese cultures are different, but they did not necessarily comprehend and respect Chinese students' social activities. They stated that drinking and parties were important for making friends and felt students should be more open to sharing their ideas without being too concerned about how they would appear in front of others. This lack of intercultural awareness sometimes led to a feeling among Chinese students that they were being discriminated against. This suggests that although participants were aware of 'possibilities for mismatch and miscommunication' in a multi-cultural environment and attempts to mediate between cultures (Baker 2011, 203), the difficulties that they experienced often remain unresolved.

This research indicates that, despite many years of discussion and debate, British universities do not provide enough or appropriate opportunities for their students to develop skills, knowledge and attitudes that are essential in negotiating and mediating effectively in intercultural communication. Indeed, the research highlights a general lack of intercultural communication among students and staff particularly in teaching and learning practice. The interviews demonstrate that there are tensions between different groups of students as a result of the lack of intercultural communication that does not lead to a positive learning and teaching environment. Discussing the impacts of language and culture is likely to help learners and their teachers to work together to negotiate and mediate between cultural understandings and learning behaviours (Ryan and Viete 2009). Universities could explore ways of integrating reflective activities to develop intercultural awareness within postgraduate programmes.

Implications for Institutional Policy and Practice

Based on these research findings, three key recommendations are proposed to universities facing similar issues with the aim of creating environments where intercultural awareness for a better learning experience will be actively developed. First, confidence in English proficiency is an important factor affecting students' integration into the new environment. Language programmes that are already available need to be more transparent and advertised from an early stage, for instance in induction courses. As Ryan and Viete (2009, 311) point out, intercultural interactions require 'all communicators, not just a few to actively search for meaning in what others say and write'. All students therefore need to be supported with intercultural communication practices that are enacted through English. Language programmes aimed at increasing the confidence of users of English as a second language are only one measure; developing wider confidence in the use of English as a lingua franca is also desirable. Conversations between speakers using English as a lingua franca in university settings have been characterised by the 'considerable effort invested [by the speakers] in preventing misunderstanding', through strategies such as clarification and peers working together to co-construct meaning (Mauranen 2006, 146). Modelling and exploring these strategies could offer all learners opportunities to communicate effectively.

Secondly, reducing class size and increasing cultural diversity within the class could increase opportunities for intercultural interactions, especially when the class has a large number of international students from the same country. A more viable solution is to increase the number of tutorials and seminars or allow tutors more time to deal with questions. These changes could assist students who lack confidence to participate more fully in discussions and offer more opportunities for all students to explore different ways of learning within a smaller and more interactive classroom.

Thirdly, increasing and diversifying university-supported social events could also contribute to enhanced intercultural awareness. As many of the Chinese student interviewees suggested, they did not wish to participate in social events which were often 'too British' and centred around drinking alcohol. Focusing on interactive and culturally diverse activities and developing cross-cultural partnerships would help students from different cultural backgrounds to get to know each other. For example, Pritchard & Skinner's (2002) research suggests that cross-cultural partnerships could help international students to overcome isolation and establish satisfactory relationships with home students abroad.

References

Adler, J. Nancy, and Allison Gundersen. 2008. *International Dimensions of Organizational Be- havior*. Mason, USA: Thomson – South Western.

Altbach, G. Philip, and Jane Knight. 2007. 'The Internationalization of Higher Education: Motivations and Realities'. *Journal of Studies in International Education* 11 (3–4): 290–305.

Ancis, R. Julie, William E. Sedlacek, and Jonathan J. Mohr. 2000. 'Student Perceptions of Campus Cultural Climate by Race'. *Journal of Counseling & Development* 78 (2): 180–185.

Baker, Will. 2011. 'Intercultural Awareness: Modelling an Understanding of Cultures in Intercultural Communication Through English as a Lingua Franca'. *Language and Intercultural Communication* 11 (3): 197–214.

Black, H. Tyrone, and David L. Duhon. 2006. 'Assessing the Impact of Business Study Abroad Programs on Cultural Awareness and Personal Development'. *Journal of Education for Business* 81 (3): 140–144.

Boyatzis, E. Richard. 1998. *Transforming Qualitative Information: Thematic Analysis and Code Development.* Thousand Oaks, London, & New Delhi: SAGE.

Briguglio, Carmela, and Robina Smith. 2012. 'Perceptions of Chinese Students in an Australian University: Are We Meeting their Needs?' *Asia Pacific Journal of Education* 32 (1): 17–33.

Creswell, W. John, ed. 2013. *Qualitative Inquiry and Research Design: Choosing among Five Approaches.* London: Sage.

Crichton, Jonathan, and Angela Scarino. 2011. 'How are We to Understand the 'Intercultural Dimension'? An Examination of the Intercultural Dimension of Internationalisation in the Context of Higher Education in Australia'. *Australian Review of Applied Linguistics* 30 (1): 04.1–04.21.

Deardorff, K. Darla. 2006. 'Identification and Assessment of Intercultural Competence as a Student Outcome of Internationalization'. *Journal of Studies in International Education* 10 (3): 241–266.

De Vita, Glauco, and Peter Case. 2003. 'Rethinking the Internationalisation Agenda in UK Higher Education'. *Journal of Further and Higher Education* 27 (4): 383–398.

Eisenberg, Jacob, Hyun-Jung Lee, Frank Brück, Barbara Brenner, Marie-Therese Claes, Jacek Mironski, and Roger Bell. 2013. 'Can Business Schools Make Students Culturally Competent? Effects of Cross-cultural Management Courses on Cultural Intelligence'. *Academy of Management Learning & Education* 12 (4): 603–621.

Gannon, Judie. 2008. 'Developing Intercultural Skills for International Industries: The Role of Industry and Educators'. *Hospitality, Leisure, Sport and Tourism Network: Enhancing Series: Internationalisation.* Retrieved from https://www. heacademy. ac.uk/sites/default/files/e2_developing_intercultural_skills.pdf

Guo, Shibao, and Mackie Chase. 2011. 'Internationalisation of Higher Education: Integrating International Students into Canadian Academic Environment'. *Teaching in Higher Education* 16 (3): 305–318.

Hale, J. Ellen. 1986. *Black Children: Their Roots, Culture, and Learning Styles.* Baltimore and London: Johns Hopkins University Press.

Hayward, M. Fred. 2000. *Internationalization of US Higher Education. Preliminary Status Report, 2000.* Washington, D.C.: American Council on Education.

Higher Education Funding Council for England (HEFCE). 2014. *Decline in Global Demand for English Higher Education.* Retrieved from http://www.hefce.ac.uk/ news/newsarchive/2014/news86922.html.

Hofstede, Geert. 2015. *China – Geert Hofstede* [online] Retrieved from http://geer-thof- stede.com/china.html.

Holmes, Prue. 2004. 'Negotiating Differences in Learning and Intercultural Communication Ethnic Chinese Students in a New Zealand University'. *Business Communication Quarterly* 67 (3): 294–307.

Huang, Rong. 2008. 'Critical thinking: Discussion from Chinese Postgraduate International Students and their Lecturers'. *Hospitality, Leisure, Sport and Tour-*

ism Net- work: Enhancing Series: Internationalisation. Retrieved from https://www. heacad- emy.ac.uk/sites/default/files/e2_critical_thinking.pdf.

Hwang, Kwang-Kuo. 2012. *Foundations of Chinese Psychology: Confucian Social Relations*. New York, NY: Springer New York.

Iannelli, Cristina, and Jun Huang. 2014. 'Trends in Participation and Attainment of Chinese Students in UK Higher Education'. *Studies in Higher Education* 39 (5): 805–822.

Kelly, Philip, and Yvonne Moogan. 2012. 'Culture Shock and Higher Education Performance: Implications for Teaching'. *Higher Education Quarterly* 66 (1): 24–46.

Kimmel, Karen, and Simone Volet. 2012. 'University Students' Perceptions of and Attitudes Towards Culturally Diverse Group Work: Does Context Matter?' *Journal of Studies in International Education* 16 (2): 157–181.

Korzilius, Hubert, Andreu van Hooft, and Brigitte Planken. 2007. *A Longitudinal Study on Intercultural Awareness and Foreign Language Acquisition in the Netherlands*. Retrieved from http://www.immi.se/intercultural/nr15/planken.htm.

Leask, Betty. 2009. 'Using Formal and Informal Curricula to Improve Interactions between Home and International Students'. *Journal of Studies in International Education* 13 (2): 205–221.

Lee, J. Jenny, and Charles Rice. 2007. 'Welcome to America? International Student Perceptions of Discrimination'. *Higher Education* 53 (3): 381–409.

Mauranen, Anna. 2006. 'Signaling and Preventing Misunderstanding in English as Lingua Franca Communication'. *International Journal of the Sociology of Language* 177: 123–150.

Mikal, P. Jude, Junhong Yang, and Amy Lewis. 2015. 'Surfing USA: How Internet Use Prior to and During Study Abroad Affects Chinese Students' Stress, Integration, and Cultural Learning while in the United States'. *Journal of Studies in International Education* 19 (3): 203–224.

Punch, F. Keith, ed. 2013. *Introduction to Social Research: Quantitative and Qualitative Approaches*. London: Sage.

Rice, G. Kenneth, Hanna Suh, Xiaohui Yang, Elise Choe, and Don E. Davis. 2016. 'The Advising Alliance for International and Domestic Graduate Students: Measurement Invariance and Implications for Academic Stress'. *Journal of Counselling Psychology* 63 (3): 331–342.

Pritchard, M. O. Rosalind, and Barbara Skinner. 2002. 'Cross-cultural Partnerships Between Home and International Students'. *Journal of Studies in International Education* 6 (4): 323–354.

Ruble, A. Rachael, and Yan Bing Zhang. 2013. 'Stereotypes of Chinese International Students Held by Americans'. *International Journal of Intercultural Relations* 37 (2): 202– 211.

Ryan, Janette, and Rosemary Viete. 2009. 'Respectful Interactions: Learning with International Students in the English-speaking Academy'. *Teaching in Higher Education* 14 (3): 303–314.

Sarath, Ed. 2005. 'Meditation Spirituality and Educational Leadership: Consciousness Studies and the Future of Academe'. In *New Directions in Higher Education*, edited by R. Nata, 73–97. New York: Nova Publishers.

Signorini, Paola, Rolf Wiesemes, and Roger Murphy. 2009. 'Developing Alternative Frameworks for Exploring Intercultural Learning: A Critique of Hofstede's Cultural Difference Model'. *Teaching in Higher Education* 14 (3): 253–264.

Soria, M. Krista, and Jordan J. Troisi. 2014. 'Internationalization at Home Alternatives to Study Abroad: Implications for Students' Development of Global, International, and Intercultural Competencies'. *Journal of Studies in International Education* 18 (3): 261–280.

Teichler, Ulrich. 2015. 'Academic Mobility and Migration: What We Know and What We Do Not Know'. *European Review* 23 (S1): S6–S37.

Tian, Mei, and John Lowe. 2009. 'Existentialist Internationalisation and the Chinese Student Experience in English Universities'. *Compare: A Journal of Comparative and International Education* 39 (5): 659–676.

Trius, Lilia, and Tatiana Shyryaeva. 2013. 'A Call for Cultural Awareness and Tolerance in Higher Education. The Case of Pyatigorsk State Linguistic University, North Caucasus, Russia'. *Revista de Cercetare şi Intervenţie Socială* 43: 255–265.

Turner, Yvonne. 2006. 'Chinese Students in a UK Business School: Hearing the Student Voice in Reflective Teaching and Learning Practice'. *Higher Education Quarterly* 60 (1): 27–51.

Volet, E. Simone, and G. Ang. 2012. 'Culturally Mixed Groups on International Campuses: An Opportunity for Inter-cultural Learning'. *Higher Education Research & Development* 31 (1): 21–37.

Wong, Grace, Barry J. Cooper, and Steven Dellaportas. 2015. 'Chinese Students' Perceptions of the Teaching in an Australian Accounting Programme – An Exploratory Study'. *Accounting Education* 24 (4): 318–340.

Wu, Wenli, and Michael Hammond. 2011. 'Challenges of University Adjustment in the UK: A Study of East Asian Master's Degree Students'. *Journal of Further and Higher Education* 35 (3): 423–438.

Wursten, Huib, and Carel Jacobs. 2013. *The Impact of Culture on Education. Can We Introduce Best Practices in Education across Countries?* ITIM International. Retrieved from http://geert-hofstede.com/tl_files/images/site/social/Culture%20and%20educa- tion.pdf

Xiao, Hong, and Eleni Petraki. 2007. 'An Investigation of Chinese Students' Difficulties in Intercultural Communication and its Role in ELT'. *Journal of Intercultural Communication*, 13 Retrieved from http://immi.se/intercultural/nr13/petraki.htm

Yin, K. Robert, ed. 2014. *Case Study Research: Design and Methods*. Los Angeles, USA: Sage Publications.

Zheng, Ping. 2014. 'Antecedents to International Student Inflows to UK Higher Education: A Comparative Analysis'. *Journal of Business Research* 67 (2): 136–143.

CHAPTER 10

The Development of Intercultural Competencies During a Stay Abroad: Does Cultural Distance Matter?

Joris Boonen, Ankie Hoefnagels and Mark Pluymaekers

The employability of young graduates is increasingly dependent on their ability to effectively adapt to international contexts (Eisenchlas and Trevaskes, 2007; Marcotte, Desroches and Poupart, 2007). Young professionals in today's globalised world should not only be able to meet today's employment opportunities but should also be ready for new yet undefined roles. In that light, it comes as no surprise that international and intercultural learning has become a key feature in all types of curricula around the world. The ability to behave and communicate appropriately and effectively in intercultural situations (Deardorff, 2006) is omnipresent in listings of so-called 21st century skills as well (Trilling and Fadel, 2009). One of the strongest advocates of fostering this ability in young professionals is the American philosopher Martha Nussbaum:

> We live in a world in which people face one another across gulfs of geography, language, and nationality. More than at any time in the past, we all depend on people we have never seen, and they depend on us. [...] The world's schools, colleges, and universities therefore have an important and urgent task: to cultivate in students the ability to see themselves as members of a heterogeneous nation (for all modern nations are heterogeneous), and a still more heterogeneous world, and to understand something of the history and character of the diverse groups that inhabit it. (Nussbaum, 2010, 79–81)

Universities have responded to this call for global citizens by developing a wide range of internationalisation activities to enable students to meet and collaborate with peers and professionals from different cultures. Most notably, opportunities are offered to study abroad as part of an exchange or an internship program. An advantage of a stay abroad in a study context is that potential clashes between values, beliefs, customs and behaviours of the home and host culture, referred to by Oberg (1954) as 'culture shocks', are experienced intensively in a relatively safe environment and can be reflected upon and discussed with an experienced supervisor. This directly relates to Allport's classic 'contact hypothesis' (Allport, Clark and Pettigrew, 1954), extensively examined and further expanded in the intergroup contact theory (Pettigrew et al. 2011). Meta-analyses of the hundreds of empirical tests of this theory demonstrate a stable positive and rather universal pattern of intergroup contact (and especially intergroup friendship) remedying and reducing (interracial) prejudice between groups (Pettigrew et al. 2011). This shows the potential positive effects of intercultural contact, but contact theory does not of course imply that all types of intergroup contact produce positive outcomes under all conditions. Some situations such as those in which threat is involved or in which participants did not choose to have the contact can enhance prejudice (Pettigrew and Tropp 2011). Intergroup contact can also have the undesired side-effect of *relative group deprivation*: a feeling that occurs when you as member of a minority ingroup learn—through intergroup contact—what a majority outgroup possesses that you are denied. In general, however, the intergroup contact theory provides a solid theoretical base for the expectation that intercultural contact (and friendship) during a stay abroad will reduce prejudice towards members of other cultures and promote the development of a 'global mindset'.

To encourage positive and effective intercultural contact for all students, it is not only the number of study abroad programmes that has increased. Higher education institutions have also seen a rise in the number of initiatives that aim at 'internationalisation at home' (van Gaalen et al. 2014). This more recent approach has gained importance because it lowers the threshold for international experiences and offers opportunities to achieve international learning outcomes for students with lower incomes for whom a stay in a faraway destination is often too costly. Examples of internationalisation at home are online international learning collaborations, also called 'virtual exchange'. The emergence of all those initiatives and investments in the international curriculum warrants measurement of the extent to which these international experiences are effective in developing the participants' intercultural competencies. When we know under which circumstances an international experience helps to develop intercultural competencies, we can focus on educational activities that contribute significantly to this international learning. We want to note that intercultural contact is relevant not only for the development of intercultural competence, but also directly relates to successful second language learning: the willingness to have social interactions with members of the foreign language group is an important success factor in foreign language learning (Gardner and Lambert 1972; Masgoret and Gardner 2003).

The most important aim of this chapter is to analyse the added value of a study abroad experience to international learning. More specifically, we would like to contribute to the debate by providing evidence whether *cultural distance* to the destination plays a role. Cultural distance is a quantification of the cultural difference between the home country and the host country, based on Hofstede's six-dimension model (1980). For this study, we make use of cultural country scores entered from the *GLOBE Culture and Leadership study* (House 2004) in which every country is scored on nine different value dimensions based on Hofstede's theory. Earlier research has already shown the positive effect of an international exchange on intercultural effectiveness (Anderson et al., 2006; Marcotte et al., 2007; Sison and Brennan, 2012). But the additional question we would like to answer with this study is whether this expected positive effect of a study stay abroad is moderated by the cultural (and geographical) distance between the home culture and the international environment (Salisbury, An and Pascarella, 2013).

In order to answer these and other similar research questions, an instrument called the Global Mind Monitor was developed. This tool offers students an individual report of the development of their international learning on the basis of a longitudinal panel survey measurement. At a higher level, the individual data allow comparison of groups of students, their experiences, and their learning outcomes. For this study, we use data collected from a pilot study of the Monitor among 320 students; they were students in the faculties of Hotel Management and International Business and Communication in the academic year 2015–2016.

In the next sections we will first elaborate on the importance of an international educational context for personal attitude development, discuss the concept of 'intercultural competence', and develop our hypotheses. After this we will present our findings and conclusions.

Literature Review and Hypotheses

THE DEVELOPMENT OF SOCIAL ATTITUDES

Our worldview is developed to a large extent in the influential period of adolescence. Core values about society and about other cultures are shaped before graduation from secondary school. The most important actors in the socialisation process are the school environment, peers, extra-curricular activities and the social family network (Flanagan, 2013).

This classic view on socialisation is supported by several longitudinal studies. Yet it underestimates the further development of young adults aged 18–25. This phase entails a number of life-changing events, such as moving to a college town, a first job, relationships, etc. (Dinas, 2010). Research has shown that social attitudes developed early tend to remain stable over time, provided they are supported by developments during the 18–25 age range. In that case, the term 'crystallisation' or 'consolidation' of early attitudes is used (Visser and Krosnick, 1998). If there are substantial social changes, these may indeed have a large impact on the further development of young people's attitudes. If we apply this argumentation to international learning as part of a study stay abroad, the following two scenarios could serve as examples. In scenario one a student participates in an exchange program because he/she is highly interested in other cultures. This student with highly educated parents has already developed a strong cultural identity during adolescence by travelling or living abroad and by being part of the parents' international social network. For this young adult, a study stay abroad is a logical step, rather than a life-changing event. This is more an example of the self-selection mechanism of 'preaching to the converted' that Kuhn (2012) described in relation to the European Erasmus Program (see also Sigalas, 2010; Wilson, 2011). In scenario two, a student from a lower income family participates in the same exchange program because he/she is motivated by the university to do so. This young person may have travelled abroad more often but lacks a strong international social network. This student's social circle is monocultural and he/she identifies most strongly with the culture of the home country.

Research about the effectiveness of study abroad programs shows that in both above-mentioned scenarios the international experience has a positive effect on attitudes and the development of identity (Kuhn 2012). However, the effect on the young adult from scenario two is significantly stronger. For him/her the exchange is more of a life-changing event than for the person from scenario one. In scenario one we see an example of 'crystallisation', in scenario two we see an example of attitude development. We can apply the same line of reasoning to the relation between an international learning experience and the development of intercultural competence. Merely establishing that the participants possess some intercultural knowledge and skills is insufficient. It is more relevant to investigate under which circumstances international learning takes place. Therefore, it is important to pre-test the students' 'global mind set' before departure and measure the impact of the stay abroad on their development. A central variable that we investigate in this study is the extent to which the culture of the destination during a study abroad differs from the home culture (Shenkar, 2001). This cultural distance may matter because it may be easier for students to integrate if the cultural distance is relatively small rather than large (e.g., a Chinese student studying in South Korea vs staying in Germany). In other words, 'When cultural distance is small, multicultural individuals may find it easier to integrate because there are fewer inconsistencies to reconcile' (Fitzsimmons 2013, 532). It is expected that learning is more substantial when students are confronted with culture shocks and clearly visible, deeper cultural differences in the host country.

INTERCULTURAL COMPETENCIES

Intercultural competence is usually defined in an education context as a broad international learning outcome; it is ability to behave effectively and appropriately in intercultural situations, on the basis of one's attitudes, knowledge and skills (Deardorff 2006). This multifaceted phenomenon is conceptualised in this study as comprising both Cultural Intelligence (or CQ), referring to the general ability to function in another culture or a culturally diverse setting (Ang and Van Dyne 2007) and dispositional dimensions (or Multicultural Personality, MPQ) referring to broad personality factors (empathy, open-mindedness, emotional stability, flexibility and social initiative) that have consistently predicted effectiveness in a multicultural environment (e.g., Mol, Van Oudenhoven et al. 2001; Van der Zee and Van Oudenhoven 2000; Van Oudenhoven and Van der Zee 2002). A study stay abroad offers an ideal environment to develop intercultural competence because the participant is immersed in both the local and professional culture.

HYPOTHESES

On the basis of previous research, our first expectation is that a study stay abroad will positively affect the development of students' intercultural competencies. The international experience meets all the conditions to have a structural impact on the development or at least the 'crystallisation' of this competence. It is a 'life-changing event' that offers many of these young adults a new window on the world. Therefore, our first hypothesis is that a study abroad experience has a consistent and positive effect on the development of students' intercultural competencies:

H1: A study abroad experience has a positive effect on the development of (the different sub dimensions of) intercultural competence of students in higher education.

A number of central components of the 'intercultural competence' concept are about knowledge/ understanding of and behavioural tendencies towards individuals from a different culture. On the basis of previous studies, we expect that the international learning effect will be larger when the cultural distance between the home and the host country is larger:

H2: The development of (the different sub dimensions of) intercultural competence during a stay abroad is stronger if the cultural distance between the student's home country and the destination where the student stays is large.

Data and Methods

The data were collected from 320 students of the Faculties of Hotel Management (255) and International Business and Communication (65) at Zuyd Hogeschool, a Dutch University of Applied Sciences. The students filled in the questionnaire prior to and after a five-month stay abroad. Thirty-one students (9.9%) stayed abroad for a study exchange at a university, 282 students (90.1%) spent an internship abroad as part of their study program; 26 students (8.1%) of the sample had a nationality other than Dutch. The pre-test was taken at least one week prior to departure, the post-test took place in the last two weeks of the stay abroad. This minimised the risk of test-retest bias.

Because of the two-wave panel structure of this dataset, we can assess to what extent a stay abroad correlates with intercultural competencies, but also analyse to what extent *change* occurs over time. Analytically, we use different indicators to measure change over time by using a lagged-dependent variable model in which the pre-test measure is used as an independent variable (Keele and Kelly 2005). That way we can assess stability or change in the different indicators of intercultural competencies, but also examine which other variables have an effect on this change over time.

DEPENDENT VARIABLE: INTERCULTURAL COMPETENCIES

We use a list of validated sub-scales to measure both the behavioural and cultural intelligence dimensions of intercultural competencies. We use the following list of indicators for Cultural Intelligence (CQ) (Ang, Van Dyne et al. 2007) and Multicultural Personality (MPQ) (Van der Zee and Van Oudenhoven 2000):

- CQ – BEHAVIOUR, including statements such as 'I adapt my non-verbal behaviour if this is necessary in cross-cultural interactions'
- CQ – COGNITIVE, including statements such as 'I know the rules regarding non-verbal behaviour in other cultures'
- CQ – METACOGNITIVE, including statements such as 'I am aware of the cultural knowledge that I apply'
- CQ – MOTIVATION, including statements such as 'I like interacting with people from different cultures'
- MPQ – CULTURAL EMPATHY, including statements such as 'Tries to understand the behaviours of others'
- MPQ – OPEN MINDEDNESS, including statements such as 'Looks for contact with people with a different cultural background'
- MPQ – EMOTIONAL STABILITY, including statements such as 'Often feels lonely'
- MPQ – FLEXIBILITY, including statements such as 'Has fixed habits'
- MPQ – SOCIAL INITIATIVE, including statements such as 'Easily finds his way in new groups'

We use these different sub-scales as a list of separate dependent variables in a series of regression models to analyse the predictive power of a stay abroad on every component.

INDEPENDENT VARIABLES

The main independent variable in this chapter is the stay abroad itself in one of the 37 countries that students visited[1]. The exceptional diversity in students' destinations ensures that we have enough variance in our main variables to compare different groups of students to one another.

---

[1] The 35 countries were: Aruba, Australia, Austria, Belgium, Canada, Chile, China, Curacao, Denmark, England, Finland, France, Germany, Gibraltar, Hong Kong, Hungary, India, Indonesia, Ireland, Japan, Malta, Mexico, Poland, Qatar, Saint-Lucia, South Africa, South Korea, Spain, Sweden, Thailand, Turkey, United Kingdom, United States, United Arab Emirates and Vietnam.

To test Hypothesis 2, we need a measure for 'cultural distance' between the home country (the Netherlands) and the country of residence. To calculate this score, we use a formula developed by Kogut and Singh (1988):

$$\text{Cultural Distance}_j = \sum_{i=1}^{9} \frac{\left(I_{ij} - I_{it}\right)^2}{V_i}$$

In which:
- I_{ij} is the cultural dimension i in host country j
- I_{it} is the cultural dimension i in home country t
- V_i is the variance in dimension i
- Cultural distance$_j$ is the cultural difference between the home country and the host country on a total of 9 different dimensions.

For every home country (the Netherlands *or* the home country of international students) and all host countries, scores were entered from the *GLOBE Culture and Leadership study (2004)*. This project uses an approach inspired by Hofstede's 6-D-model in which they examine how cultural values and norms have an influence on organisations and interaction between citizens. Every country receives a score on nine different value dimensions, from 1 to 7. We cannot stress enough that this quantification is inevitably a strong simplification of a complex reality that hopefully can provide insight into how learning experiences of students can differ from one another. In a second step, the same regression models are estimated again, but with a dummy variable to directly compare European (=1) with all other countries (=0). This way, we can make an additional comparison between destinations that are subsidised by the European Erasmus program and non-European destinations.

CONTROL VARIABLES

Finally, we included a number of control variables. First of all, we control for the faculty in which students study (International Business & Communication or Hotel Management School). We do not have a specific expectation for this variable because both faculties are internationally oriented, but as we are working with two diverse student populations who study abroad for diverse purposes, we wanted to control for possible structural differences. Furthermore, we control for the nationality of the students (dummy Dutch vs. non-Dutch nationality), their gender and their reason for studying abroad (internship vs. study).

Findings

CHANGE OVER TIME

Firstly, we assessed the reliability of all scales with a list of principal component analyses. In Table 10.1 we summarise the main indicators for every scale. All survey items in these analyses were included twice in both the pre- and post-measures. The Cronbach's alpha indicator for every sub scale is larger than .80, also for scales with more than ten items, such as Flexibility and Social Initiative. This is a clear indication of the reliability of our main measures.

Table 10.1 Principal component analyses sub scales: Global Mind Monitor

	Number of indicators	Eigen-value	Variance explained	Cronbach's alpha
CQ Behaviour				
Wave 1	4	2.82	70.48 %	0.86
Wave 2	4	2.91	72.78 %	0.87
CQ Cognitive				
Wave 1	7	3.80	54.32 %	0.85
Wave 2	7	3.93	56.19 %	0.86
CQ Metacognitive				
Wave 1	7	4.23	60.44 %	0.89
Wave 2	7	4.36	62.24 %	0.90
CQ Motivation				
Wave 1	6	3.35	55.77 %	0.84
Wave 2	6	3.43	57.24 %	0.85
MPQ Cultural empathy				
Wave 1	12	5.87	48.91 %	0.90
Wave 2	12	5.68	47.32 %	0.89
MPQ Emotional stability				
Wave 1	12	4.83	40.25 %	0.86
Wave 2	12	4.43	36.94 %	0.84

	Number of indicators	Eigen-value	Variance explained	Cronbach's alpha
MPQ Flexibility				
Wave 1	12	5.30	44.13 %	0.88
Wave 2	12	5.19	43.24 %	0.87
MPQ Open mindedness				
Wave 1	14	6.04	43.11 %	0.89
Wave 2	14	6.39	45.65 %	0.90
MPQ Social initiative				
Wave 1	12	6.53	36.30 %	0.88
Wave 2	12	5.54	46.17 %	0.89

Source: Global Mind Monitor pilot, 2015

Subsequently, we transformed all sub scales to averaged scales with a range of 1 to 10. That way, we could compare totals and difference scores (pre and post) to one another. In Figure 10.1, we plotted the average scores for both waves. What stands out immediately is that the mean score for all attitudes increases over time. A list of paired samples t-tests shows that all these differences are statistically significant (p<.001 for all sub scales).

Figure 10.1 Mean scores sum scales Wave 1 and Wave 2

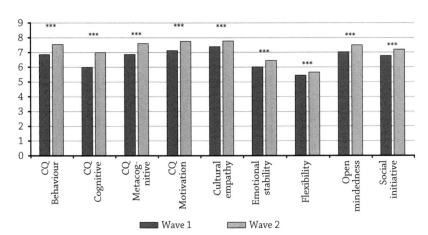

When comparing the different measures, we can see that the four CQ sub scales show the biggest change over time. The largest difference between Wave 1 and 2 is found in CQ Cognitive (+1.05). A possible explanation for this pattern is that the CQ scales are directly related to intercultural experiences, whereas the other scales are more generally linked to personal development.

EXPLANATORY FACTORS

Now we know that change over time occurs for all indicators, we need to assess which individual factors can contribute to this change. As stated in our hypotheses, cultural distance is the main factor which we expect to moderate development over time.

To effectively measure change over time, we use a series of multi-variate regression models in which the measure in Wave 2 is used as the dependent variable (0–10) and the respective measure in Wave 1 as a first control variable, a 'lagged-dependent variable' model. By adding the Wave 1 variable as a control variable, we can interpret the other effects of the independent variables in the regression models as effects on *change* over time. Lagged dependent variable models are very conservative models, because controlling for the Wave 1 measure inevitably explains a substantial amount of variance in the dependent variable[2] (Keele and Kelly 2005).

The change models are listed next to each other in Table 10.2. For every dependent variable, we ran two models: a first model (A) in which we use the dummy variable for Western-Europe (=1) vs. other destinations (see description above) and a second model (B) in which we use the full measure for cultural distance.

First of all, the results in Table 10.2 of course show a very strong effect of the Wave 1 measure on the Wave 2 dependent variable. However, we can see some interesting differences in these stability coefficients as well. For the CQ scales, for instance, the explanatory power of the initial measure is weaker (e.g., .46*** for CQ behaviour) than for the more general personality measures, such as social initiative (.81***) and flexibility (.78***), confirming the trend we saw in the descriptive models above.

---

[2] An alternative way to build this model is to use difference scores as a dependent variable and examine whether we can explain any variance in these scores. We have not used this approach, as these models have a strong tendency for *regression to the mean*, increasing the odds that we would underestimate the explanatory power of our independent variables.

If we then assess the effect of cultural distance, we see a clear and relatively stable effect in the expected direction: the larger the cultural distance to the host country, the stronger the development of the student's intercultural competencies (see Figure 10.2). The effect is clear and stable, except for cultural empathy, emotional stability and CQ Behaviour. This last variable is a remarkable exception, particularly because we do find significant effects for other measures related to cross-cultural interactions. Another exception for CQ Behaviour is that only for this variable can we observe significant effects for the other independent variables such as gender (.20★★★).

Figure 10.2 Positive (significant) effects of cultural distance
(beta coefficients from multivariate regression models)

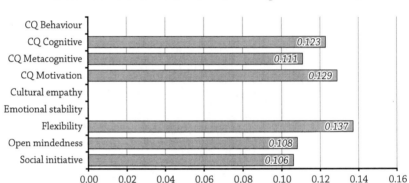

For the other regression analyses, we do find significant effects in the expected direction, and as we are using lagged dependent variable models, we can interpret these coefficients as *change over time*. What is remarkable is that the dummy variable 'Western-Europe' shows a similar explanatory pattern to that of our cultural distance indicator (models A and B). Both are of course very strongly connected, but this indicates that a study stay outside Western Europe has a stronger effect on the development of intercultural competencies than a stay within Western-Europe.

We find no effects of the faculty in which the students study, probably because both faculties have a similar and strong focus on internationalisation and a similar exchange program. Also for the other control variables, effects are weak to entirely absent, apart from the exceptions mentioned above. We did not have any specific expectations regarding the effects of these variables; these results indicate that indeed gender, nationality and the reason for the study stay abroad do not have a direct influence on intercultural competence development.

Table 10.2 Linear regression models

	CQ Behaviour		CQ Cognitive		CQ Metacognitive		CQ Motivation		Cultural empathy		Emotional stability		Flexibility		Open mindedness		Social initiative	
	Ia	Ib	IIa	IIb	IIIa	IIIb	IVa	IVb	Va	Vb	VIa	VIb	VIIa	VIIb	VIIIa	VIIIb	IXa	vIXb
Lagged DV Wave 1	.458***	.387***	.556***	.543***	.631***	.596***	.631***	.627***	.750***	.714***	.660***	.648***	.784***	.760***	.586***	.669***	.811***	.809***
Gender (female=1)	.202***	.187**	.081ns	.068ns	.081ns	.091ns	.077ns	.076ns	.037ns	.043ns	.003ns	-.038ns	-.031ns	-.037ns	.033ns	.007ns	-.026ns	-.031ns
Nationality (Non-Dutch=1)	.108*	.101*	.054ns	.024ns	.041ns	.026ns	.024ns	.029ns	-.006ns	.032ns	.020ns	.048ns	-.034ns	-.060ns	.033ns	.020ns	.016ns	.020ns
Faculty (FIBC=1)	-.097ns	-.116ns	-.096ns	-.049ns	-.034ns	.044ns	-.037ns	.003ns	-.089ns	-.050ns	-.064ns	-.087ns	.011ns	.032ns	-.094ns	-.053ns	-.040ns	-.016ns
Reason for stay (exchange=1)	.136*	.160*	.133*	.130*	.003ns	-.027ns	.017ns	.005ns	.015ns	.000ns	-.014ns	.008ns	-.024ns	-.021ns	.055ns	.038ns	.010ns	-.009ns
Region (Western Europe=1)	-.053ns		-.101*		-.095*		-.101*		.004ns		-.048ns		-.082*		-.100*		-.075*	
Cultural distance		.031ns		.123*		.111**		.129**		.050ns		.058ns		.137***		.108*		.106**
N	312	281	312	281	312	281	312	281	312	281	312	281	312	281	312	281	312	281
R²	.321	.252	.348	.325	.444	.393	.438	.440	.594	.540	.473	.462	.662	.636	.530	.488	.671	.692

Standardised linear regression coefficients (Betas)

* = p<.05

** = p<.01

*** = p<.001

Conclusions

The current study yields a number of interesting results and conclusions. Firstly, we conclude that a study stay abroad generally has a positive effect on the development of the different dimensions of intercultural competence. The students included in this analysis stayed in 35 different countries, and regardless of their purpose or their destination, the experience abroad had a consistently positive impact on both the development of attitude and knowledge. Thus, our first hypothesis (H1) is confirmed: also without taking into account the cultural context of the host institution, a study abroad experience *as such* has a structural positive effect on international learning outcomes. These results can provide additional justification for the investments that academic institutions keep on making to cooperate internationally with exchange partners. Successful international collaboration can indeed facilitate a type of intercultural learning that is not easily replaced by modules or courses at home.

Secondly, the cultural distance between the home country and the destination has a significant moderating effect on the relation between the stay abroad and the development of intercultural competencies. This means that immersion in a foreign culture that is very different from one's home culture has a stronger effect on a student's intercultural development, thus confirming our second hypothesis (H2).

In this study, the cultural distance between the two cultures is based on a very general and relatively arbitrary measure, which is based on the six cultural dimensions of Hofstede (Hofstede et al. 2010) and the related GLOBE project. Such aggregate quantitative measures inevitably simplify the complex reality of intercultural contact. Obviously, learning about other cultures does not happen at a country level, but at an interpersonal level. Cultural distance is a complex concept that is, for instance, not symmetric (reconciling host and home culture for a Dutch student staying in China may be different from that of a Chinese student staying in the Netherlands); and not stable either (since cultures may change over time (Korzilius, Bucker et al. 2017; Shenkar 2001). We are aware of the many nuances that are lost when we quantify the differences between two countries in one average.

At this point, one of the most important—and yet under-researched—themes is the learning effect of *'internationalisation at home'* experiences that we briefly discussed earlier in this chapter. For many universities, a stay abroad is not self-evident and therefore much is expected from international classrooms, virtual exchange programs and international activities within the home university. These cooperative programs could also use the current insights to promote internationalisation at home experiences in which the cultural distance between the different student populations is maximised. Our results suggest that when an institution wants to set up a virtual collaboration to promote intercultural learning, a certain level of 'alienation' is desirable. If we apply the same logic to internationalisation at home experiences, we could recommend that working together with a partner that is culturally more distant will probably result in a stronger intercultural learning effect among participating students. Empirical evidence for this recommendation can hopefully be part of future research with new data from the Global Mind Monitor or a similar longitudinal study.

Organizing international institutional collaboration can be a time-consuming and intensive process for educational institutions, both for more traditional exchange programs and for virtual variants. This is especially the case when cooperation concerns partners that are culturally (and often geographically) further removed from one another. Fortunately, these investments seem to turn out as very valuable for promoting individual development of the intercultural skills that are essential for future professionals.

References

Allport, Gordon W., Kenneth Clark, and Thomas Pettigrew. 1954. *The Nature of Prejudice*. Cambridge: Addison-Wesley Publishing Company.

Anderson, Phil H., Lei Lawton, Richard J. Rexeisen, and Ann C. Hubbard. 2006. 'Short-term Study Abroad and Intercultural Sensitivity: A Pilot Study'. *International Journal of Intercultural Relations* 30 (4): 457–469.

Ang, Soon, Linn Van Dyne, Christine Koh, Kok Yee Ng, Klaus J. Templer, Cheryl Tay, and Natarajan Chandrasekar. 2007. 'Cultural Intelligence: Its Measurement and Effects on Cultural Judgment and Decision Making, Cultural Adaptation and Task Performance'. *Management & Organisation Review* 3 (3): 335–371.

Deardorff, Darla. 2006. 'Identification and Assessment of Intercultural Competence as a Student Outcome of Internationalisation'. *Journal of Studies in International Education* 10 (3): 241–266.

Dinas, Elias. 2010. *The Impressionable Years: The Formative Role of Family, Vote and Political Events During Early Adulthood*. Doctoral dissertation, Florence: European University Institute.

Eisenchlas, Susana, and Sue Trevaskes. 2007. 'Developing Intercultural Communication Skills Through Intergroup Interaction'. *Intercultural Education* 18 (5): 413–425.

Flanagan, Constance A. 2013. *Teenage Citizens. The Political Theories of the Young.* Cambridge, MA: Harvard University Press.

Fitzsimmons, Stacey R. 2013. 'Multicultural Employees: A Framework for Understanding How They Contribute to Organizations'. *Academy of Management Review* 38 (4): 525–549.

Gardner, Robert C., and Wallace E. Lambert. 1972. *Attitudes and Motivation in Second-Language Learning.* Rowley, MA: Newbury House.

Hofstede, Geert. 2001. *Culture's Consequences: Comparing Values, Behaviours, Institutions, and Organisations Across Nations.* Second Edition, Thousand Oaks CA: Sage Publications.

Hofstede, Geert, Gert Jan Hofstede, and Michael Minkov. 2010. *Cultures and Organisations: Software of the Mind* (3rd ed.). New York: McGraw-Hill.

Keele, Luke, and Nathan J. Kelly. 2005. 'Dynamic Models for Dynamic Theories: The Ins and Outs of Lagged Dependent Variables'. *Political Analysis* 14 (2): 186–205.

Kogut, Bruce, and Harbir Singh. 1988. 'The Effect of National Culture on the Choice of Entry Mode'. *Journal of International Business Studies* 19 (3): 411–432.

Korzilius, Hubert, Joost L.E. Bucker, and Sophie Beerlage. 2017. 'Multiculturalism and Innovative Work Behaviour: The Mediating Role of Cultural Intelligence'. *International Journal of Intercultural Relations* 56: 13–24.

Kuhn, Teresa. 2012. 'Why Educational Exchange Programmes Miss Their Mark: Cross- Border Mobility, Education and European Identity'. *JCMS: Journal of Common Market Studies* 50 (6): 994–1010.

Marcotte, Claude, Jocelyne Desroches, and Isabelle Poupart. 2007. 'Preparing Internationally Minded Business Graduates: The Role of International Mobility Programs'. *International Journal of Intercultural Relations* 31 (6): 655–668.

Masgoret, Anne-Marie, and Robert C. Gardner. 2003. 'Attitudes, Motivation, and Second Language Learning: A Meta analysis of Studies Conducted by Gardner and Associates'. *Language learning* 53 (1): 123–163.

Mol, Stefan, Jan Pieter van Oudenhoven, and Karen Van der Zee. 2001. 'Validation of the Multicultural Personality Questionnaire Among an Internationally Oriented Student Population in Taiwan'. In *Multicultural Education: Issues, Policies and Practices*, edited by Farideh Salili and Rumjahn Hoosain, 167–187. Connecticut: Information Age Publishing.

Nussbaum, Martha C. 2010. *Not for Profit: Why Democracy Needs the Humanities.* Princeton, N.J: Princeton University Press.

Oberg, Kalervo. 1954. *Culture Shocks.* Indianapolis IN: Bobbs-Merrill.

Pettigrew, Thomas F., and Linda R. Tropp. 2011. *When Groups Meet: The Dynamics of Intergroup Contact.* Philadelphia, PA: Psychology Press

Pettigrew, Thomas F., Linda R. Tropp, Ulrich Wagner, and Oliver Christ. 2011. 'Recent Advances in Intergroup Contact Theory'. *International Journal of Intercultural Relations* 35 (3): 271–280.

Salisbury, Mark H., Brian P. An, and Ernest T. Pascarella. 2013. 'The Effect of Study Abroad on Intercultural Competence among Undergraduate College Students'. *Journal of Student Affairs Research and Practice* 50 (1): 1–20.

Shenkar, Oded. 2001. 'Cultural Distance Revisited: Towards a More Rigorous Conceptualization and Measurement of Cultural Differences'. *Journal of International Business Studies* 32 (3): 519–535.

Sigalas, Emmanuel. 2010. 'Cross-border Mobility and European Identity: The Effectiveness of Intergroup Contact During the ERASMUS Year Abroad'. *European Union Politics* 11 (2): 241–265.

Trilling, Bernie, and Charles Fadel. 2009. *21st Century Skills: Learning for Life in Our Times*. San Francisco: Wiley & Sons.

Van der Zee, Karen, and Jan Pieter van Oudenhoven. 2000.' The Multicultural Personality Questionnaire: A Multidimensional Instrument of Multicultural Effectiveness'. *European Journal of Personality* 144 (4): 291–309.

Van Gaalen, Adinda, Hendrik Jan Hobbes, Sjoerd Rodenburg, and Renate Gielesen. 2014. *Studenten internationaliseren in eigen land. Nederlands Instellingbeleid.* [Students internationalise in their own country. Dutch Institutional Policy]. Nuffic, Nederlandse Organisatie voor Internationale Samenwerking in het Hoger Onderwijs.

Van Oudenhoven, Jan Pieter, and Karen Van der Zee. 2002. 'Predicting Multicultural Effectiveness of International Students: The Multicultural Personality Questionnaire'. *International Journal of Intercultural Relations* 26 (6): 679–694.

Visser, Penny S., and Jon A. Krosnick. 1998. 'Development of Attitude Strength Over the Life Cycle: Surge and Decline'. *Journal of Personality and Social Psychology* 75 (6): 1389–1410.

Wilson, Iain. 2011. 'What should We Expect of "Erasmus Generations"?' *Journal of Common Market Studies* 49 (5): 1113–1140.

*Engaging Student
Diversity*

CHAPTER 11

Cultivating Voter Participation among First-Generation College Students: The Relationship of Study Abroad Participation to Post-College Voting Behaviour

Radomir Ray Mitic

Civic participation is a prerequisite for a strong democratic society. At the same time, in a world that is rapidly globalising, there exists a tension between looking beyond one's borders and being active within them. One of the behaviours most commonly associated with civic participation at home is voting, but in Western democracies, voter participation leaves something to be desired. With less than 56 percent of the eligible age cohort voting in the 2016 presidential election, the US lags behind countries such as Belgium and Sweden (well over 80 percent) and even countries that have had recent controversial election results such as the UK and Hungary (just over 60 percent) (DeSilver 2017). For over a century, scholars such as Dewey (1916) and Putnam (2000) have argued that education is vital for civic engagement and, in turn, civic engagement promotes a strong democratic society. In particular, higher education still maintains a local focus while also recognising the necessity of preparing citizens to live in a globalised world (Knight 2015). In particular, Mayhew et al. (2016) observe that a college education is linked to post-college civic engagement. What is unclear, however, is how certain elements of a college education, including studying abroad as an undergraduate, are linked with civic engagement. Furthermore, interest has increased in how college affects first-generation college students (those students of whom neither parent attended college). This study brings these concepts together.

It addresses two broad aims. The first aim is to better understand the ways in which a college education prepares engaged citizens by specifically focusing on students' study abroad participation and subsequent voting behaviour. Second, this chapter seeks to provide new information on whether or not study abroad may be uniquely advantageous to first-generation college students. In terms of the conference themes, examining civic engagement aligns with the social dimension of higher education, as well as with aspects of out-of-classroom teaching and learning.

In the US context, the 18–24 age group has been much maligned for a lack of voting in national elections as well as in state and local elections (Wattenberg 2015). In general, college attendance has been reported as being a positive factor in promoting voting; after graduating from college, graduates typically remained engaged in terms of voting and political action (Pascarella and Terenzini 2005). What remains to be understood, however, is the relationship between certain educational experiences and post-college voting. Organisations across the US such as the Association of American Colleges and Universities (2007) have advocated 'high-impact educational practices' such as study abroad and service-learning opportunities to prepare active citizens. The end goal is to promote civic action that can help alleviate problems of inequality, discrimination and apathy (Cantor 2018). What is unclear is whether study abroad influences political participation through voting. Against this backdrop, the present study addresses the following research questions:

1) What is the relationship between studying abroad during college and voting behaviour within the first few years following college?
2) Are these relationships moderated by first-generation college status?

The hypothesis is that there is a positive relationship between study abroad and voting behaviour and that this relationship is stronger for first-generation college students. By investigating the relationships between participation in study abroad during college and voting after college, and whether or not those relationships are conditional on first-generation student status, this study seeks to contribute to a better understanding of how, and for whom, specific college experiences may affect voting behaviour after college.

Background

This study has been conceptually situated by drawing from two theoretical frameworks and incorporating elements from models of college choice and post-college outcomes. First, human capital theory's emphasis on decision-making based on a cost-benefit analysis informs research on study abroad as students make similar calculations when deciding to study abroad (Becker 1994). Moreover, human capital theory has been used in studies of non-market public outcomes (McMahon 2009), including inter-cultural competence related to study abroad (Salisbury et al. 2013). How-ever, human capital theory does not adequately take into account the ways in which differences in social contexts—such as those formed by gender, class, or race—influence students' educational decision-making (Granovet-ter 1985; Grodsky 2007). Second, status attainment theory (Tinto 1975) is relevant for studying the effects of college on first-generation students, as this population tends to be upwardly mobile. Because this theory accounts for pre-college characteristics such as first-generation status, status attain-ment theory allows for examination of study abroad as an environmental factor after which the participants are expected to have developed in cer-tain ways, including post-college voting behaviour.

Overall, education attainment correlates highly with civic engagement (Astin and Sax 1998; Coley and Sum 2012). Civic engagement includes actions such as voting, donating and volunteering (Bowman 2011; Brand 2010; Ishitani and McKitrick 2013; Lott 2013). McMahon (2009) notes that a civically engaged population leads to a larger middle class, a respect for the rule of law, democratisation and human rights. In their critique of the higher education system, Astin and Astin (2000) lament a decline in civic engagement and a loss of higher education's civic mission. This disen-gagement with higher education's civic mission has led to an emphasis on empirically studying civic learning in college.

The factors within college that associate with post-college civic engage-ment, however, are unclear. Long (2010) found that institutional selectiv-ity correlated negatively with voting, while Hillygus (2005) found no such relationship. Students' academic majors also show an association with civic engagement. Lower civic participation has been tied to business, science, and engineering majors (Mayhew et al. 2016), and Hillygus (2005) found a positive relationship between social science majors and civic participation. Ishitani and McKitrick (2013) also found a negative relationship between alumni of engineering, maths, & physical sciences and civic participation, while showing no relationship for alumni of the social sciences.

In terms of study abroad alumni, the Study Abroad for Global Engage-ment (SAGE) study used a retrospective tracer study to find that alumni felt that their study abroad experience influenced international civic engage-ment more than domestic civic engagement (Paige et al. 2009). The study notes that these alumni felt that study abroad had a much stronger influ-ence on political engagement such as voting than on other forms such as volunteering and donating. Overall, prior research indicates that the long-term effects of college on civic engagement are unclear or inconsistent.

The empirical research into the benefits of study abroad have focused on the individual gains after the experience, but research has not delved into civic participation at the local or national level. Much of the literature on the impact of study abroad focuses on student development domains, one of Hoffa and DePaul's (2010) four main rationales for study abroad participation. The development argument advocates that study abroad leads to gains in intrapersonal and interpersonal skills beyond simple cognitive gains. Studies examine growth in language skills (Jochum 2014; Cubillos and Ilvento 2013), intercultural competence (Salisbury et al. 2013), intercultural communication (Williams 2005), and global citizenship (Stoner et al. 2014). Few studies, however, explicitly name civic learning as one of these educational outcomes.

At the same time, with the increase of first-generation college students in higher education, there is a need to explore the learning and involvement of this group of students. Of particular interest in this study is civic learning and participation in study abroad. Many first-generation students do not have access to these activities due to various factors (e.g., financial, academic, etc.). Kuh (2008) finds that non-first-generation students tend to research with faculty, participate in study abroad, and engage in internships at a higher rate than first-generation students. Walpole (2003) also

Figure 11.1. Proposed conceptual model on the effects of study abroad on post-college civic engagement

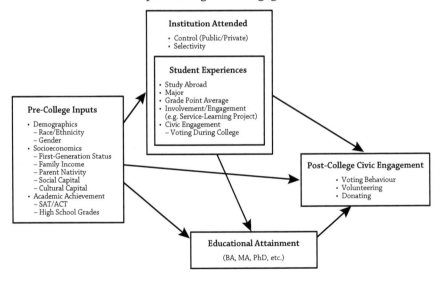

notes that low SES students are less involved on campus when it comes to contact time with faculty, studying, volunteer work and student groups. Because first-generation students often come from low SES backgrounds, they lack the social, cultural, and financial capital to take advantage of educational opportunities such as study abroad.

Build on past research, the present study relies on the following conceptual model based on human capital theory and status attainment theory. The model helps explain the student's learning from high school through post-college life. Framed by this model, analyses have been tailored to explore whether, first, certain precollege inputs relate to study abroad participation, and second, to examine post-college voting behaviour.

This study brings together three domains (civic engagement, study abroad, and first-generation college students) to explore the relationships between these important social and learning aspects of a college education.

Research Methods

DATA

Deploying the restricted-use Educational Longitudinal Survey (ELS), this study is based on data collected from 2002 to 2012, following students from the sophomore year of high school in the United States until about age 26. The ELS surveyed a national sample of students at ages 16, 18, 20, and 26 and combined data from high school and postsecondary transcripts to show growth from high school to post-college life. Using information on pre-college characteristics, the college experience (including study abroad participation), and post-college outcomes, this study uses statistical techniques (propensity score analysis, multivariate linear regression, logistical regression, and factor analysis) to find the relationships and causes of study abroad participation and post-college civic engagement.

The analytical sample consists of approximately 8,460 college attendees (rounded to the nearest 10 as per National Center for Education Statistics requirements), of which 19% identify as first-generation college students. In addition, approximately 11% of the sample indicate that they studied abroad which is consistent with national figures provided by the Institute of International Education (2017). Furthermore, 42% of the sample indicate that they had voted in either national, state, or local elections in the last two years while 61% of the sample say that they voted during college. Full descriptive statistics are presented in Table 11.1.

Table 11.1 Descriptive statistics of study variables (N=8,460)

	Min	Max	Mean	SE
Pre-College Characteristics				
Female	0	1	0.565	0.005
Male	0	1	0.435	0.005
American Indian/Alaskan Native	0	1	0.006	0.001
Asian/Pacific Islander	0	1	0.098	0.003
Black	0	1	0.113	0.003
Hispanic	0	1	0.118	0.004
Multiracial / Other	0	1	0.042	0.002
White	0	1	0.622	0.005
Income (in thousands of USD)	0	392.37	79.603	0.876
First-Generation College Student	0	1	0.194	0.004
Parent Nativity (at least one foreign-born parent)	0	1	0.197	0.004
Missing: Parent Nativity	0	1	0.086	0.003
Parental Involvement	0	22	12.622	0.050
Social Capital	0	4	1.580	0.014
High School Grade Point Average	0.17	4.00	2.839	0.008
SAT Composite Score (in 100-point increments)	4.2	16	9.929	0.022
Family Vacations: Never	0	1	0.036	0.002
Family Vacations: Rarely	0	1	0.108	0.003
Family Vacations: Sometimes	0	1	0.523	0.005
Family Vacations: Frequently	0	1	0.333	0.005
College Environment and Experiences				
College Type: Public	0	1	0.670	0.005
College Type: Private	0	1	0.215	0.004
College Type: For-Profit	0	1	0.115	0.003

	Min	Max	Mean	SE
College Selectivity: Highly Selective	0	1	0.197	0.004
College Selectivity: Moderate	0	1	0.269	0.005
College Selectivity: Inclusive	0	1	0.093	0.003
College Selectivity: Other	0	1	0.441	0.005
Major: STEM	0	1	0.112	0.003
Major: Social Science	0	1	0.130	0.004
Major: Education	0	1	0.060	0.003
Major: Business	0	1	0.143	0.004
Major: Arts & Humanities	0	1	0.074	0.003
Major: Health & Human Services	0	1	0.170	0.004
Major: Other	0	1	0.127	0.004
Major: Missing	0	1	0.185	0.004
College Grade Point Average	0	4.00	2.866	0.009
Study Abroad	0	1	0.111	0.003
First-Generation College Student in Study Abroad	0	1	0.010	0.001
Post-College Civic Engagement Outcomes				
Voting	0	1	0.424	0.005
Volunteering	0	1	0.457	0.005
Donating	0	1	0.756	0.005
Control Variables				
Volunteered in High School	0	1	0.703	0.005
Volunteered in College	0	1	0.512	0.005
Voted in College	0	1	0.613	0.005
Community-Based Project	0	1	0.192	0.004
Unweighted N = 8,460 Weighted N =1,942,650				

Source: ELS 2002 Restricted Dataset.

MEASURES

Dependent Variable. The dependent variable was participants' self-reported voting in any local, state, or national election from 2009 to 2011, represented as a binary (0/1) variable with voting assigned a value of 1.

Independent Variables. A number of independent variables were used in the analytic model. Using hierarchical logistic regression, we regressed the voting variable on sets of variables entered incrementally in blocks to understand the relationship of each block with voting behaviour (Keith 2015). The first block contained the precollege variables, including first-generation college student status, race/ethnicity, gender, parental nativity (having at least one foreign-born parent) and income. The demographic variables were dummy-coded with whites and males as the referent groups. In addition, this block included students' pre-college academic achievement, including ACT/SAT scores and high school grades. Finally, this block included the frequency at which students went on family vacations through high school (Simon and Ainsworth 2012).

The second block contained postsecondary institutional measures for selectivity and control of the college attended. In addition, the second block included the students' majors and undergraduate GPA, as collected in the postsecondary transcript.

For predicting post-college voting behaviour, we introduced a third block for the key college high-impact experiences of interest in this study, service-learning and study abroad participation. With study abroad participation being the 'treatment' of interest, an approach that goes beyond controlling for selected covariates through regression analysis is necessary to account for the decision to study abroad (Murnane and Willett 2011). A fourth block included the propensity score to account for selection bias. The propensity score was calculated using a logistic regression model based on the first two blocks that include variables commonly used to predict study abroad participation. Variables such as parental nativity and family vacations which may make it more likely that a first-generation student might pursue an overseas experience are thus controlled for in the overall regression model and the propensity score.

The base logistic regression equation for voting behaviour is as follows:

$$\ln(\text{Prob(Voting)})/(1\text{-Prob(Voting)}) = b_0 + b_1 P + b_2 C + b_3 E,$$

where the probability of voting is a function where P is the set of all precollege variables, C is the set of all college variables, and E is the set of college environmental variables.

LIMITATIONS

Although a longitudinal database such as ELS has many advantages in that it tracks a large number of students over four points in time from ages 16 to 26, the database does have some drawbacks. First, both of the outcome variables (study abroad participation and voting behaviour) are crude in that they elicit simple yes/no responses without any further exploration into the quality or intensity of the experience. For example, there is no difference in the data between a year-long immersive-language with a host family study abroad experience versus a one-week excursion to a country where (in this case) English is spoken and the student stays in a hotel with other Americans. Similarly, there is no indication whether voting behaviour extended beyond one vote in a national election or a consistent pattern of voting behaviour across all local, state, and national elections.

Second, because this study relied on observational data, any causal claims must come with a caveat that unobserved factors are not accounted for (Mann, 2003). The use of propensity scores, a proxy pre-test for voting and volunteering, and controlling for a variety of institutional and personal characteristics improves the analysis but cannot account for all potential unobserved variables that distinguish those who choose to study abroad from those who do not. These unobserved variables could include whether students travelled internationally prior to college, whether they already owned a passport, intercultural competence or appreciation of diversity, or levels of risk-taking or adventurousness. As a result, these findings are limited by not capturing these important factors that could help explain the relationship between study abroad participation and post-college civic engagement and thus we refrain from making causal claims.

Analyses

The first phase of analysis included data cleaning and an examination of missing data. For any substantial amount of missing data in a variable (e.g., greater than 10%), a chained regression approach was used to impute values for those that are missing (Manly and Wells 2015). At this point, univariate and bivariate descriptive statistics were computed on all the items to be used in this study.

Given that the dependent variable for this question is binary (whether or not a student voted in any election from 2009–2011), logistic regression was used as the method of analysis (Osborne 2015; Weinberg and Abramowitz 2016).

In order to determine that a conditional (or moderation) analysis for first-generation college student status was appropriate, an interaction term was added for first-generation college students who studied abroad. A significant result of this interaction term was the signal to conduct the conditional analysis.

To ascertain the conditional effects of first-generation college student status on voting behaviour, sub-group analyses were performed by splitting the sample by first-generation status and testing them for differences. This approach provided a means to examine whether the effects of the independent variables were conditional on first-generation status. We utilised z-tests for all estimated coefficients to formally examine the moderating influence of first-generation status (see Cohen et al. 2003; Clogg, Petkova, and Haritou 1995; Hayes 2013; Jose 2013 for discussion and justification for this test). For application of this method in college impact research, see Mayhew et al. (2016, 615–616).

In order to account for selection bias, a propensity score analysis was performed. Because the subsample of first-generation college students who studied abroad was somewhat small (N=90 cases), the propensity score was introduced as a covariate in a fourth block of the voting behaviour regression model in order to preserve the original sample size and to achieve the desired correction (Murnane and Willett 2010; Reynolds and DesJardins 2009; Yang and Schafer 2007). One limitation of this study is that in order to preserve the relatively small number of cases where first-generation college students studied abroad, we did not use a propensity score matching method that would completely remove bias from the sample. As a result, we interpret results in a non-causal way, and use the propensity score as a covariate merely to help gain greater precision in the regression estimates.

Results

The results of the statistical analyses show that while there is no main effect for study abroad on post-college voting behaviour, there is a moderation effect when accounting for first-generation college student status.

GENERAL EFFECTS

The first step was to run a full binary logistic regression model to predict study abroad participation; this was intended to ascertain an appropriate propensity score model when predicting post-college voting behaviour. As expected, many of the often-cited characteristics (Salisbury 2009; Salisbury 2011; Stroud 2010) such as being female, coming from a higher income background, attending a highly selective private institution, and majoring in either the humanities or social sciences were significant predictors. Of particular interest is that having a foreign-born parent is a positive predictor of study abroad participation ($OR = 1.467$, $p < 0.01$) and that going on family vacations frequently made students nearly twice more likely to study abroad than their peers who only went on family vacations rarely ($OR = 0.558$, $p < 0.01$). Table 11.2 presents the general effects model for predicting study abroad participation.

Table 11.2 Estimated general effects predicting study abroad

	Model I		Model II	
	B	OR	B	OR
Pre-College Characteristics				
Female	0.627***	1.871	0.613***	1.847
American Indian/Alaskan Native	−1.968	0.140	−2.038	0.130
Asian/Pacific Islander	−0.680**	0.507	−0.749***	0.473
Black	0.277	1.319	0.301	1.351
Hispanic	0.004	1.004	-0.041	0.960
Multiracial / Other	−0.307	0.735	-0.360	0.697
First-Generation College Student	−0.294	0.746	-0.197	0.822
Income (in thousands of USD)	0.002***	1.002	0.001*	1.001
Parent Nativity (at least one foreign-born parent)	0.324*	1.383	0.383**	1.467
Missing: Parent Nativity	0.151	1.162	0.152	1.164
Parental Involvement	0.014	1.014	0.008	1.008

	Model I		Model II	
	B	OR	B	OR
Social Capital	0.026	1.026	0.014	1.014
High School Grade Point Average	0.328**	1.388	0.034	1.034
SAT Composite Score (in 100-point increments)	0.378***	1.459	0.242**	1.274
Family Vacations: Never	−0.466	0.627	−0.523	0.593
Family Vacations: Rarely	−0.521**	0.594	−0.583**	0.558
Family Vacations: Sometimes	−0.182	0.834	−0.207*	0.813
College Environment and Experiences				
College Type: Public			−0.508***	0.601
College Type: For-Profit			−0.047	0.954
College Selectivity: Moderate			−0.530***	0.588
College Selectivity: Inclusive			−1.213***	0.297
Major: STEM			−0.593**	0.553
Major: Education			−0.789***	0.454
Major: Business			−0.495**	0.609
Major: Arts & Humanities (A&H)			0.233	1.262
Major: Health & Human Services (H&HS)			−0.638***	0.528
Major: Other			−0.929***	0.395
College Grade Point Average			0.391***	1.478
Model Fit (*Nagelkerke-R^2*)		0.178		0.246
Model Fit (AIC, lower is better)		5129.347		4829.346
Unweighted N = 8,460 Weighted N = 1,942,650				

SOURCE: ELS 2002 Restricted Dataset.

*NOTES: Reference categories are Race/Ethnicity: White=0; Family Vacations: Frequent=0; College Type: Private=0; College Selectivity: High=0; Major: Social Sciences=0. Additional variables for 'Missing' major and 'Other' selectivity were included in the model but not shown in the table. `p<0.10; *p<0.05; **p<0.01***p<0.001.*

Table 11.3 Estimated general effects predicting post-college voting

	Model I		Model II		Model III		Model IV	
	B	OR	B	OR	B	OR	B	OR
Pre-College Characteristics								
Female	0.033	1.034	-0.002	0.998	0.012	1.012	0.057	1.059
American Indian/Alaskan Native	0.184	1.202	0.144	1.155	0.037	1.038	0.009	1.009
Asian/Pacific Islander	-0.302*	0.739	-0.297*	0.743	-0.181	0.835	-0.223	0.800
Black	0.384***	1.468	0.388***	1.475	0.335***	1.398	0.345***	1.412
Hispanic	0.027	1.027	0.047	1.048	0.065	1.067	0.070	1.072
Multiracial / Other	0.018	1.019	0.024	1.024	0.047	1.049	0.024	1.025
Income (in thousands of USD)	0.001	1.001	0.000	1.000	0.000	1.000	0.000	1.000
First-Generation College Student (FGCS)	-0.127	0.881	-0.107	0.899	-0.051	0.950	-0.052	0.949
Parent Nativity (at least one foreign-born parent)	-0.263**	0.768	-0.278**	0.757	-0.094	0.910	-0.078	0.925
Missing: Parent Nativity	-0.225*	0.798	-0.244*	0.784	-0.133	0.875	-0.123	0.884
Parental Involvement	0.037***	1.037	0.034***	1.035	0.029***	1.030	0.030***	1.030
Social Capital	0.046*	1.047	0.047*	1.048	0.017	1.017	0.018	1.019
High School Grade Point Average	0.123*	1.131	0.058	1.060	-0.028	0.973	-0.028	0.972

	Model I		Model II		Model III		Model IV	
	B	OR	B	OR	B	OR	B	OR
SAT Composite Score (in 100-point increments)	0.049*	1.050	0.031	1.032	0.008	1.008	0.024	1.025
Family Vacations: Never	−0.286	0.751	−0.291	0.747	−0.162	0.850	−0.190	0.827
Family Vacations: Rarely	0.042	1.043	0.042	1.043	0.114	1.121	0.073	1.076
Family Vacations: Sometimes	−0.051	0.950	−0.049	0.952	−0.019	0.981	−0.037	0.964
College Environment and Major								
College Type: Public			0.079	1.082	0.072	1.075	0.015	1.015
College Type: For-Profit			−0.113	0.893	−0.055	0.947	−0.093	0.911
College Selectivity: Moderate			0.100	1.105	0.073	1.075	−0.021	0.979
College Selectivity: Inclusive			0.052	1.054	0.044	1.045	−0.073	0.930
Major: STEM			−0.225*	0.798	−0.182	0.833	−0.260*	0.771
Major: Education			0.009	1.009	−0.013	0.987	−0.089	0.915
Major: Business			−0.439***	0.644	−0.354**	0.702	−0.405**	0.667
Major: Arts & Humanities			−0.178	0.837	−0.183	0.833	−0.164	0.848
Major: Health & Human Services			−0.217*	0.805	−0.233*	0.792	−0.310*	0.734
Major: Other			−0.308**	0.735	−0.271*	0.763	−0.347**	0.707
College Grade Point Average			0.047	1.048	0.068	1.071	0.088*	1.093

	Model I		Model II		Model III		Model IV	
	B	OR	B	OR	B	OR	B	OR
College Experiences								
Study Abroad					0.013	1.013	0.047	1.049
Community-Based Project					0.235**	1.265	0.235**	1.265
Voted in College					1.169***	3.220	1.173***	3.232
Propensity Score							-0.920	0.398
Model Fit (*Nagelkerke-R²*)		0.043		0.052		0.140		0.141
Model Fit (AIC, lower is better)		11293.59		11259.62		10670.02		10669.93
Unweighted *N* = 8,460 Weighted *N* = 1,942,650								

Source: ELS 2002 Restricted Dataset.

Notes: Reference categories are Race/Ethnicity: White=0; Family Vacations: Frequent=0; College Type: Private=0; College Selectivity: High=0; Major: Social Sciences=0. Additional variables for 'Missing' major and 'Other' selectivity were included in the model but not shown in the table. *p<0.05; **p<0.01***p<0.001.

The general effects model for predicting post-college voting behaviour while accounting for selection bias for study abroad yielded several interesting findings. Table 11.3 presents the general effects model for predicting post-college voting behaviour. While gender was not a significant predictor, black students were 40% ($OR = 1.412$, $p < 0.01$) more likely to have voted after college than their white colleagues. The only other precollege characteristic that proved significant was parental involvement ($B = 0.030$, $p < 0.001$) defined as checking homework, discussing high school classes, and college preparation.

Students majoring in business ($OR = 0.667$, $p < 0.01$), health and human services ($OR = 0.734$, $p < 0.05$), and other majors ($OR = 0.707$, $p < 0.05$) were significantly less likely to vote after college than their social science major counterparts. Neither postsecondary institutional control nor selectivity yielded significant results. College grade point average also did not play a significant role.

Of particular interest to this study, the interaction term of first-generation college students who studied abroad was highly significant; first-generation college students were nearly two-and-a-half times more likely to vote than their counterparts ($OR = 2.453$, $p < 0.01$). While study abroad itself was not a significant predictor, the results are particularly striking as they held with a control for voting in college ($OR = 3.232$, $p < 0.001$) and participating in a community-based project while in college ($OR = 1.265$, $p < 0.01$). The study abroad experience for this subsample of students has a unique relationship to post-college voting behaviour that already accounts for selection bias into study abroad and other civic-minded behaviour. The findings point to the lasting influence of a study abroad experience in post-college civic engagement.

CONDITIONAL EFFECTS

Given the significant relationship between first-generation college students who studied abroad and post-college voting behaviour, the next set of analyses focused on whether any of the other predictors of post-college voting behaviour were moderated by first-generation college status. Table 11.4 presents the conditional effects model for predicting post-college voting behaviour on first-generation college student status. The general effects among race and parental involvement disappeared in the conditional model. The general effects among STEM, business, and other majors disappeared while a relationship emerged among arts and humanities majors ($OR = 0.401$, $p < 0.05$) indicating that first-generation arts and humanities majors were significantly less likely to vote than their non-first-generation counterparts.

Table 11.4 Estimated effects predicting post-college voting by first-generation college student status

	First-Generation		Non-First-Generation	
	B	*OR*	*B*	*OR*
Pre-College Characteristics				
Female	−0.007	0.993	0.075	1.078
American Indian/Alaska Native	0.856+[n]	2.354	−0.384[f]	0.681
Asian/Pacific Islander	−0.309	0.734	−0.204	0.816
Black	0.387+	1.472	0.323**	1.382
Hispanic	−0.062	0.940	0.119	1.126
Multiracial/Other	−0.342	0.710	0.108	1.114
Income (in thousands of USD)	0.001	1.001	0.000	1.000
Parent Nativity (at least one foreign-born parent)	0.109	1.115	−0.124	0.883
Missing: Parent Nativity	−0.132	0.877	−0.106	0.900
Parental Involvement	0.015	1.015	0.035***	1.035
Social Capital	0.060	1.062	0.007	1.007
High School GPA	0.001	1.001	−0.047	0.954
SAT Composite	0.085	1.089	0.012	1.012
Family Vacations: Never	−0.479+	0.619	−0.004	0.996
Family Vacations: Rarely	−0.392+[n]	0.676	0.202[f]	1.224
Family Vacations: Sometimes	−0.183	0.832	−0.003	0.997
College Environment and Major				
Public	0.199	1.220	−0.006	0.994
For-profit	−0.030	0.971	−0.057	0.945
Selectivity, Moderate	0.276	1.318	−0.057	0.944
Selectivity, Inclusive	0.011	1.011	−0.057	0.945
STEM	−0.290	0.749	−0.252	0.777
Education	−0.183	0.833	-0.066	0.936
Business	−0.591+	0.554	−0.367**	0.693

	First-Generation		Non-First-Generation	
	B	*OR*	*B*	*OR*
Arts & Humanities	-0.913^{*n}	0.401	-0.103^{f}	0.902
Health & Human Services	$-0.581+$	0.559	-0.235	0.790
Other	-0.465	0.628	-0.318^{*}	0.728
College GPA	0.075	1.078	0.097	1.102
College Experiences				
Study Abroad	0.897^{**n}	2.453	-0.056^{f}	0.946
Community-Based Project	0.099	1.104	0.257^{**}	1.293
Voted in College	1.338^{***}	3.813	1.147^{***}	3.148
Model Fit (*Nagelkerke-R^2*)	0.181		0.130	
Model Fit (AIC, lower is better)	1973.938		8729.027	
Unweighted *N*	1,640		6,820	
Weighted *N*	428,370		1,514,280	

Source: ELS 2002 Restricted Dataset.

Notes: 'OR' represents estimated Odds Ratios (Exp(B)). Reference categories are Race/Ethnicity: White=0; Family Vacations: Frequent=0; College Type: Private=0; College Selectivity: High=0; Major: Social Sciences=0. Additional variables for 'Missing' major and 'Other' selectivity were included in the model but not shown in the table. $^{+}p<0.10$; $^{*}p<0.05$; $^{**}p<0.01$ $^{***}p<0.001$.
^{n} Estimated effect is significantly ($p<0.10$) different from non-First-Generation estimate.
^{f} Estimated effect is significantly ($p<0.10$) different from First-Generation estimate.

As seen in the general model, study abroad participation was significantly different between first-generation and non-first-generation students. First-generation students who studied abroad were nearly two-and-a-half times more likely to vote than their non-first-generation counterparts. These results point to the increased importance of participating in study abroad when thinking of post-college civic-mindedness.

Discussion and Implications

The current study's finding that study abroad is a significant pathway to post-college voting among first-generation college students supports Granovetter's (1985) argument of the embeddedness of social relations in decision-making. Whereas students make the decision whether to study abroad based on a cost-benefit analysis as noted by human capital theory (Becker, 1994; Salisbury, Umbach, Paulsen, & Pascarella, 2009; Schmidt & Pardo, 2017), the family environment, as seen in having at least one foreign-born parent and frequently going on family vacations, demonstrates how status is attained given these background characteristics. In other words, the development expected of college students is dependent on more than income, academic achievement, and the type of institution one attends. Experiences such as study abroad feature a selection process that goes beyond these indicators and requires an exploration of where these students truly come from, including their families.

With this study, study abroad has been identified as a significant pathway to post-college voting behaviour among first-generation college students. With colleges and universities already trying to expand access to study abroad programs as well as promoting civic education both within and outside the curriculum, these findings indicate a strong link between these two activities. This study represents some of the first evidence in support of the aims of organisations such as the Association of American Colleges and Universities (2007).

As Kuh (2008) noted, and as was confirmed by the current study, first-generation students are less likely to study abroad. But this current study also finds that comparing those who studied abroad with those who did not, the difference in the odds of voting for first-generation students is approximately 2.4 times what it is for non-first-generation students. As this is the first known study to examine the relationship of study abroad with civic engagement among first-generation students, this finding provides insight into the importance of the participation of first-generation college students in high-impact practices such as study abroad. This finding suggests that study abroad helps to bridge a gap between first-generation and non first-generation students in terms of post-college voting.

Tied to first-generation college students is parental involvement. Prior research has shown that parental involvement is associated with student success, particularly among first-generation students (Bui and Rush, 2016; McCarron and Inkelas, 2006). When situating the examination of parental involvement in terms of post-college outcomes like voting behaviour, it is important to address how parental involvement may be linked with these outcomes. Dumais and Ward (2010) may be correct in asserting that there are elements of high culture absent in first-generation college student families. By uncovering an interaction between parental involvement and first-generation status on study abroad, this study suggests that study abroad may be a possible mechanism for reducing long-term differences in civic outcomes between first-generation and non first-generation students.

The interaction effect uncovered in the current study suggests that parental involvement is an additional factor for predicting study abroad participation and post-college civic engagement beyond a simple identification of first-generation college student status. An increased level of parental involvement reduces the difference in the odds of studying abroad thereby indicating a possible barrier not widely cited in the literature. And because lower levels of parental involvement can be a barrier to study abroad for first-generation college students, we may be observing a bottleneck effect as fewer first-generation students are studying abroad, they will be less exposed to an educational experience that is associated with a 2.4 times higher likelihood of voting compared to their non first-generation peers.

Because first-generation college students are an underrepresented student group in higher education, practitioners must give special attention to this group. For the outcomes of this study, we see that first-generation college students are less likely to study abroad and to vote. It is important, however, to understand the inner workings of this diverse group of students.

In addition, practitioners must consider the intersectionality of first-generation college students. The group is sizable; our analytic sample comprised approximately 19% first-generation college goers, which mirrors national figures (Chen 2005; Engle and Tinto 2008). Within this group, we see that they are largely female, students of colour, and the less wealthy or members of less affluent families. The lower levels of parental involvement and social capital evident in first-generation college students serve as a barrier to success in college. Research has shown that low socioeconomic groups, including first-generation students, are less involved on campus when it comes to contact time with faculty, studying, volunteer work, and student groups (Walpole 2003). Having an office or a program that targets first-generation students early after college acceptance, through orientation, and into the undergraduate experience, can help level the playing field through providing resources to assist these students and their families. First-generation students may uniquely benefit from being connected with student services related to finances and advising, student clubs and groups, and post-college opportunities such as graduate school.

In terms of study abroad for first-generation students, it is clear from the present study that experience abroad is associated with post-college voting. This finding suggests that study abroad may have an even stronger effect on first-generation students given their other deficits upon entering college. Therefore, colleges and universities should be more diligent in encouraging first-generation participation in study abroad programs in order to reap the reported benefits. Given the socioeconomic disadvantages of this diverse group, such initiatives should involve more funding but also a deeper effort to promote the cultural capital gained by an experience abroad. We see that students with at least one foreign-born parent study abroad more and first-generation students have a higher proportion of parents that are foreign-born so there is a natural connection that can be exploited to promote more first-generation involvement in study abroad.

When putting these findings within the context of civic engagement, we see that in a country that does not have compulsory voting laws such as the United States, the educational system is in a central position to promote civic participation. Higher education institutions have long attempted to encourage students to vote through direct efforts such as voter registration drives but more emphasis is being placed on less direct efforts. While most of the literature has found links between volunteering and civic outcomes (Bowman 2011; Brand 2010), the current study suggests there is a relationship between study abroad and voting for first-generation college students. Given that first-generation college students are less likely to vote in general, the study abroad experience may be filling in the civic participation gap possibly due to being a part of an immigrant family or simply being from a household where their parents did not vote. The experience of living abroad may be exposing the students to living conditions or policies in another country that cause them to reflect on the situation in their home country and to use their political voice upon returning home.

The question though still remains for the large number of students, particularly first-generation college students, that do not have an opportunity to study abroad. While the present study does not address this issue, scholars and practitioners must consider parallel opportunities within the home country to promote civic engagement. One example that was used as a control variable in this study, participation in a community-based project, was a significant predictor of post-college voting behaviour although only about 20% of students partook in this type of service-learning experience. Although this study focused on study abroad, practitioners must take an all-of-the-above approach in trying to reach this large segment of the college student population.

Future Research

As with all studies, this study manifested several limitations that should be addressed in future research. First, information about the length of time spent in a study abroad program was not available and therefore could not be assessed for its links to post-college voting behaviour. Corker et al. (2018) note that short-term study abroad programs (ranging from one-week to a summer term) may not be as advantageous as semester-long or year-long study abroad. Future work should interrogate differences by the length of the study abroad experience.

Second, future work should consider the conditional effects of participating in a study abroad program. While the current study explores the conditional effects of first-generation college student status, studying the conditional effects of study abroad participation can help understand whether or not there are the differences between study abroad and non-study abroad participants in terms of post-college outcomes such as civic engagement. Such work, while accounting for selection bias, can help researchers and practitioners understand key differences between these student populations.

Third, future work should also consider additional aspects of the first-generation college student experience that may be advantageous for study abroad participation and post-college voting behaviour. For example, while this study takes into account parental nativity and family travel, there may be elements such as reasons for parental immigration that may be formative in a student's life. For example, parents coming to the United States to leave a non-democratic home country may make that student more inclined to be civically engaged knowing that such freedom is not common in their parents' home country.

Conclusion

As nations struggle with intense political battles, the ballot box remains democracy's method of hearing the voice of the people. Unfortunately, the United States lags behind its peer Western democracies in terms of the percentage of voting age population that vote. As college impact researchers, we are interested in understanding the link between parts of the college experience, such as study abroad, and post-college voting behaviour. This study demonstrates that for first-generation college students, an underrepresented student group, there is a compensatory effect in terms of a link between study abroad participation and voting behaviour. The hope is that more first-generation college students can find themselves in a study abroad program to receive the benefits of this educational experience.

References

Association of American Colleges and Universities. 2007. *College Learning for the New Global Century: A Report from the National Leadership Council for Liberal Education America's Promise* (LEAP). Washington, DC: AAC&U.

Astin, Alexander W., and Helen S. Astin. 2000. *Leadership Reconsidered: Engaging Higher Education in Social Change*. Battle Creek, Michigan: W.K. Kellogg Foundation.

Astin, Alexander W., and Linda J. Sax. 1998. 'How Undergraduates are Affected by Service Participation'. *Journal of College Student Development* 39 (3): 251–263.

Becker, Gary S. 1994. *Human Capital: A Theoretical and Empirical Analysis with Special Reference to Education* (3rd ed.). Chicago, IL: University of Chicago Press.

Bowman, Nicholas A. 2011. 'Promoting Participation in a Diverse Democracy: A Meta-Analysis of College Diversity Experiences and Civic Engagement'. *Review of Educational Research* 40 (1): 29–68.

Brand, Jennie E. 2010. 'Civic Returns to Higher Education: A Note on Heterogeneous Effects'. *Social Forces* 89 (2): 417–433.

Bui, Khanh, and Ryan A. Rush. 2016. 'Parental Involvement in Middle School Predicting College Attendance for First-Generation Students'. *Education* 136 (4): 473–489.

Cantor, Nancy. 2018. 'Of Mutual Benefit: Democratic Engagement between Universities and Communities'. *Liberal Education* 104 (2): 6–13.

Chen, Xianglei, and Carroll C. Dennis. 2005. *First Generation College Students in Postsecondary Education: A Look at Their College Transcripts*. (NCES 2005-171). U.S. Department of Education, National Center for Education Statistics. Washington, DC: U.S. Government Printing Office.

Clogg, Clifford C., Eva Petkova., and Adamantios Haritou. 1995. 'Statistical Methods for Comparing Regression Coefficients between Models'. *The American Journal of Sociology* 100 (5): 1261–1293.

Cohen, Jacob, Patricia Cohen, Stephen G. West, and Leona S. Aiken. 2003. *Applied Multiple Regression/Correlation Analysis for the Behavioral Sciences* (3rd ed.). Mahwah, NJ: Lawrence Erlbaum Associates.

Coley, Richard J., and Andrew M. Sum. 2012. *Fault Lines in Our Democracy: Civic Knowledge, Voting Behavior, and Civic Engagement in the United States*. Princeton, NJ: Educational Testing Service.

Cubillos, Jorge H., and Thomas Ilvento. 2013. 'The Impact of Study Abroad on Students' Self-Efficacy Perceptions'. *Foreign Language Annals* 45 (4): 494–511.

DeSilver, Drew. 2017. *U.S. Trails Most Developed Countries in Voter Turnout*. Pew Research Center.

Dewey, John. 1916. *Democracy and Education*. Carbondale, IL: Southern Illinois University.

Dumais, Susan A., and Aaryn Ward. 2010. 'Cultural Capital and First-Generation College Success'. *Poetics* 38 (3): 245–265.

Engle, Jennifer, and Vincent Tinto. 2008. *Moving Beyond Access: College Success for Low-Income, First Generation Students*. Washington, DC: The Pell Institute for the Study of Opportunity in Higher Education.

Granovetter, Mark. 1985. 'Economic Action and Social Structure: The Problem of Embeddedness'. *American Journal of Sociology* 91 (3): 481–510.

Grodsky, Eric. 2007. 'Compensatory Sponsorship in Higher Education'. *American Journal of Sociology* 112 (6): 1662–1712.

Hayes, Andrew F. 2013. *Introduction to Mediation, Moderation, and Conditional Process Analysis: A Regression-Based Approach*. Guilford Press, New York.

Hillygus, D. Sunshine. 2005. 'The Missing Link: Exploring the Relationship between Higher Education and Political Engagement'. *Political Behavior* 27 (1): 25–47.

Hoffa, William W., and Stephen C. DePaul. 2010. *A History of U.S. Study Abroad: 1965 to Present*. A Special Publication of *Frontiers: The Interdisciplinary Journal of Study Abroad* and The Forum on Education Abroad.

Institute of International Education. 2017. Open Doors Data. Accessed August 6, 2018. http://www.iie.org/Research-and-Publications/Open-Doors/Data/US-Study-Abroad#.WGa_JvkrKUl.

Ishitani, Terry T, and Sean A. McKitrick. 2013. 'The Effects of Academic Programs and Institutional Characteristics on Postgraduate Civic Engagement Behavior'. *Journal of College Student Development* 54 (4): 379–396.

Jochum, Christopher J. 2014. 'Measuring the Effects of a Semester Abroad on Students' Oral Proficiency Gains: A Comparison of At-Home and Study Abroad'. *Frontiers: The Interdisciplinary Journal of Study Abroad* 24: 93–104.

Jose, Paul E. 2013. *Doing Statistical Mediation and Moderation*. Guilford Press, New York.

Keith, Timothy Z. 2015. *Multiple Regression and Beyond: An Introduction to Multiple Regression and Structural Equation Modelling*. New York, NY: Routledge.

Knight, Jane. 2015. 'International Universities: Misunderstandings and Emerging Models?' *Journal of Studies in International Education* 19 (2): 107–121.

Kuh, George D. 2008. *High-Impact Educational Practices: What They Are, Who Has Access to Them, and Why They Matter*. Washington, DC: Association of American Colleges and Universities.

Long, Mark C. 2010. 'Changes in the Returns to Education and College Quality'. *Economics of Education Review* 29 (3): 338–347.

Lott, Joe L., II. 2013. 'Predictors of Civic Values: Understanding Student-Level and Institutional-Level Effects'. *Journal of College Student Development* 54 (1): 1–16.

Manly, Catherine A., and Ryan S. Wells. 2015. 'Reporting the Use of Multiple Imputation for Missing Data in Higher Education Research'. *Research in Higher Education* 56 (4): 397–409.

Mayhew, Matthew J., Alyssa N. Rockenbach, Nicholas A. Bowman, Tricia A. Seifert, Gregory C. Wolniak, Ernest T. Pascarella, and Patrick T. Terenzini. 2016. *How College Affects Students: 21st century Evidence that Higher Education Works* (Vol. 3). San Francisco, CA: Jossey-Bass.

McCarron, Graziella P., and Karen K. Inkelas. 2006. 'The Gap Between Educational Aspirations and Attainment for First-Generation College Students and the Role of Parental Involvement'. *Journal of College Student Development* 47 (5): 534–549.

McMahon, Walter W. 2009. *Higher Learning, Greater Good: The Private and Social Benefits of Higher Education*. Baltimore, MD: Johns Hopkins University Press.

Murnane, Richard J., and John B. Willett. 2011. *Methods Matter: Improving Causal Inference in Educational and Social Science Research*. New York: Oxford University Press.

Osborne, Jason W. 2015. *Best Practices in Logistic Regression*. Thousand Oaks, CA: SAGE Publications.

Paige, R. Michael, Gerald W. Fry, Elizabeth M. Stallman, Jasmina Josic, and Jae-Eun Jon. 2009. 'Study Abroad for Global Engagement: The Long-Term Impact of Mobility Experiences'. *International Education* 20 (sup1): S29–S44.

Pascarella, Ernest T., and Patrick T. Terenzini. 2005. *How College Affects Students: A Third Decade of Research* (Vol. 2). San Francisco, CA: Jossey-Bass.

Putnam, Robert D. 2000. *Bowling Alone: The Collapse and Revival of the American Community*. New York, NY: Simon & Schuster.

Reynolds, C. Lockwood, and Stephen L. DesJardins. 2009. 'The Use of Matching Methods in Higher Education: Answering Whether Attendance at a 2-Year Institution Results in Differences in Educational Attainment.' In *Higher Education: Handbook of Theory and Practice* edited by C. Lockwood Reynolds and Stephen L. DesJardins, 47–97. London: Springer.

Salisbury, Mark H., Brian T. An, and Ernest T. Pascarella. 2013. 'The Effect of Study Abroad on Intercultural Competence Among Undergraduate College Students'. *Journal of Student Affairs Research and Practice* 50 (1): 1–20.

Salisbury, Mark H., Michael B. Paulsen, and Ernest T. Pascarella. 2011. 'Why Do All the Study Abroad Students Look Alike? Applying an Integrated Student Choice Model to Explore Differences in the Factors that Influence White and Minority Students' Intent to Study Abroad'. *Research in Higher Education* 52 (2): 123–150.

Salisbury, Mark H., Paul D. Umbach, Michael B. Paulsen, and Ernest T. Pascarella. 2009. 'Going Global: Understanding the Choice Process of the Intent to Study Abroad'. *Research in Higher Education* 50 (2): 119–143.

Schmidt, Stephen & Manuel Pardo. 2017. 'The Contribution of Study Abroad to Human Capital Formation'. *The Journal of Higher Education* 88 (1): 135–157.

Simon, Jennifer, and James W. Ainsworth. 2012. 'Race and Socioeconomic Status Differences in Study Abroad Participation: The Role of Habitus, Social Networks, and Cultural Capital'. *International Scholarly Research Notices* 2012: 1–21.

Stoner, Krystina R., Michael A. Tarrant, Lane Perry, Lee Stoner, Stephen Wearing, and Kevin Lyons. 2014. 'Global Citizenship as a Learning Outcome of Educational Travel'. *Journal of Teaching in Travel & Tourism* 14 (2): 149–163.

Stroud, April H. 2010. 'Who Plans (not) to Study Abroad? An Examination of U.S. Student Intent'. *Journal of Studies in International Education* 14(5): 491-507.

Tinto, Vincent. 1975. 'Dropout from Higher Education: A Theoretical Synthesis of Recent Research'. *Review of Educational Research* 45 (1): 89–125.

Walpole, MaryBeth. 2003. 'Socioeconomic Status and College: How SES Affects College Experiences and Outcomes'. *The Review of Higher Education* 27 (1): 45–73.

Wattenberg, Martin P. 2015. *Is Voting for Young People?* New York: Routledge.

Weinberg, Sharon L. and Sarah K. Abramowitz. 2016. *Statistics Using STATA: An Integrative Approach.* New York, NY: Cambridge University Press.

Williams, Tracy R. 2005. 'Exploring the Impact of Study Abroad on Students' Intercultural Communication Skills: Adaptability and Sensitivity'. *Journal of Studies in International Education* 9 (4): 356–371.

Yang, Joseph D.Y. and Joseph L. Schafer. 2007. 'Demystifying Double Robustness: A Comparison of Alternative Strategies for Estimating a Population Mean from Incomplete Data'. *Statistical Science* 22 (4): 523–539.

Encouraging Entrepreneurial
Spirit among Students

CHAPTER 12

Developing Students' Innovation Capacities: A Comparison between US and Germany

Benjamin S. Selznick, Lini Zhang, Matthew J. Mayhew, Carolin Bock and Daniel Dilmetz

Introduction and Definitions

As the need for innovative cooperation in the connected global economy accelerates (see Marti and Cabrita 2013), how to best develop innovators has become an increasingly international concern. Evidence of this trend includes policies articulated to promote innovation as a national priority (e.g., Innovation Union Initiative) and touches on recent research inquiries into educational system differences and their effects on graduating innovators (e.g., Moriano et al. 2012). Can good teaching and makerspaces (e.g., fabrication labs designed for broad-based usage; see Hynes and Hynes 2018) be vehicles not only for coordinating national innovation but also for educating innovators? As an extension of previous research that focused on innovative entrepreneurship (e.g., Mayhew et al. 2012; Mayhew et al. 2016), this study focuses on understanding the impact of university and its role in influencing innovation capacity development in the US and Germany, respectively.

We wish to define two key terms used in this study and throughout our line of research. First, drawing on a multidisciplinary perspective spanning education, entrepreneurship, management, and leadership, we define innovation as the process of generating and executing contextually beneficial new ideas. Second, building on research from education and human development work, we define innovation capacities as a set of attributes students can develop to better engage in all aspects of innovation (see Baumol 2004, 2010; Selznick 2017; Selznick and Mayhew 2019).

Literature Review

International research into education that promotes undergraduates' innovation capacities has typically emerged from two academic fields: higher education and entrepreneurship studies. Within higher education (e.g., Mars and Rhoades 2012; Selznick and Mayhew, in press), scholarship has examined the influence of pedagogical and curricular practices on promoting students' innovation capacities. Findings in this domain have demonstrated that forms of assessment and positive interactions with faculty can develop such capacities, cultivating 'creative ecosystems' (Hulme, Thomas, and DeLaRosby 2014, 14) that radiate out into economic regions and nations. Literature emerging from entrepreneurship studies supports such findings, conclusively demonstrating that taking coursework associated with innovation and entrepreneurship can develop aspects of students' innovation skills and intentions on an international scale (Moriano et al. 2012; see also Antal et al. 2014; Duval-Couetil 2014). Cutting across both the educational and entrepreneurship spaces, we note that research has progressed in the past decade from contested notions of innovation as being purely a function of personality (Fisher and Koch, 2008) toward an understanding that innovation capacities can be developed over and above personality traits (e.g., extraversion, openness; see Selznick and Mayhew, 2018).

Important to note is that the concept of *innovation* in these studies—as in our own—is broadly applied, encompassing both ideas, products and processes that lead to for-profit ventures (e.g., in technology, engineering, business) and also common, contextually beneficial applications (e.g., social venturing, community organising, non-market). Furthermore, our research reflects an international push that seeks to expand innovation beyond its traditional home in management, instead emphasizing the notion that *all* students should at least have the opportunity to gain insight into their own processes that can help realise their contextually beneficial insights (see Mayhew et al. 2016; Selznick 2017).

Research Methods

SAMPLE AND PROCEDURE

For this study, students were survey-sampled from six diverse institutions in the United States (three private research, one public research, and two private liberal arts) and one Technical University (TU) in Germany. To acquire longitudinal data, all participating undergraduate students were sampled twice: once near the beginning of the academic year (i.e., September, October) and once near the end of the academic year (i.e., March, April). A total of 7,927 students were invited to participate in this survey at the pre-test phase. After cleaning, screening and matching procedures were completed a total of 27.4% (n = 834) complete time-two cases persisted: 489 were from US institutions and 345 were from the German institution.

MEASUREMENTS

The primary measure used for this study was a theoretically-derived, reliable and valid instrument designed to assess students' innovation capacities (see Selznick and Mayhew 2018). Drawing on Kegan's (1994) theoretical model, nine constructs representing three lines of personal development were incorporated. Specifically, intrinsic motivation, proactivity, and innovation self-concept represented the intrapersonal dimension; networking, persuasive communication and teamwork across difference measured the social dimension; and creative cognition, intention to innovate, and risk taking/tolerance covered the cognitive dimension of the innovation capacity. Total innovation capacity scores were generated using a second-order confirmatory factor model which incorporated all conditioned first-order constructs into a single second-order factor. This factor demonstrated unidimensionality and score normality (see Selznick 2017).

In addition to the measure of innovation capacity, various measures of environmental factors, including faculty challenge, faculty interaction, assessments that encourage argument development, functional experiences, and connecting experiences were also assessed in this study. All the measures were rated on a 5-point Likert scale. Additionally, students were asked to indicate their personality traits (extraversion and openness to new experience), their family innovation history (including family business and family inventors), and innovation course experiences in the survey.

DESCRIPTIVE STATISTICS

The descriptive results shown in Table 12.1 describe the 489 students from US and the 345 students from Germany. More than 55% of the US students in the sample were male, while more than 60% of the German students in the sample were female. Most students in the sample were between ages 17 and 22, with the largest group between ages 19 to 20, followed by those students aged 17 to 18. Nearly one-half of the US respondents (44.58%) pursued Bachelor of Arts followed by those who pursued Bachelor of Science (39.26%). However, for the German sample, most respondents (83.48%) pursued Bachelor of Science.

Table 12.1 Descriptive statistics of the sample

	US (N = 489)		Germany (N = 345)	
	n	%	n	%
Gender				
Male	273	55.83	129	37.39
Female	205	41.92	212	61.45
No information	11	2.25	4	1.16
Age				
17 – 18	178	36.40	74	21.45
19 – 20	284	58.08	149	43.19
21 – 22	11	2.25	70	20.29
23 – 25	5	1.02	18	5.22
26 – 30	3	0.61	22	6.38
31+	8	1.64	12	3.47
Degree Type				
Bachelor of Arts	218	44.58	24	6.96
Bachelor of Science	192	39.26	288	83.48
Joint Bachelor	64	13.09	19	5.50
Bachelor of Education	15	3.07	14	4.06
Extraversion				
Extrovert	167	34.15	92	26.67
Introvert	322	65.85	253	73.33
Openness to Experiences				
Open	458	93.66	319	92.46
Reserved	31	6.34	26	7.54

	US (N = 489)		Germany (N = 345)	
	n	%	n	%
Family Innovation History				
Yes	212	43.35	123	35.65
No	277	56.65	222	64.35
Participation in Innovation Courses				
Yes	107	21.88	33	9.57
No	382	78.12	312	90.43

For the two personality traits (extraversion and openness) examined in this study, more than 65% of US students and more than 73% of German students reported themselves as being introverted. In addition, most students (more than 90% for both US and German sample) reported themselves as being open to new experiences. For family innovation history, nearly one-half (43.35%) of the US students and more than one-third (35.65%) of the German students reported they have a family member who has started a new business/non-profit organisation or invented a new product, service, or process. For innovation course-taking experience, more than 20% of the US students took a college-level course focused on innovation, while less than 10% of the German students took a similar college-level innovation course.

MEASUREMENT MODEL

All multi-item variables were evaluated for reliability and validity.[1] The reliability test is performed through calculating Cronbach's α values of the Likert-type scales adapted from the previous research. Leong et al. (2013) suggested the following interpretations for reliability coefficients: 0.90 or higher = excellent, 0.80 to 0.89 = good, 0.70 to 0.79 = adequate, and 0.69 and below = may have limited applicability. As shown in Table 12.2, the α values ranged from 0.74 to 0.83, suggesting high internal consistency of the scales.

---

[1] Due to the length of the innovation capacity measures (42 items in total), detailed items and reliability and validity test information are not presented in this study. However, all items met accepted standards for reliability and validity. Please refer to Selznick and Mayhew (2018) for detailed information.

Table 12.2 Properties of measurement items

Measurement Items	Standardised Factor Loadings	Composite Reliability (CR)	Average Variance Extracted (AVE)
Faculty challenge (Cronbach's α = 0.79)		0.82	0.54
1. Faculty ask me to show how a particular course concept could be applied to an actual problem.	0.56		
2. Faculty challenge my ideas in class.	0.68		
3. Faculty encourage me to explore my own original ideas.	0.83		
4. Faculty challenge me to think in new ways in order to create solutions to problems presented in class.	0.83		
Faculty interaction (Cronbach's α = 0.81)		0.84	0.64
1. My non-classroom interactions with faculty have had a positive influence on my personal growth, attitudes, and values.	0.87		
2. My non-classroom interactions with faculty have had a positive influence on my career goals and aspirations.	0.90		
3. Since coming to this institution, I have developed a close personal relationship with at least one faculty member.	0.69		
Assessments encourage argument development (Cronbach's α = 0.83)		0.85	0.60
1. Exams or assignments that required me to create new solutions to presented problems.	0.59		
2. Exams or assignments that required me to argue for or against a particular point of view and defend an argument.	0.84		

Measurement Items	Standardised Factor Loadings	Composite Reliability (CR)	Average Variance Extracted (AVE)
3. Exams or assignments that required me to compare or contrast topics or ideas for a course.	0.79		
4. Exams or assignments that required me to point out the strengths and weakness of a particular argument or point of view.	0.83		
Functional experiences (Cronbach's α = 0.74)		0.79	0.57
1. My campus provides enough physical spaces for individuals to work collaboratively on new projects.	0.50		
2. The library resources at this school encourage me to explore connections across academic disciplines.	0.86		
3. The library resources at this school help me come up with ideas for academic projects, papers, and/or other course assignments.	0.84		
Connecting experiences (Cronbach's α = 0.83)		0.89	0.62
1. My out-of-class experiences have helped me connect what I learned in the classroom with life events.	0.76		
2. My out-of-class experiences have had a positive influence on my personal growth, attitudes, and values.	0.76		
3. My out-of-class experiences have had a positive influence on my intellectual growth and ideas.	0.82		
4. My out-of-class experiences have provided me with opportunities to translate knowledge and understanding acquired in the classroom into action.	0.80		

Confirmatory factor analysis (CFA) was conducted to test for the validity of the multi-item constructs to examine convergent and the discriminant validity. Convergent validity tests whether measures of constructs that theoretically should be related to each other are in fact observed to be related. Convergent validity is manifested if all factor loadings are larger than 0.50, the composite reliability (CR) exceeds 0.70, and the average variance extracted (AVE) exceeds 0.50 level (Fornell and Larcker 1981). Table 12.2 illustrates that all of the convergent validity criteria had been met. Discriminant validity tests whether constructs that theoretically should not be related to each other are in fact observed to be unrelated. Discriminant validity is met when there is low correlation between constructs or the square root of AVE is larger than the surrounding values in the correlation table (Leong et al. 2013). The correlation matrix presented in Table 12.3 shows that all constructs passed the discriminant validity test. Thus, both the convergent validity and discriminant validity were statistically verified and confirmed.

Table 12.3 Correlation matrix of model constructs

	1	2	3	4	5	6	7
1. Faculty challenge	**0.73**						
2. Faculty interaction	0.49	**0.80**					
3. Argument development	0.47	0.51	**0.77**				
4. Functional experiences	0.35	0.39	0.37	**0.75**			
5. Connecting experiences	0.35	0.31	0.28	0.22	**0.79**		
6. Pre-test innovation score	0.15	0.23	0.15	0.08	0.19	**0.71**	
7. Post-test innovation score	0.27	0.33	0.29	0.20	0.35	0.66	**0.74**

Note. Square root of AVE is shown on the diagonal of the correlation matrix (in bold).

STRUCTURAL MODEL

Structural Equation Modeling (SEM) was conducted to investigate the relationship between personality traits and students' innovation capacities and explore the impact of college positive environmental factors on promoting innovators. With consideration of differences regarding number and types of institutions sampled in each nation, two structural models using maximum likelihood estimation were constructed separately for US students and German students. The robust maximum likelihood estimator was utilised in this study.

A series of fit indices were used to determine the acceptance of the model. The incremental fit indices Comparative Fit Index (CFI) and Tucker-Lewis Index (TLI) indicate an optimal fit when their values are greater than 0.95; for the Parsimony Fit Index Root Mean Square Error of Approximation (RMSEA), the cut-off suggested is 0.08 (Hu and Bentler 1999). The suggested cutoff value of absolute fit index Standardised Root Mean Square Residual (SRMR) is 0.05 to identify good models (Leong et al. 2013).

In the model using US data, the model fit indices were χ^2 (554) = 764.07, p < 0.001; CFI = 0.970; TLI = 0.958; RMSEA = 0.028 (90% confidence interval = [0.023, 0.033]); SRMR = 0.040 (see Table 12.4 and Figure 12.1). For the model employing German data, the model fit indices were χ^2 (554) = 711.91, p < 0.001; CFI = 0.968; TLI = 0.955; RMSEA = 0.029 (90% confidence interval = [0.022, 0.035]); SRMR = 0.048 (see Table 12.5 and Figure 12.2). The model fit indices indicate that the overall model fit of the measurement model was good for both US data and German data.

Table 12.4 SEM analysis results for US students

Path	Est.	S. Est.	S.E.	p-value
Extraversion -> pre-test innovation score	0.171	0.293	0.036	0.000***
Openness -> pre-test innovation score	0.279	0.246	0.064	0.000***
Family innovation history –> pre-test innovation score	0.074	0.132	0.027	0.006**
Extraversion –> faculty challenge	−0.009	−0.009	0.058	0.874
Openness –> faculty challenge	0.170	0.081	0.111	0.127
Family innovation history –> faculty challenge	0.018	0.018	0.052	0.730
Pre-test innovation score –> faculty challenge	0.385	0.208	0.127	0.002**
Extraversion –> faculty interaction	−0.052	−0.037	0.077	0.494
Openness –> faculty interaction	−0.147	−0.053	0.147	0.318
Family innovation history –> faculty interaction	0.023	0.017	0.069	0.736

Path	Est.	S. Est.	S.E.	p-value
Pre-test innovation score –> faculty inter-action	0.667	0.272	0.178	0.000***
Extraversion –> argument	−0.005	−0.005	0.052	0.929
Openness –> argument	−0.000	−0.000	0.100	0.998
Family innovation history –> argument	0.044	0.046	0.048	0.361
Pre-test innovation score –> argument	0.258	0.153	0.110	0.019*
Extraversion –> functional experiences	−0.063	−0.077	0.043	0.146
Openness –> functional experiences	0.075	0.047	0.082	0.362
Family innovation history –> functional experiences	0.016	0.020	0.039	0.684
Pre-test innovation score –> functional experiences	0.128	0.092	0.085	0.131
Extraversion –> connecting experiences	0.066	0.045	0.074	0.375
Openness –> connecting experiences	0.063	0.022	0.142	0.659
Family innovation history –> connecting experiences	0.031	0.022	0.067	0.649
Pre-test innovation score –> connecting experiences	0.351	0.141	0.151	0.020*
Extraversion –> innovation courses	−0.052	−0.060	0.042	0.215
Openness –> innovation courses	−0.087	−0.051	0.080	0.277
Family innovation history –> innovation courses	0.000	0.000	0.038	0.997
Pre-test innovation score –> innovation courses	0.182	0.122	0.084	0.029*
Extraversion –> post-test innovation score	0.044	0.052	0.031	0.153
Openness –> post-test innovation score	0.046	0.028	0.059	0.438
Family innovation history –> post-test innovation score	0.027	0.034	0.027	0.316
Pretest innovation score –> post-test innovation score	0.795	0.556	0.132	0.000***
Faculty challenge –> post-test innovation score	0.122	0.158	0.043	0.005**

Path	Est.	S. Est.	S.E.	p-value
Faculty interaction –> post-test innovation score	0.048	0.082	0.037	0.191
Argument –> post-test innovation score	0.109	0.128	0.041	0.008**
Functional experiences –> post-test innovation score	0.016	0.016	0.046	0.726
Connecting experiences –> post-test innovation score	0.071	0.123	0.029	0.014*
Innovation courses –> post-test innovation score	0.080	0.084	0.032	0.013*

Note. Est. = parameter estimate; S. Est. = standardised estimate of parameter; S.E. = standard error.
N = 489, χ^2 (554) = 764.07, p < 0.001; CFI = 0.970; TLI = 0.958; RMSEA = 0.028; SRMR = 0.040.
*p < .05, **p < .01, ***p < .001.

Table 12.5 SEM analysis results for German students

Path	Est.	S. Est.	S.E.	p-value
Extraversion –> pre-test innovation score	0.065	0.108	0.033	0.047*
Openness –> pre-test innovation score	0.350	0.346	0.063	0.000***
Family innovation history –> pre-test innovation score	0.075	0.135	0.030	0.014*
Extraversion –> faculty challenge	−0.028	−0.024	0.069	0.686
Openness –> faculty challenge	−0.078	−0.040	0.123	0.525
Family innovation history –> faculty challenge	−0.060	−0.056	0.064	0.349
Pre-test innovation score –> faculty challenge	0.158	0.082	0.134	0.239
Extraversion –> faculty interaction	−0.096	−0.060	0.103	0.350
Openness –> faculty interaction	−0.228	−0.085	0.186	0.220
Family innovation history –> faculty interaction	−0.017	−0.011	0.095	0.861
Pre-test innovation score –> faculty interaction	0.928	0.349	0.226	0.000***
Extraversion –> argument	−0.162	−0.120	0.087	0.061

Path	Est.	S. Est.	S.E.	p-value
Openness –> argument	0.033	0.014	0.152	0.831
Family innovation history –> argument	0.044	0.035	0.079	0.573
Pre-test innovation score –> argument	0.225	0.100	0.168	0.180
Extraversion –> functional experiences	−0.019	−0.028	0.039	0.628
Openness –> functional experiences	0.032	0.029	0.070	0.648
Family innovation history –> functional experiences	−0.016	−0.025	0.036	0.667
Pre-test innovation score –> functional experiences	0.103	0.093	0.079	0.195
Extraversion –> connecting experiences	0.054	0.037	0.086	0.533
Openness –> connecting experiences	−0.143	−0.059	0.155	0.357
Family innovation history –> connecting experiences	−0.028	−0.021	0.080	0.728
Pre-test innovation score –> connecting experiences	0.903	0.379	0.207	0.000***
Extraversion –> innovation courses	0.012	0.018	0.036	0.736
Openness –> innovation courses	−0.005	−0.005	0.065	0.937
Family innovation history –> innovation courses	0.049	0.079	0.033	0.145
Pre-test innovation score –> innovation courses	0.055	0.050	0.069	0.429
Extraversion –> post-test innovation score	0.035	0.063	0.021	0.098
Openness –> post-test innovation score	0.016	0.017	0.039	0.676
Family innovation history –> post-test innovation score	0.011	0.021	0.019	0.565
Pre-test innovation score –> post-test innovation score	0.747	0.811	0.094	0.000***
Faculty challenge –> post-test innovation score	−0.025	−0.052	0.027	0.356
Faculty interaction –> post-test innovation score	−0.000	−0.000	0.022	0.995
Argument –> post-test innovation score	0.016	0.038	0.023	0.491

Path	Est.	S. Est.	S.E.	p-value
Functional experiences –> post-test innovation score	0.006	0.008	0.035	0.855
Connecting experiences –> post-test innovation score	0.060	0.155	0.023	0.008**
Innovation courses –> post-test innovation score	0.085	0.101	0.032	0.007**

Note. Est. = parameter estimate; S. Est. = standardised estimate of parameter; S.E. = standard error.
N = 345. χ^2 (554) = 711.91, p < 0.001; CFI = 0.968; TLI = 0.955; RMSEA = 0.029; SMR = 0.048.
*p < .05, **p < .01, ***p < .001.

Figure 12.1 Summary of SEM results from US data

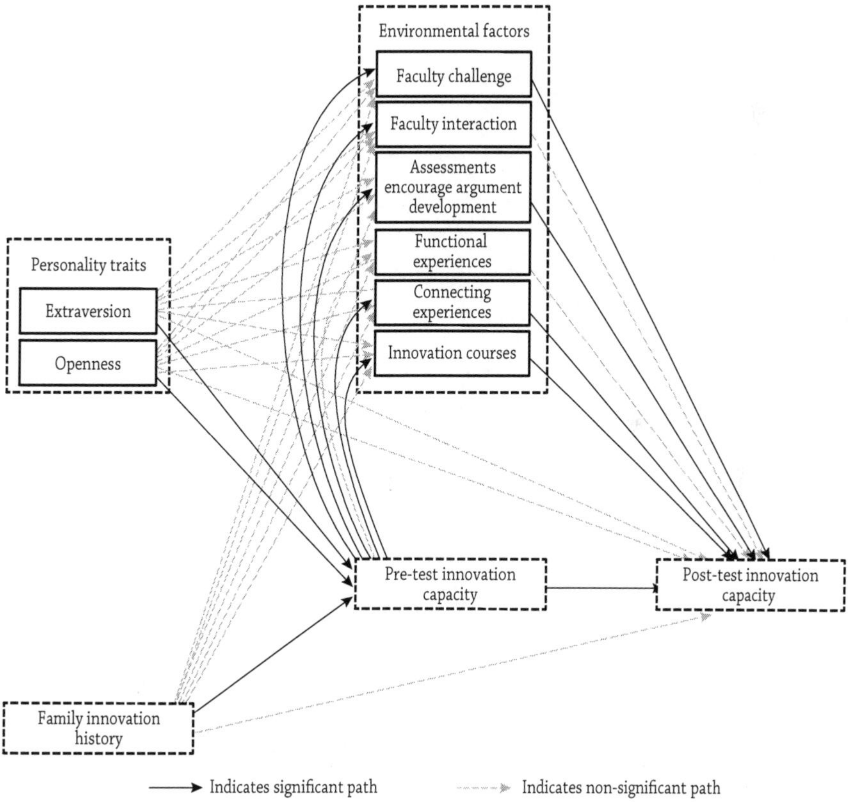

Note. N = 489. χ^2(554) = 764.07, p<0.001; CFI = 0.970; TLI = 0.958; RMSEA = 0.028; SMR = 0.040.

Figure 12.2 Summary of SEM results from German data

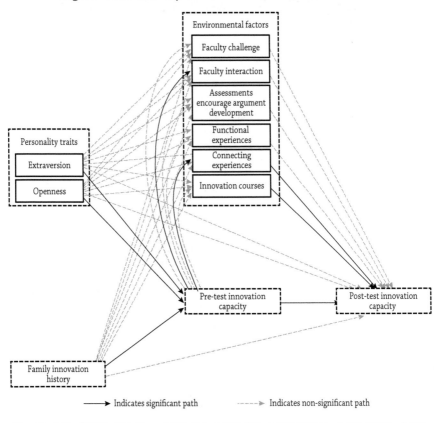

Note. N = 345. $\chi^2(554)$ = 711.91, p < 0.001; CFI = 0.968; TLI = 0.955; RMSEA = 0.029; SRMR = 0.048.

RESULTS

The two self-reported personality traits were both found to have positive re-lationships with students' pre-test innovation capacities among US students (extraversion: β = 0.293, p < 0.001 and openness: β = 0.246, p < 0.001) and German students (extraversion: β = 0.108, p = 0.047 and openness: β = 0.346, p < 0.001). Similarly, family history was also found to have a positive relationship with students' pre-test innovation capacities among US stu-dents (β = 0.132, p = 0.006) and German students (β = 0.135, p = 0.014).

It was also found that students who had higher original innovation capacities had positive perceptions of curricular and co-curricular supports for innovation on their campus. For US students, those who had higher initial innovation capacities had positive perceptions of faculty challenge

(β = 0.208, p = 0.002), faculty interaction (β = 0.272, p < 0.001), assessments that encourage argument development (β = 0.153, p = 0.019), and connecting experiences (β = 0.141, p = 0.020). In addition, US students who had higher initial innovation capacities were also found more likely to take innovation courses (β = 0.122, p = 0.029). For German students, those who had higher initial innovation capacities were observed to have a positive perception of faculty interactions (β = 0.349, p < 0.001) and benefit from connecting experiences (β = 0.379, p < 0.001).

Most importantly, positive environmental factors were found to have positive impacts on promoting students' innovation capacities. For US students, faculty challenge (β = 0.158, p = 0.005), assessments that encourage argument development (β = 0.128, p = 0.008), connecting experiences (β = 0.123, p = 0.014), and innovation courses (β = 0.084, p = 0.013) were found to have significant positive effects on US students' post-test innovation capacities. Similarly, connecting experiences (β = 0.155, p = 0.008) and innovation courses (β = 0.101, p = 0.007) were also found to have significant impact on promoting German students' innovation capacities. In addition to the positive environmental factors, students' initial innovation capacities were also observed to play a significant role in forming their innovation capacities based on the analyses of both US data (β = 0.556, p < 0.001) and German data (β = 0.811, p < 0.001).

It is also worth noting that once positive environmental factors were taken into consideration, personality traits, which were found to have a positive relationship with pre-test innovation capacities, did not have significant influences on students' post-test innovation capacities any more. Among US students, extraversion (β = 0.052, p = 0.153) and openness to new experience (β = 0.028, p = 0.438) did not have significant impact on students' post-test innovation capacities. The same results were found in the German data; extraversion (β = 0.063, p = 0.098) and openness to new experience (β = 0.017, p = 0.676) did not influence students' post-test innovation capacities. In addition, the significant relationship between family history and students' innovation capacities also disappeared when taking the positive campus environmental factors into the model (US data: β = 0.034, p = 0.316; German data: β = 0.021, p = 0.565).

Discussion

With strong indicators of fit, the theoretical model designed to examine college and its role in influencing innovation capacities may serve as an empirically-based starting point for generating discussions about the best learning to spur creativity among US and German students. Indeed, it is a critical finding that neither personality or family history significantly influences innovation capacity scores beyond the pre-test measure; exposure to and participation in college does influence innovation capacities, further confirming that innovators are developed and that an 'innovative personality' is, at best, only part of the story. This said, effects differed between US and German students, respectively.

For US students, innovation capacity development was related to a series of environmental factors, including student perceptions of their curricular environments as challenging and frequent exposure to assessments that required students to develop and defend arguments. In addition, students who reported engaging in productive faculty relationships were also more likely to develop innovation capacities. These trends echo those in other college impact research (see Mayhew et al. 2016); academically challenging environments—when properly supported through productive relationships with educators—are a cornerstone of student learning.

Messages were not as clear for the sample of German students. Although a positive relationship was found between initial innovation pre-test scores and productive relationships with faculty, the effect did not exert influence on the post-test measure, after other theoretical variables were considered. Perhaps an artifact of this sample (i.e., differences in course-taking patterns) of students or of a system that tracks students based on assessed career interests, the lack of significant findings is surprising, given the strength of indicators for model fit. However, the theoretical model has some explanatory power for explaining German students' innovation capacity and can be used for generating conversations about environmental factors hypothesised to exert influence among German students. German educators must ask: What are the optimal ways to help *our* students develop innovation capacities?

Conclusion

As nations increasingly strive to leverage existing Higher Education infrastructures in service of promoting innovation, we believe it is essential not to lose sight of educating *innovators*—the students who will graduate into the modern labour market equipped with those skills needed to generate and execute contextually beneficial new ideas in their regions, states, nations, and beyond. We offer this study as an initial step in nuancing such research by country, understanding that while systematic, organisational, and strategic leadership differences exist both intra- and internationally, exploring how innovation capacities can be developed among populations of students can be a starting point to potentially unleashing enormous synergistic and unexpected positive benefits for societies and ecologies on a global scale. We further hope that reframing innovation using the language of student capacities and positive externalities—a shift from purely competitive notions of *innovation* toward inspired visions of *innovators*—may in turn motivate effective collaborations between postsecondary institutions across borders and help uncover previously unrecognised avenues for authentic complementarity and mutually beneficial partnership.

References

Antal, Natalie, Bruce Kingma, Duncan Moore, and Deborah Streeter. 2014. 'University-wide Entrepreneurship Education'. In *Innovative Pathways for University Entrepreneurship in the 21st Century* (*Advances in the Study of Entrepreneurship, Innovation and Economic Growth,* Volume 24), edited by Sherry Hoskinson, Donald F. Kuratko, 227–254. Bingley: Emerald Group Publishing Limited.

Baumol, William J. 2005. 'Education for Innovation: Entrepreneurial Breakthroughs versus Corporate Incremental Improvements'. *Innovation Policy and the Economy* 5: 33–56.

Baumol, William J. 2010. *The Microtheory of Innovative Entrepreneurship*. Princeton, NJ: Princeton University Press.

Duval–Couetil, Nathalie. 2013. 'Assessing the Impact of Entrepreneurship Education Programs: Challenges and Approaches'. *Journal of Small Business Management* 51 (3): 394–409.

Fisher, James L., and James V. Koch. 2008. *Born, Not Made: The Entrepreneurial Personality*. Westport, Conn.: Praeger.

Fornell, Claes, and David F. Larcker. 1981. 'Evaluating Structural Equation Models with Unobservable Variables and Measurement Error'. *Journal of Marketing Research* 18 (1): 39–50.

Hu, Litze, and Peter M. Bentler. 1999. 'Cutoff Criteria for Fit Indexes in Covariance Structure Analysis: Conventional Criteria versus New Alternatives'. *Structural Equation Modeling: A Multidisciplinary Journal* 6 (1): 1–55.

Hulme, Eileen, Ben Thomas, and Hal DeLaRosby. 2014. 'Developing Creativity Ecosystems: Preparing College Students for Tomorrow's Innovation Challenge'. *About Campus* 19 (1): 14–23.

Hynes, Morgan M., and Wendy J. Hynes. 2018. 'If You Build It, Will They Come? Student Preferences for Makerspace Environments in Higher Education'. *International Journal of Technology and Design Education* 28 (3): 867–883.

Kegan, Robert. 1994. *In over Our Heads: The Mental Demands of Modern Life*. Cambridge, Mass.: Harvard University Press.

Leong, Lai-Ying, Teck-Soon Hew, Garry Wei-Han Tan, and Keng-Boon Ooi. 2013. 'Predicting the Determinants of the NFC-enabled Mobile Credit Card Acceptance: A Neural Networks Approach'. *Expert Systems with Applications* 40 (14): 5604–5620.

Mars, Matthew M., and Gary Rhoades. 2012. 'Socially Oriented Student Entrepreneurship: A Study of Student Change Agency in the Academic Capitalism Context'. *The Journal of Higher Education* 83 (3): 435–459.

Marti, José Maria Viedma, and Maria do Rosário Cabrita. 2013. *Entrepreneurial Excellence in the Knowledge Economy: Intellectual Capital Benchmarking Systems.* New York: Palgrave Macmillan.

Mayhew, Matthew J., Jeffrey S. Simonoff, William J. Baumol, Batia M. Wiesenfeld, and Michael W. Klein. 2012. 'Exploring Innovative Entrepreneurship and Its Ties to Higher Educational Experiences'. *Research in Higher Education* 53 (8): 831–859.

Mayhew, Matthew J., Jeffrey S. Simonoff, William J. Baumol, Benjamin S. Selznick, and Stephen J. Vassallo. 2016. 'Cultivating Innovative Entrepreneurs for the Twenty-First Century: A Study of US and German Students'. *The Journal of Higher Education* 87 (3): 420–455.

Moriano, Juan A., Marjan Gorgievski, Mariola Laguna, Ute Stephan, and Kiumars Zarafshani. 2012. 'A Cross-cultural Approach to Understanding Entrepreneurial Intention'. *Journal of Career Development* 39 (2): 162–185.

Selznick, Benjamin S. 2017. 'Higher Education for Undergraduate Innovation'. Unpublished PhD diss., New York University.

Selznick, Benjamin S., and Matthew J. Mayhew. 2019. 'Developing first-year students' innovation capacities'. *Review of Higher Education,* 42 (4): 1607–1634.

Selznick, Benjamin S., and Matthew J. Mayhew. 2018. 'Measuring Undergraduates' Innovation Capacities'. *Research in Higher Education* 59 (6): 744–764.

Conclusion: The 'Three Cs' in Practice

CHAPTER 13

The Virtues of Cooperation, Complementarity and Competition in Higher Education in Time of Crisis

Liviu Matei

The 'CEU Affair': Democracy Recession and the Restriction of Academic Freedom and University Autonomy

Starting in 2010, the Hungarian government introduced a series of regulatory and legislative measures that significantly reduced the freedom of the higher education and research institutions in the country. They included, for example, a restrictive reformulation of the provisions regarding academic freedom and university autonomy in the Constitution (Kenesei 2017; Chikan 2017). The constitutional protection of these two principles in Hungary was all but abolished. Soon thereafter, the Government appointed external administrators, officially called 'chancellors', often not academics, to exercise direct control on its behalf over the elected governance bodies, faculty and students, and the operations of the public universities (Kováts 2015). Surprisingly, these regulatory and legislative changes, complemented by a drastic reduction of the public budget for higher education[1], did not generate significant opposition or protest domestically, nor much concern internationally. This might be explained by the fact that the restriction of freedoms in higher education was only a partial story in the erosion of democracy; it was possibly overshadowed by broader more severe developments in the body politic. Along with the officially declared intention of Prime Minister Viktor Orbán to build an 'illiberal regime' (Wilkin 2018, 22–23), Hungary experienced dramatic legislative, regulatory and practical restrictions on the

---

[1] The public budget for higher education was reduced by almost 40% between 2008 and 2014, according to the EUA Public Funding Observatory (http://efficiency.eua.eu/public-funding-observatory). The situation has improved, at least in nominal terms, after 2014.

freedom of the media (currently all but abolished in Hungary), the freedom of the judiciary, the freedom of speech and the freedom of association. Like the domestic monster from a Hungarian folk tale—a pork belly sausage that swallows consecutively a young girl, her mother, the neighbours, everybody from the village and in the end an entire army sent by the king to rescue them—the Hungarian regime built by Viktor Orbán fed on freedoms, 'swallowing' them one after the other until almost nothing was left (Matei 2019). The Hungarian case is an extreme but not isolated case of what could be called 'democratic recession' in Europe. Sadly, this replaces the previous period of 'democratic growth' and exuberance experienced for about two decades after the fall of the Berlin Wall and the end of the Cold War. This democratic recession has an impact on the work of higher education institutions in many European countries and in other parts of the world (Matei 2018).

CEU is a small international graduate university that has been operating in Budapest since 1995. Events affecting it have helped to expose to public view what was really happening in Hungary. CEU enrols about 1,500 Master's and doctoral students coming from over 110 countries. Faculty members and staff are from 40 countries. Accredited both in the US and in Hungary, CEU is highly international. The largest national group in the student body consists of Hungarians, but they represent less than 20% of the total. In many classes there are not even two students from the same country. CEU's mission is to promote open society and democracy through advanced research and research-based teaching and learning in the social sciences, humanities, law, public policy and management. CEU ranks among the top 50 universities in the world on several global measures (see, for example, QS World Rankings by Subject 2019). A private university, CEU provides full financial support to all its doctoral students and at least partial support to all its master's students.

Beginning in spring 2017, CEU became a target of attacks from institutions of the Hungarian state, in particular the Hungarian Government and the office of the Prime Minister (Matei and Orosz 2017). Direct attacks from the top of the political and state administrative hierarchies were complemented by a sustained barrage of government-sponsored criticism and political condemnation from government-obedient media outlets. The accusations levelled against CEU were numerous, grave and often mutually contradictory. They included, for example, the published lists of alleged traitors and 'agents of foreign interests', many of whom, although not all, were CEU academics (Slaughter, in this volume). CEU was accused of promoting a global conspiracy aiming at corrupting, through the mass immigration of Muslims, the 'Christian fibre' of the Hungarian nation; of being at the same time not serious academically— a 'political enterprise' rather than a 'real university'—and 'too elitist' or 'cosmopolitan intellectualist'. The founder of CEU, George Soros, a Hungarian-American Jewish philanthropist, was accused of being the master puppeteer of innumerable cabals and was figured in oversized anti-Semitic posters around the country for almost two years.[2] New legislation was passed in higher education, nominally regulating in new ways all international universities operating in Hungary, but in reality specifically targeting CEU.[3] These attacks put at risk not only the autonomy and institutional integrity of the University, but its very existence. CEU fought back vigorously, but in the end, for lack of a resolution to the crisis, it was obliged to choose between closing down altogether or moving to another country. It decided to open a campus in neighbouring Austria in autumn 2019, answering an invitation by the Viennese regional authorities (Witte 2018; Enyedi 2018).

An important question that can be asked is why was CEU attacked? In answering this question, it is important to note that CEU was not the only institution under siege. The attacks against CEU took place in a marked erosion of democracy and disregard for the rule of law and human rights that affected the entire Hungarian society. The responsibility for these developments lies with the new regime that emerged in the country and its leader, Prime Minister Viktor Orbán. It is also true, at the same time, that CEU became a prime target and, rapidly, a highly visible one. The regime called itself 'illiberal' and, for a time, 'Christian democrat'. It was analysed by others as being populist, anti-democratic or at the extreme-right end of the political spectrum (Wilkin 2018). Slaughter (in this volume) calls it neo-nationalist. Although really a small institution, in particular when compared to a powerful quasi-totalitarian regime, CEU

---

[2] In Spring 2018, Viktor Orbán promoted the adoption of a legislative package targeting NGOs, which he and his Government called 'Stop Soros'. It was noted at that time that '"Soros" refers to George Soros, the Hungarian American and Jewish financier, government-accountability advocate and pro-migrant philanthropist, whom Orbán has cast as an evil puppet master, pulling strings that spell Hungary's demise' (McAuley 2018).

[3] An article published in *The Guardian* was quick to observe that the new law *was* targeting CEU and noted ironically, referring to Prime Minister Orbán, on the margin of a meeting in Brussels: 'PM in truculent mood as he rejects claims Hungary's education laws designed to close institution founded by US billionaire' (Boffey 2017).

was perceived as standing in the way of the new program of political construction in the country. Everything CEU stood for looked wrong, dangerous and larger than life in Viktor Orbán's regime. CEU cultivated critical thinking. It promoted advanced knowledge as an international public good and as a tool for socio-economic emancipation; tolerance for diversity, including diversity of opinions; international education and peaceful European integration. Viktor Orbán's regime promoted a recycled national myth of Hungarian economic and cultural supremacy based on 'manual labour' (as opposed to a knowledge-based economy), isolation, or 'Eastern-opening' (as opposed to globalism or Western-European integration) (Csáky 2018;[4] Göbl 2018; Mercier 2018). All this made CEU if not a genuine enemy, a useful symbolic target. Engulfed by its own logic, the regime decided to take on this small institution that it perceived as a thorn in its ideological flesh.

The history of these attacks, how the CEU case unfolded, is surprising for a European Union country in the 21st century.

In April 2017, the Hungarian Parliament adopted a set of modifications to the national higher education law. These modifications were passed through an expedited procedure in disregard of the formal rules governing the legislative process in Hungary (Matei and Orosz, 2017). The Hungarian Rectors' Conference and the Hungarian Academy of Sciences immediately protested at not being involved, although the higher education law itself mandated that they be consulted prior to any modification (there was no public consultation anyway). The law was not explicitly *about* CEU, but it was clear from the beginning that it did target that institution and it was dubbed 'Lex CEU' by everybody. The modifications consisted of prohibitive, new provisions for the operation of international higher education institutions like CEU; they included the requirement for an intergovernmental treaty between Hungary and 'the country of origin', specifically and individually for each university under consideration[5]. In the US, where CEU is accredited, the central, federal government is prevented under the Constitution from negotiating and signing such a treaty.

---

[4] In her article, Csáky writes that 'As the European Union takes long overdue measures to punish the Hungarian regime, the prime minister appears to be moving from rhetorical to real repression'.

[5] It was never clear how many such universities were operating in the country at that time. Government sources mentioned varying numbers, usually between a dozen and 16–18, at different times. With the exception of CEU, they were all local extensions of universities from other countries.

One could, however, be signed with a state government; indeed, New York State, where CEU is chartered, would have had the authority to sign such a document. In fact, the Hungarian Government eventually entered into negotiations with the Governor of New York and even provisionally came to an agreement on a draft treaty about CEU but refused to sign it after months of deferrals and contradictory justifications vis-à-vis their American counterparts in 2017–2018.

Resorting to New Types of Targeted Cooperation in Higher Education to Address Challenges in Time of Crisis

The attacks generated a large wave of sympathy and support for CEU, domestically and internationally. Hundreds of thousands of Hungarian citizens took to the streets in 2017 and 2018 in an unprecedented movement to protest against the Government; they demanded the right to education and defended CEU under the motto 'free country, free university'. Universities from around the world joined in a global expression of solidarity and concern for the restriction of academic freedom and university autonomy. Foreign governments and international organisations protested as well and asked for the law to be rescinded. The European Commission sued Hungary in 2017 over the CEU case, for infringement of academic freedom and of the right of establishment and the freedom to provide services. As of March 2019, the case is still pending at the European Court of Justice.

The effect of this domestic and international mobilisation was that the Hungarian government extended the deadlines for reaching compliance with the new law by a year, but that was not sufficient to avoid CEU closing down or being forced to move another country. That was because the substance of Lex CEU remained unchanged and after the expiration of the extended deadline on 1 January 2019 the University was no longer allowed to enrol new students in Budapest onto its US accredited programs. CEU itself tried to address this crisis in a number of practical ways, beyond just relying on public expressions of support. One of these was starting targeted cooperation with other higher education institutions.

Another requirement of Lex CEU was to have educational activities in the country of origin. Although CEU is a US-accredited institution, like other American universities, such as the American University of Cairo or the American University of Paris, it did not have an operation on the US soil. Several US universities immediately offered their support to start joint programs with CEU in the US and help it in this way to ensure compliance with this new provision of Lex CEU. CEU decided to enter into a partnership with Bard College, another New York State-chartered institution and a privileged long-term partner in the US, and started joint educational activities at the certificate and degree levels, authorised by the New York State Education Department through a procedure similar to program accreditation in Europe. Taking advantage of Bard College's offer, CEU established a physical presence at two locations in New York State, with educational and administrative facilities (buildings, classrooms, offices), professors, students and administrators. New York educational authorities confirmed repeatedly and in writing to their Hungarian counterparts that CEU fulfilled the condition in Lex CEU of having educational activities in the US. Moreover, in April 2018, the Hungarian Government sent a large official delegation led by a State Secretary to inspect CEU in the US. On this visit, the Hungarian delegation inspected CEU's premises and met CEU and Bard students, faculty and administrators, members of the Board of Trustees of CEU and representatives of the New York State educational authorities. The team declared itself satisfied that CEU met this condition. At the same time, however, several members of the Hungarian delegation made it clear during the visit that while they would convey their positive assessment back to Hungary, there was only one person who could decide on that matter, at his will, and that person was Viktor Orbán himself, the Prime Minister. After the team's return to Budapest and a few months of ensuing silence, the Government refused to accept that CEU was in compliance.

In short, this cooperation meant to ensure compliance with a new provision of Lex CEU did not help to address the crisis. CEU and Bard have made significant financial efforts to get a US CEU branch up and running. Although it failed to convince Viktor Orbán and his Government, the two institutions decided to maintain and enhance their cooperation, which was pedagogically and professionally of mutual benefit and included elements of innovation. For example, CEU and Bard launched a joint advanced certificate program which promoted a new interdisciplinary approach to research on Inequalities and to the teaching of Economics of Inequalities. As another example, special internship opportunities with international organisations were created in New York for students of the Master's degree in International Relations that CEU started offering in this city, also in cooperation with Bard.

One lesson learned by CEU during the crisis was that the University was somewhat too small and isolated to flourish or possibly even survive. Moreover, while short-term partnerships can be extremely useful, the creation of stable, long-term partnerships could be of greater help. Accordingly, the leadership and members of the CEU community started to explore the possibility of creating or joining 'university networks'. Two specific initiatives have been considered.

The first was the creation of a global Open Society University Network (OSUN), with partner universities from around the world who share an interest in and dedication to values of the open society and are willing to promote them through the means that are normally available to universities: teaching and learning, research and outreach. A very ambitious concept was developed by CEU. It also envisaged that such a network could become the first genuinely global university, as opposed to local, regional, national or international higher education institutions. Over the years, CEU has established partnerships and worked together with other institutions from Europe, North America, the Middle East, Central and South East Asia, that became potential partners for such a network. New partners from Africa and Latin America are being considered. The OSUN project is in progress, including working towards the finalisation of an overall concept, the design of governance and operational structures, and mobilisation of the necessary funding. When CEU developed its plans for the new campus in Vienna, considerations about how this new campus would support a global university network were central to the planning process.

The second project aiming at building networks is a lot more advanced and practical. It took advantage of a new, promising and also difficult development in Europe: the launch of the European Universities Initiative by the European Commission, based on the vision of the French president Emmanuel Macron, announced at Sorbonne University in 2017 (Myklebust and O'Malley 2018). The Commission announced a plan to support the creation of European university networks beginning in autumn 2019, supported by a significant budget, in the billions of Euros over several years. CEU was invited by partners with a similar institutional profile to join in preparing an application for the creation of a network intended to become the 'European University of Social Sciences', to be named 'CIVICA'.[6] The consortium includes European universities that have openly supported CEU during the crisis in Hungary: Sciences Po Paris, European University Institute Florence, Bocconi University Milan,

---

[6] https://www.civica.eu/

Stockholm School of Economics, Hertie School of Governance Berlin and the National University of Public Administration Bucharest. An important potential partner from the UK, the London School of Economics, was eventually prevented from joining because of Brexit. This is a prestigious group. CEU was happy to take an active part in the preparation of the proposal and is looking forward to becoming a founding member of the European University of Social Sciences. This is an exciting, even unprecedented, academic initiative on the European higher education scene. It is ambitious and potentially highly impactful, in particular in terms of promoting a new type of European cooperation in teaching and learning, and to some extent also in research and outreach to society. These are the main reasons for CEU to join. At the same time, however, members of the CEU community are looking forward to creating a strong European network that might become in due course a network university, helping not only with the advancement of education and research in the social sciences and related disciplines, but at the same time providing trans-national protection against the eventual whims of particular national political regimes.

In an even less expected development, which illustrates how cooperation can be used to address political challenges, in March 2019 the government of the *Land* of Bavaria offered to support financially a cooperation plan between CEU and the Technical University Munich (TUM). TUM is a highly respected university specialising primarily in engineering, with a few strong departments in the social sciences. In a letter to the Hungarian Government, the Prime Minister of Bavaria insisted as a condition for funding this partnership that Hungary should provide legal guarantees for CEU's continuation as a US-accredited institution in Budapest. Moreover, the European People's Party, the European political organisation including the governing parties of both Bavaria and Hungary, threatened to exclude the Hungarian party led by Prime Minister Orbán (Fidesz) from this organisation if he refused to meet this condition and allow the CEU-TUM network to proceed (Zubașcu 2019a).

CEU greatly welcomed the possibility of a cooperation with TUM and other partners, such as Stanford University, identified under this Bavarian initiative. Obviously, apart from the clear academic and professional virtues of this possible cooperation, it was also intended, by its promoters, as a *political means* to address a *political crisis* and commit German and European politicians to academic freedom and university autonomy. At the time when this chapter is being written, it is not known whether this worthy attempt will end up being 'too little and too late'.

Complementarity in Higher Education in Time of Crisis

The CEU affair shows that the need to utilise complementary assets and characteristics of higher education institutions can become more acute in time of crisis. Concurrently, it also shows that political interference can result in costly losses by bringing to a halt productive cooperative endeavours based on complementarity.

As CEU is preparing to move to Austria, a major planning consideration relates to cooperation with Viennese universities in the context of complementarities. CEU has advanced academic units and resources in several areas, including some that are highly innovative and even unique in Europe. For example, CEU is currently running the only PhD program in Network Science in Europe and one of the very few in the world. At the same time, however, most CEU academic units are small, often working hard to achieve critical mass, be it in terms of human resources or disciplinary coverage. Excellent areas of complementarity have been identified between CEU and Viennese universities and research institutions. For example, CEU has a very strong department of cognitive science, largely using approaches from psychology. Likewise, a strong cognitive science centre exists in Vienna, which in turn is specialising in brain research. The two groups are discussing putting together their complementary research approaches and resources. Similarly, the prestigious Complexity Science Hub Vienna and the new CEU Department of Data and Network Science are looking forward to cooperating, based on their existing similarities of profiles and resources. CEU specialises in network approaches in the Social Sciences and Humanities, not in the Natural Sciences, and recently obtained a multi-million Euro European Research Grant in this area. In general, CEU brings to Vienna several elements of academic complementarity to what specialisms are already available there and also a degree of internationalisation that is greatly appreciated. Although current complementarity with Viennese institutions is in no way politically motivated (not even partially, unlike the cooperation examples discussed in the previous section), Viennese and Austrian federal authorities are well aware of these possibilities and have repeatedly and openly stated that they see CEU as a great contribution to the Viennese academic landscape, by virtue of the complementarity aspects that it is bringing.

However, leaving Hungary creates significant barriers in terms of taking advantage of complementarities in higher education and research in Budapest. There are clear negative outcomes that result from political interference. The following three short examples illustrate this.

Since 2000, CEU has run an innovative PhD program in Mathematics and the Applications of Mathematics. This program was designed and offered jointly with the Alfréd Rényi Institute of Mathematics of the Hungarian Academy of Sciences, one of the most prestigious mathematics institutes in the world. Enrolment of new students is currently suspended, as a result of Lex CEU. The continuation of this cooperation, which has taken advantage intelligently of elements of complementarity for almost 20 years, is uncertain once CEU moves to Vienna. Rényi researchers cannot easily commute from Budapest to Vienna to teach and cannot provide continuous supervision for the PhD students of the joint program. In addition, the very future of the Rényi Institute itself is uncertain. In 2018, the Hungarian Government announced a plan to cut about 75% of the budget of the Academy and eventually simply disband all its research institutes (Zubaşcu 2019b). The elements of complementarity between CEU and Rényi were clear and important. CEU wanted to create a program in mathematics to complement its social sciences and humanities profile, and to promote new synergies across its entire disciplinary palette. However, CEU did not have the financial and symbolic resources to attract first class mathematicians. The Rényi Institute, on the other hand, had world class mathematicians who did not have a chance to teach or work with students more generally, let alone with students and academics in the Social Sciences. CEU's forced move out of the country might result in bringing this innovative cooperation to an end.

Though CEU has no undergraduate programs, it cooperates with several Hungarian undergraduate institutions, so-called advanced colleges, building on elements of complementarity with them. CEU offers them some financial support but its main contribution is in terms of providing access to its educational, research activities and facilities. These are made available to some of the best undergraduate students from Budapest within these local advanced colleges, which operate in cooperation with and build on the regular undergraduate programs of local Budapest universities. CEU offers advanced education in English in an international environment, not otherwise available for these students. In turn, CEU gets direct access to undergraduate students and a recruitment avenue to some of the top students in the country. This cooperation will most probably also cease when CEU moves to another country.

The third example is in the area of library services cooperation. CEU is a young institution, created in 1991. Since then, it has built the best English-language library in the entire region for Social Sciences and Humanities. The CEU Library is open to and intensively used by members of the Budapest and Hungarian academic community, as well as by professionals and academics from the entire Central and Eastern European region. One difficulty that CEU faces is that all its resources, the books for example, are new: produced after 1991. There are no older books in the CEU Library, let alone rare books. For some disciplines, such as History and Medieval Studies, for example, older resources are needed, indeed they are a must. To address this challenge, CEU has created links with other institutions, building on their respective strengths in this area. For example, CEU and Eötvös Loránd University Budapest (ELTE), the main Hungarian public university, have created a joint Medieval Library. CEU is responsible for the salaries of the librarians and acquisition of new materials. ELTE offers premises as well as access to its materials that significantly go back in time. CEU and ELTE students and researchers have access to the joint resources of this Library. This is another form of cooperation based on complementarity that will end, as a consequence of politically motivated attacks restricting academic freedom and university autonomy.

These three examples illustrate how innovative and effective cooperation in higher education will be disrupted or even made impossible by political interference. When moving to another country, CEU could eventually build similar links based on similar complementarities in Vienna. For the local Budapest partners, however, as well as for the border local academic community, the loss appears to be severe and irreplaceable.

Competition in Higher Education—A Political Tool in Time of Crisis?

CEU's experience during the crisis that erupted in 2017 has been significantly shaped by instances of solidarity from and cooperation with other universities. No threats or other hostile acts have come from other universities, be they in the name of competition or anything else that might put universities at odds with each other in normal times. The Government and its subservient media, by contrast, have on occasion used the competition argument as part of their attacks. They have argued, for example, that Lex CEU was adopted in order to level the playing field in Hungary, because, allegedly, CEU has unfair competitive advantage given its double accreditation, the internationality of the student body and staff, and its resources as a private university. Even CEU's remarkable success in access-

ing EU funds (always based on open competition) has been presented as
an unfair competitive advantage vis-à-vis local Hungarian universities. The
same has been said about CEU's good cooperation with other institutions
around the world: CEU was criticised for building effective academic relations with many other higher education institutions and becoming stronger
and more competitive in this way, and for having benefited from the backing of Hungarian, European and worldwide coalitions of supporters (a real
'conspiracy', in the words of the Hungarian Government). The most blis-
tering rebuttal of this invalid and unfair 'competition' argument, based, as
it is, on pseudo-fact, has been delivered by the President of the Hungarian
Academy of Sciences, László Lovász, a world class mathematician, winner
of the Wolf, Knuth and Kyoto Prizes in mathematics. In a public debate
with the Secretary of State for Higher Education (the same one who first
acknowledged, then denied, that CEU did have a presence in the US),
Lovász famously stated that wanting to restrict CEU's autonomy or close
it down in the name of levelling the playing field to ensure fair competition
in the Hungarian higher education is as irrational and ridiculous as wanting to cut off the legs of a famous Hungarian swimmer, a multiple Olympic
gold medallist, in the name of giving a chance to other swimmers in the
country (Joób 2017).

Conclusions

The CEU case is the case of a particular university in a particular country. Yet, it is highly relevant for new trends and developments in higher
education, in particular in the area of academic freedom and university
autonomy. Although in many ways quite extreme, this case is also relevant
to the evolving relationship between higher education institutions and the
state in a time of democratic recession.

The CEU case shows that cooperation in higher education can be
useful in order to address crises that have a political nature or origin. By
necessity, such cooperation initiatives acquire a clear, even possibly primarily political dimension, in addition to genuinely promoting academic and
professional advancement in the participating institutions. Universities are
not and should not be political organisations, but a political crisis in higher
education requires political solutions.

The CEU case also shows that cooperation based on complementarity in higher education can be seriously affected by political interference,
resulting in significant loses for the participating institutions and for the

broader academic and professional communities. The CEU case further shows that enlightened political organisations and individuals can promote inclusive cooperation based on complementarity as a means to strengthening the educational and research environments nationally and internationally. For this, however, an acceptance of democratic standards and principles is a pre-requisite; foremost amongst these are the principles of academic freedom and university autonomy.

Finally, while cooperation can significantly help during a political crisis, competition does not appear to be a danger, except when the political power tries to instrumentalise it.

References

Boffey, Daniel. 2018. 'Orbán on offensive after EU takes legal action over Soros university'. *The Guardian.* 24 Apr 2017. Accessed at https://www.theguardian.com/world/2017/apr/26/eu-launches-legal-action-against-hungary-higher-education-law-university on 25 March 2019.

Chikán, Attila. 2017. 'Key Developments in Hungarian Higher Education'. In *Academic Freedom. The Global Challenge,* edited by Michael Ignatieff and Stefan Roch, 113–123. Budapest–New York: CEU Press.

Csáky, Zselyke. 2018. 'The End of Viktor Orbán's Peacock Dance'. *Foreign Policy,* 14 Sep 2018. Accessed at https://foreignpolicy.com/2018/09/14/the-end-of-viktor-orbans-peacock-dance-hungary-eu-article-7-epp-european-parliament/ on 25 March 2019.

Enyedi, Zsolt. 2018. 'Hungarian Government's Spectacular Phase of Attacks Against Academia'. *The Globe Post,* 15 Oct. 2018. Accessed at https://theglobepost.com/2018/10/15/hungary-ceu-academia/ on 25 March 2019.

Gőbl, Gabi. 2018. 'Democracy is Out of Order: CEU Forced to Leave Hungary'. *Henrich Böll Stiftung,* 5 Dec 2018. Accessed at https://www.boell.de/en/2018/12/05/democracy-out-order-central-european-university-forced-leave-hungary on 25 March 2019.

Joób, Sándor. 2017. 'Nyírjuk ki Hosszú Katinkát, hogy a többi úszó jobb legyen?' *Index,* 11 May 2017. Accessed at https://index.hu/belfold/2017/05/11/ceu_ceu-torveny_mta_palkovics_laszlo_enyedi_zsolt_lovasz_laszlo_felsooktatas_verseny/ on 22 March 2019.

Kenesei, István. 2017. 'University Autonomy in Hungary in Perspective'. In *Academic Freedom. The Global Challenge,* edited by Michael Ignatieff and Stefan Roch, 123–129. Budapest–New York: CEU Press.

Kováts, Gergely. 2015. 'Recent Developments in the Autonomy and Governance of Higher Education Institutions in Hungary: the Introduction of the "Chancellor System"'. In *Central European Higher Education Cooperation Conference Proceedings,* edited by József Berács, Julia Iwinska, Gergely Kováts, and Liviu Matei, 26–39. Budapest: Corvinus University of Budapest Digital Press.

McAuley, James. 2018. 'Viktor Orban, after Soaring to Reelection Win in Hungary, to Target George Soros and NGOs'. *The Washington Post,* 9 Apr 2018, accessed at https://www.washingtonpost.com/world/europe/viktor-orban-after-soaring-to-reelection-win-in-hungary-to-target-george-soros-and-ngos/2018/04/09/268d314e-3b9d-11e8-955b-7d2e19b79966_story.html?utm_term=.39dfc7a47aa3 on 31 March 2019.

Matei, Liviu. 2018. 'Governance and Funding of Universities in the European Higher Education Area: Times of Rupture'. In: *European Higher Education Area: The Impact of Past and Future Policies*, edited by Adrian Curaj, Ligia Deca, and Remus Pricopie, 591–602. Cham: Springer.

Matei, Liviu. 2019. 'Ungarn Erlebt Augenblick der Klarheit und Brutalität'. *Die Zeit*, 4/2019, 17. Januar 2019, accessed at https://www.zeit.de/2019/04/central-european-university-budapest-ungarn-viktor-orban on 22 March 2019.

Matei, Liviu, and Kata Orosz. 2017. 'Central European University: An Exceptional Moment for Hungary, and for International Higher Education'. *World Education News + Reviews*, June 6, 2017. Available at https://wenr.wes.org/2017/06/central-european-university-an-exceptional-moment-for-hungary-and-higher-educations-international-ambitions, accessed February 25, 2019.

Mercier, Laura. 2018. 'Academic Freedom Flouted in Hungary'. *The New Federalist*, 29 Dec 2018. Accessed at https://www.thenewfederalist.eu/academic-freedom-flouted-in-hungary on 25 March 2019.

Myklebust, Jan Petter, and Brendan O'Malley. 2018. 'Macron's Vision of Universities Networks Moves Forward'. *University World News*, 05 May 2018. Accessed at https://www.universityworldnews.com/post.php?story=20180505051434124 on 22 March 2019.

QS World Rankings by Subject. 2019. Accessed at https://www.topuniversities.com/subject-rankings/2018 on 22 March 2019.

Rupnik, Jacques. 2017. 'The Illiberal Democracy in Central Europe'. *Esprit* 6: 69–85.

Wilkin, Peter. 2018. 'The Rise of "Illiberal" Democracy: The Orbánization of Hungarian Political Culture'. *Journal of World-Systems Research* 24 (1): 5–42.

Witte, Griff. 2018. 'Amid Illiberal Revolution in Hungary, a University with U.S. Roots Fights to Stay'. *The Washington Post*, Sep 3, 2018. Accessed at https://www.washingtonpost.com/world/europe/amid-illiberal-revolution-in-hungary-a-university-with-us-roots-fights-to-stay/2018/09/03/7061771c-a547-11e8-a656-943eefab5daf_story.html?noredirect=on&utm_term=.2cdb492fe4f7 on 25 March 2019.

Zubașcu, Florin. 2019a. '"Start of a Kind of Hope" for Central European University to Stay in Budapest, Weber says'. *Science Business*, 21 Mar 2019. Accessed on 22 March 2019 at https://sciencebusiness.net/news/start-kind-hope-central-european-university-stay-budapest-weber-says.

Zubașcu, Florin. 2019b. 'Government Continues Crackdown on Academic Freedom in Hungary. The Academy of Sciences Battles Research Minister over Control of Research Funding'. *Science Business*, 22 January 2019. Accessed on 22 March 2019 at https://sciencebusiness.net/news/government-continues-crackdown-academic-freedom-hungary.

List of Contributors

ADEKOLA, OLALEKAN ADEBAN, Lecturer, School of Humanities, Religion and Philosophy, York St John University, York, England.

BEHRMANN, LAURA, Research Assistant, German Centre for Higher Education Research and Science Studies (DZHW), Hannover, Germany.

BOCK, CAROLIN, Professor of Entrepreneurship, Technical University Darmstadt, Germany.

BOONEN, JORIS, Postdoctoral Researcher and Senior Lecturer, Zuyd University of Applied Sciences, Maastricht, The Netherlands.

BORDEN, VICTOR M. H., Professor of Higher Education, Indiana University School of Education, USA.

CARVALHO, TERESA, Associate Professor and Researcher, University of Aveiro and CIPES – Centre for Research in Higher Education Policies, Portugal.

CHENG, MING, Professor of Higher Education, Faculty of Education, Edge Hill University, Lancashire, United Kingdom.

COGSWELL, CYNTHIA A., Director of Strategic Planning and Assessment, Ohio University, Athens, USA.

DEGN, LISE, Assistant Professor, Danish Centre for Studies in Research and Research Policy, Aarhus University, Denmark.

DILMETZ, DANIEL, Research Associate. Department of Entrepreneurship, Technical University, Darmstadt, Germany.

FRIEDHOFF, CAROLINE, Project Manager for U-Multirank, Centre for Higher Education, Gütersloh, Germany.

HOEFNAGELS, ANKIE, Senior researcher, lecturer and research director, Zuyd University of Applied Sciences, Maastricht, The Netherlands.

KOBLER-WEISS, MICHAELA, Assistant to the Rector's Council, Vienna University of Economics and Business, Vienna, Austria.

LEDERMÜLLER, KARL, Head of Evaluation and Quality Enhancement, Vienna University of Economics and Business, Vienna, Austria.

LINGHI, TIAN, Associate Professor, Research Institute for Higher Education; Fudan University, Shanghai, China.

MACHADO-TAYLOR, MARIA DE LOURDES, Researcher, A3ES – Agency for Assessment and Accreditation of Higher Education and CIPES – Centre for Research in Higher Education Policies, Portugal.

MAYHEW, MATTHEW J., William Ray and Marie Adamson Flesher Professor of Educational Administration, Ohio State University, Columbus, USA.

MATEI, LIVIU, Co-Editor, Provost and Professor of Higher Education Policy at the School of Public Policy, Central European University, Budapest, Hungary.

MILSOM, CLARE V., Co-Editor, Professor of Academic Practice and Director of the Teaching and Learning Academy, Liverpool John Moores University, Liverpool, United Kingdom.

MITIC, RADOMIR RAY, Postdoctoral Researcher, Council of Graduate Schools, USA.

MORDHORST, LISA, Advisor to the Executive Directors, Centre for Higher Education, Gütersloh, Germany.

O'HARA, MARK, Co-Editor, Professor and Associate Dean, Faculty of Health, Education and Life Sciences, Birmingham City University, United Kingdom.

PLUYMAEKERS, MARK, Professor of International Relationship Management, Zuyd University of Applied Sciences, Maastricht, The Netherlands.

PRINGLE BARNES, GAYLE, College International Student Learning Officer, College of Social Sciences, University of Glasgow, Scotland, United Kingdom.

PRITCHARD, ROSALIND M.O., Co-Editor, Emeritus Professor of Education, Ulster University, Coleraine, Northern Ireland, United Kingdom.

ROMAN, JOHN, Communications and PR Manager for U-Multirank, Centre for Higher Education, Gütersloh, Germany.

SÁ, MARIA JOSÉ, Researcher, CIPES – Centre for Research in Higher Education Policies, Portugal.

SELZNICK, BENJAMIN S., Assistant Professor, James Madison University, Harrisonburg, Virginia, USA.

SEMBRITZKI, THORBEN, Research Assistant, German Centre for Higher Education Research and Science Studies (DZHW), Hannover, Germany.

SLAUGHTER, SHEILA, Louise McBee Professor of Higher Education, University of Georgia, Athens, USA.

TROILO, FOX, Senior Research Advisor, Higher Education, Hanover Research, Arlington, USA.

WERNER, DEBORAH, Project Manager for U-Multirank, Centre for Higher Education, Gütersloh, Germany.

WILLIAMS, JAMES, Co-Editor, Senior Research Fellow, Social Research and Evaluation Unit, Birmingham City University, Birmingham, United Kingdom.

ZEEH, JULIA, Senior Analyst, Evaluation and Quality Enhancement, Vienna University of Economics and Business, Vienna, Austria.

ZHANG, LINI, Postdoctoral Researcher, Ohio State University, Athens, USA.

ZIEGELE, FRANK, Executive Director of the Centre for Higher Education, Gütersloh, Germany and Professor of Higher Education and Research Management at the Osnabrück University of Applied Sciences.

Index

A

academic capitalism 30, 31, 44, 45
academic freedom, 4, 7, 27, 29, 32, 37–44, 45, 46, 253, 257, 260, 263–265
academic identity, 55, 65
academic performance, 134, 151, 152, 155
Academic Ranking of World Universities, 89, 91, 97–98, 109
academic support, 151, 154, 156, 157, 158, 163
access to higher education, 131
admission procedures, 131
American Association of University Professors (AAUP) 28, 40, 43, 45
Association of American Colleges and Universities (AAC&U), 206
Austria, 41, 78, 131, 135

B

basic funding, 21
Belgium, 78, 205

C

Campus of International Excellence Programme, 20
Carnegie Classification of Institutions of Higher Education, 89–92, 94–95, 98
Centres of Excellent Research, 19
Central European University (CEU), 1, 2, 3, 7, 40, 253–265
Chinese students, 6, 102, 169, 176, 177, 174, 179
civic engagement, 205–209, 213, 220, 223–226
classification, 19, 58, 59, 76, 89, 92, 94, 99, 103, 104
collaboration, 2, 11, 12, 13, 16, 19, 21, 102, 186, 198
competition 1, 2, 11, 12, 13, 16, 19, 21, 22, 23, 44, 57, 61, 84, 107, 109, 113, 115, 119, 120, 121, 124, 131, 132, 134, 263, 264, 265
Competition, Collaboration and Complementarity (CCC), 2, 3, 5, 11–23
competitive funding, 19, 20
complementarity, 11, 12, 13, 16, 19, 20, 22
contact hypothesis, 186
critical mass, 13, 15, 21, 261
cultural distance, 185–189, 192–199
Cultural Intelligence (CQ), 189, 191, 195–197
Czech Republic, 17, 78

D

'dark money', 28, 34, 37
Dartmouth College, 93–96
democratic recession 254, 264
Denmark, 18, 41, 79, 191
digitalisation, 11, 13, 14
diversity, 5, 6, 12, 15, 18, 21–23, 93, 99, 135, 142–147, 170, 181, 191, 213, 256
dropout, 132, 151

E

Educational Longitudinal Survey (ELS), 209, 213
employability support, 159, 163
England, 17, 191
Erasmus, 2, 188, 192
European Tertiary Education Register (ETER) 74, 75, 76
European Union (EU), 6, 11, 22, 23, 27, 28, 29, 31, 32, 38, 39, 40, 42, 46, 76, 78, 172, 176, 178, 256, 264
European University Initiative, 22
Eurostat, 75, 76, 77, 80, 81
evaluation system, 108, 109
excellence cluster, 16
Excellence Initiative, 17, 19
Excellence scheme 23
Exzellenzstrategie (Excellence Strategy), 17
Exzellenzinitiative, 17

F

faculty interaction, 235, 238, 240, 241, 242, 243, 244, 245, 246, 247
financial support, 151, 154, 156, 159, 163, 254, 262
Finland, 18, 20, 41, 79, 191
first-generation college students, 205, 220, 224, 226, 227
France, 19, 41, 78, 79, 109–111, 114–117, 122–125, 191
funding incentives, 19, 21

G

gender balance, 71, 73, 75, 78, 80, 82, 83
gender equality, 71, 73, 74, 76, 110, 112
gender imbalance, 71, 72, 73, 74, 75, 76, 79, 84
German students, 235, 237, 241, 243, 246, 247, 248
Germany, 13, 15, 16, 17, 36, 41, 78, 79, 109–113, 114, 120–125, 233, 234, 235, 236, 237
global challenges, 13, 14
Global Mind Monitor, 187, 193, 199
globalisation, 11, 13, 14
governance, 4, 66, 72, 107, 108, 114–125
government initiatives, 11
group work, 173, 175, 176, 177, 179

H

Hanover Research, 99–103
High Commission for the Evaluation of Research and of Higher Education (HCERES), 107, 110–117, 122–123
Higher Education Alliance for Small and Medium Enterprises, 16
Higher Education Institutions (HEIs), 53–66, 75, 84, 90, 93, 96, 99, 100, 104, 109, 114–125, 131–135, 146, 147, 148, 152, 154, 155, 158–164
higher education policies, 11, 12, 22
higher education system, 3, 11, 12, 13, 15, 16, 17, 20, 21, 22, 23, 107–113, 207
Hochschulallianz für den Mittelstand, 16
horizontal diversity, 12, 15, 21, 22, 23
human capital theory, 206–207, 209, 223
Hungary, 39, 40, 78, 79, 191, 205, 253–265

I

Iceland, 17, 78, 79
identification, 55, 58–66, 156, 224
Indiana University, 96–99, 104
innovation capacities, 233, 234, 235,
    240, 246, 247, 248, 249
Institute of International Education,
    209
intellectual property 29, 30
intercultural awareness, 3, 5, 169, 170,
    175, 177, 178, 179, 180, 181
intercultural competencies, 5, 185–
    189, 196, 198
intermediating organisations, 27, 28,
    30-37, 39, 44
international comparison, 110, 113,
    125
internationalisation, 5, 22, 169, 185,
    186, 196, 198, 199, 261
Italy, 17, 41, 79

L

Leading National Research Centres,
    19–20
legal regulation of institutional
    typologies, 19
Lex CEU, 40, 256–258, 262–263
Lisbon Agenda, 32
logistic regression 212, 215
loosely coupled organisations, 62, 65

M

massification 13, 15
Memorandum of Understanding
    (MOU), 36
merger, 16–23, 53, 64, 111, 114
merger policies 18, 23
merger reform 17, 18
money-follows-students-approach, 16
monitoring, 41, 74, 154, 157, 161,
    162, 163
Multicultural Personality (MPQ),
    190–191

multidimensional performance
    measurement, 19

N

neoliberalism, 30, 31
neo-nationalism, 27, 28, 29, 30,
    37–44, 45
Netherlands, 18, 41, 78, 192, 198,
new regionalism, 14
non-university research institution, 16,
    18, 19
North-Rhine Westphalia (NRW),
    109–113, 114, 120–125
Norway, 19, 78

O

organisational actorhood, 5, 108,
    114–125
organisational identity, 56–57, 61, 63

P

parental involvement, 210, 215, 220,
    223, 224
peer interaction, 169, 171, 172
performance-based funding (PBF),
    112, 120, 123
performance-oriented salaries, 16, 19
personal statements, 133, 136, 137,
    139, 142, 143, 145, 146, 148
personality traits, 234, 235, 237, 240,
    245, 246, 247
Poland 17, 19, 20, 39, 40, 41, 78, 79,
    191
policy instruments, 11, 19, 20, 21
Portugal, 17, 79, 153
propensity score analysis, 209, 214
public formula funding, 16, 19
public-private partnership funding,
    19

Q

qualitative methods, 136, 155

R

rankings, 13, 15, 19, 21
rankings, critique, 89–92, 103–104
Research Excellence Framework
  (REF), 20, 109–113, 117–120,
  123–125
research funds, 2, 15, 16, 17, 19

S

Scale Enlargement, Task division, and
  Concentration, 18
Scotland, 17
sector consolidation process, 19
sensemaking, 53, 54, 60–63
sex ratio, 71, 78
Slovakia, 17, 78, 79
social dimension, 131, 135, 142–147,
  206, 235
social identity theory, 58
social support, 151, 156, 158, 159, 163
status attainment theory, 207, 209
strategic capacity, 108, 114–125
structural reforms, 11
student persistence, 151, 152, 153,
  154, 162
student success, 151, 153
student support, 95, 151, 154, 156,
  157, 159, 162, 163
study abroad, 6, 102, 158, 185–189,
  192, 198, 205–227
study motivation, 139
study success, 5, 82, 132, 140–141,
  146, 147, 148
Sweden, 36, 41, 79, 191, 205

T

target/performance agreements, 19
text mining, 136–137
'Third Sector', 36, 37
Times Higher Education World
  University Rankings, 89, 91, 113,
  172
traditional excellence concept, 21
transfer, 14, 21, 22
transparency 19, 22, 73, 92

U

U-Multirank 22, 71, 74, 75, 79, 80,
  81, 82, 83
United Kingdom, 6, 13, 18, 20, 37,
  73, 109–113, 122–125, 201, 205
United States, 89, 90, 91, 191,
  205, 209, 225, 233, 235, 236, 237,
  248
universalism, 29. 30
universities of applied science, 15, 17
university autonomy 21, 253, 257, 260,
  263–265
university network, 259, 260
US News & World Report Rankings
  (USNWR), 89–95, 97–101, 103–104
US Students, 235, 237, 241, 246, 247,
  248

V

vertical diversity, 22
virtual exchange, 186, 199
voting, 6, 38, 205–227